LESSONS OF HOPE

LESSONS OF HOPE

How to Fix Our Schools

JOEL KLEIN

HARPER

An Imprint of HarperCollins*Publishers*

LESSONS OF HOPE. Copyright © 2014 by Joel Klein. All rights reserved. Printed in the United States of America. No part of this book may be used or reproduced in any manner whatsoever without written permission except in the case of brief quotations embodied in critical articles and reviews. For information, address HarperCollins Publishers, 195 Broadway, New York, NY 10007.

HarperCollins books may be purchased for educational, business, or sales promotional use. For information, please e-mail the Special Markets Department at SPsales@harpercollins.com.

FIRST EDITION

Designed by Janet M. Evans

Library of Congress Cataloging-in-Publication Data has been applied for.

ISBN: 978-0-06-226864-8

14 15 16 17 18   OV/RRD   10 9 8 7 6 5 4 3 2 1

FOR NICOLE AND JULIA

CONTENTS

PREFACE

March 28, 2008: The day brings grim news; an eighteen-year-
old honor student is brutally stabbed at Brooklyn's Paul Robeson High
School. His life hangs in the balance.

In the wake of the stabbing, teachers at Robeson—already anxious and
often discouraged—are horrified, angry, and mournful. Students and
parents around the city are concerned. I had known the school was a
mess—low graduation rates, gang violence bleeding into the school from
a neighborhood now often a battleground, and a faculty close to the breaking point. As the boy fights to survive, I'm tense. Each moment feels shaky.

Thank god, the boy survives, but the fate of the others at Robeson
is uncertain. I set out for the school to assess the situation firsthand and
to show my support for the people dealing with the aftermath, trying to
rally their courage and perseverance. As I drive from lower Manhattan
across the Brooklyn Bridge through the gentrified neighborhoods on
the other side, I am reminded of Brooklyn's transformation into a borough of haves and have-nots. Newly affluent communities rim the borough while some parts remain burned-out and decayed. Neighborhoods
such as Crown Heights, where Robeson is located, resist the progress
that propels the rest of the city.

Fear and frustration are palpable in the halls of the school. Nobody knows why the kid was targeted. Teachers say they are scared just to walk through the Robeson doors. After six years on the job as New York City's schools chancellor, I know the scenario and how this will play out: Robeson will have to be closed and replaced.

FEBRUARY 12, 2013: I'M WATCHING PRESIDENT OBAMA DELIVER his State of the Union address, turning his attention to the problems of American education. I lean forward, listening attentively as he tells the story of a school I know well, P-Tech, in Brooklyn—housed in what had once been Robeson, the school where the boy was stabbed. He praises it for putting "our kids on a path to a good job," noting that students there "will graduate with a high school diploma and an associate's degree in computers or engineering."

Change had come, kicking and screaming. How did it happen? How had the place that was once Robeson, where basic safety was imperiled, been transformed in fewer than five years into a national showcase? This seeming miracle was brought about by a strategy of change we had inaugurated years before, a program of replacing large, dysfunctional high schools in high-poverty communities with new, smaller schools built from scratch with strong community partnerships. P-Tech itself had grown out of a discussion I had with Sam Palmisano, then CEO of IBM, in late 2010, who told me the tech industry was having difficulty finding students with the skills it currently needed.

I proposed we open a six-year institution in partnership with the City University of New York that would include four years of high school and two years of community college. The goal would be the development of those technology skills too often missing in students looking for work. IBM would partner with us on developing the curriculum, while also supporting the school financially and providing internships for its students. After completing their coursework, students would be eligible to take a certification test, prepared by IBM. If they passed, they would get priority placement for hiring by IBM. Palmisano agreed, and with lots of work by the teams at my department, City University, and IBM, P-Tech opened in September 2011, as my department simultaneously began the process of closing the old Robeson school.

Most remarkable is the resistance we encountered when shuttering Robeson. Despite the school's wretched performance, the students, community, and teachers union rallied behind it, angrily protesting the closure as they had in so many similar instances around the city. The students are too proud to acknowledge their school's failure, the community clings to its memories, and the teachers worry about their jobs. This is why school reform is so tough in America: the status quo, even when irreparably broken, has many defenders who will fiercely resist change.

In his speech, President Obama made clear that P-Tech's success story could not be repeated without a major overhaul of public education. "We need to give every American student opportunities like this," Obama noted, stating the obvious. What is not obvious to many is this: to succeed, public education needs radical rethinking. That is why I wrote this book.

I WAS A CAREER LAWYER, FRESH FROM THE CLINTON ADMINIS-tration, with little background in education before these matters became my life's work. In August 2002, I was selected as New York City's schools chancellor. Michael Bloomberg had become the city's 108th mayor on January 1 of that year. One of his first acts was to persuade the state legislature in Albany to give him operational control over the schools, then run by thirty-two separately elected community school boards. My appointment as head of the newly created department of education surprised many, but Bloomberg wanted innovation, a leader who could bring fresh ideas from other walks of life into the discussion. He and I worked together for almost eight and a half years, profoundly changing the face of public education in the city. At virtually every turn, we encountered strong resistance by the politicians, unions, bureaucrats, and other entrenched opponents of reform.

Why did we do it? America is at a crossroads. Economic inequality is tearing at the fabric of our society, as the gap between rich and poor becomes a chasm, social mobility stalls, and for the first time a majority of Americans grow more and more pessimistic about their future and their children's ability to make their way successfully in the world. Many things need to be done to address these issues, but none is more important than improving public education.

Our problems have now become our crisis. First, despite decades of trying to improve our schools—and more than doubling the financial outlay earmarked for them—only slightly more than a third of U.S. students are being well educated. For kids growing up in poverty and for black and Latino children, the number is less than half that. Notably, today's high-school graduates perform no better than students who graduated forty years ago. When compared with students in other industrialized countries, ours are in the middle levels in reading and science, and near the bottom rung in math.

Today's global high-tech economy—and the job market it has spawned—demand much more of most American workers. Consequently, even given the high incidence of unemployment, many positions remain unfilled because applicants lack the requisite skills.

The perplexing question is: Why is it so hard to improve our schools? Ardent defenders of the status quo say the schools are doing as well as they can and the real problem is the kids, many of whom come from poor and challenged backgrounds. The realities of students' lives, argue these people, limit their capacity to become educated and successfully navigate the job market. This argument is easily proven wrong. Any observer can see that it's not just poor kids who are being left behind. Compared with kids in countries that do a good job in education, our middle-class and wealthy students are underperforming as well.

As for the more economically and socially challenged kids, of course family circumstances matter, but the best research and much firsthand experience show that children with similar economic and social challenges often fare quite differently in school, usually owing to the quality of the schools they attend and the teachers they encounter. In some instances, the differences are quite astonishing. For example, even though they educate mostly poor and minority students, the Success Academy charter schools in New York City perform at the same level as the best schools in the wealthiest communities anywhere in New York State. The performance of the Success schools has fostered much discussion about why other schools with similar students fail to produce remotely similar results.

The issue of poverty and its effect on our ability to educate kids dominates the contemporary debate on school reform and improvement. From the day I became chancellor, many people told me, "You'll never fix education in America until you fix poverty." I've always believed that the reverse is true: we'll never fix poverty until we fix education. Sure, a strong safety net and support programs for poor families are appropriate and necessary. But we've recently celebrated the fiftieth anniversary of Lyndon Johnson's war on poverty, and it seems fair to say that we must seek new approaches as our problems increase.

Safety-net and support programs can never do what a good education can; they can never instill in a disadvantaged child the belief that society can and will work for him in the same way that it works for middle- and upper-class children. It is the sense of belonging—the feeling that the game is not rigged from the start—that allows a child to find autonomy, productivity, and, ultimately, happiness. That's what education did for me. And that's why, whenever I talk about education reform, I like to recall the wise, if haunting, words of Frederick Douglass, himself a slave, who said, "It is easier to build strong children than to repair broken men."

If we want to build strong children, we must not allow family or community circumstances to dictate whether a child gets a good school and good teachers. Yet that's what's happening to millions of kids today: all too often zip codes determine the quality of a child's education. The reason for this has nothing to do with our kids. It stems from the fact that our public schools are structured and organized in exactly the wrong way. School systems in America are government-run monopolies dominated by unions and political interests and not subject to the kinds of accountability and competitive incentives that breed successful organizations. Steve Jobs, certainly one of the greatest entrepreneurs ever, lamented that, because most families have no choices when it comes to public education, the "monopoly gets control" and, when that happens, "the service level almost always goes down." Analogizing the public schools to the old AT&T telephone monopoly, he added: "I remember seeing a bumper sticker with the Bell Logo on it and it said, 'We don't care. We don't have to care.'"

You might expect a die-hard capitalist like Jobs to criticize a government monopoly such as our public education system. But the same sentiments coming from Albert Shanker, the most influential teachers union leader ever, are more of a surprise. Much like Jobs, Shanker argued, "It's time to admit that public education operates like a planned economy, a bureaucratic system in which everyone's role is spelled out in advance and there are few incentives for innovation and productivity. There's no surprise that our school system doesn't improve. It more resembles the communist economy than our market economy."

Jobs and Shanker found unexpected common ground, but too many people continue to insist that schools must be run differently from businesses or other organizations. They believe that schools provide a public service and must, by definition, remain a public monopoly. This insistence ignores the innovation and progress that competition has brought to every other sector of our society. Our four-year colleges and graduate schools have always had to compete for students and faculty and have long been considered the best in the world, something no one can say of our K–12 system.

To make matters worse, public education is not only a government-run monopoly, but also a terrain where change occurs mainly at the local level. The historically quaint notion that communities should control their kids' education—long a hobby horse of conservatives who fear anything originating from the federal government—has led neither to active citizen involvement nor to real experimentation at the local level. It has instead produced a multitude of small, balkanized fiefdoms, easily controlled by special interests with political expertise. As a result, we have almost fourteen thousand separate school districts practicing precious little innovation and exhibiting little differentiation, even though many are doing a poor job. This is hardly surprising; the powerful forces protecting the status quo in one community are doing the same thing in all the others. Preserving these small political units only continues to empower special interests and perpetuate failure.

Plainly, we need to get our national act together. In an era of global, high-tech competition, the notion that it is fitting for students in different states to meet different academic standards, no matter how low, makes no sense. Our kids will compete with kids in China, India,

Europe, and the rest of the world. As a country, we need to take responsibility for all of our children and prepare them for what they will encounter. This is precisely what nations that have high-performing education systems do. If school choice—new, smaller schools or charter schools, for example—is good for kids in New York, it's hard to see why kids in Atlanta shouldn't have the same range of high-quality choices as well.

Although I believed from the start that competition and school choice for all students should be our ultimate goal, such a system can't be created overnight. There aren't nearly enough available seats out there to provide good options for the more than 50 million kids in U.S. public schools. Aware of that reality in New York, from the beginning we identified two core values—equity and excellence—that would inform everything we did. We would fight at every turn to treat all kids fairly and give them opportunities that they hadn't had previously. During the eight years, we adopted four basic reform strategies to implement those values. We initiated these strategies at different times—each building on what came before—in the following order.

First, we seized control of the system we inherited, a highly politicized mess of thirty-two disparate school districts, each doing its own thing in terms of academic standards and curriculum. We dubbed this phase the three C's (control, coherence, and capacity building). We dismantled the former district offices, rolled them up into a centralized management structure, established a citywide curriculum in reading and math, and invested heavily in professional development for our teachers. We did this principally to break down the sclerotic, politically controlled bureaucracy and begin the process of replacing it with a culture based on merit and innovation. Even as we set up this new management structure, however, we knew it would be transitional; it was still too top-down and bureaucratic for long-term success. But before we could make the other changes we wanted, we had to get control of the system across the city.

Once we established control, we began two major long-term initiatives to create choice. During the course of my tenure, we shut down dozens of failing high schools like Robeson and replaced them with hundreds of new smaller schools. We gave all students the opportunity to list up to twelve high schools they would like to attend and then matched them to schools based on fair and objective criteria. We also broadly expanded charter schools—public schools operated by outside groups that serve all students, without bureaucratic or union interference—by opening more than one hundred of them. Together, these programs amounted to the most dramatic expansion of school choice ever in America. Before we arrived, schools were almost never closed, new ones were rarely opened, and charter schools were few and far between.

Third, we put in place policies and programs that empowered principals and enabled them to be the real leaders of their schools, rather than puppets of the bureaucracy. We focused heavily on recruiting and training excellent principals and gave them substantially more control over key decisions in their schools, like hiring teachers, contracting with outside support and training programs, and making overall budgetary decisions. We also held them accountable for meeting academic performance targets based largely on student progress. In essence, we replaced the bureaucratic command-and-control management that traditionally governs the public schools with the kind of freedoms and accountability seen in the best private and charter schools. This was unprecedented in public education.

Our last major initiative was to jump-start innovation, something that doesn't come naturally to monopoly service providers such as public schools. To do this, we established a cluster of some two hundred schools, called the iZone (for innovation), and gave them additional funding so they could try new ways of organizing themselves, teaching students, and using technologies. In so doing, we created several new and very different school models and novel approaches to classroom teaching and learning. Nothing like this level of innovation had ever been tried in public schools.

Coupled with these were many other initiatives—ending social promotion by requiring students to show basic academic mastery before being promoted; putting a parent coordinator in each school to get parents more involved; establishing a "fair student funding" formula to ensure that school budgeting was based on individual student needs and not on other arbitrary or political considerations; surveying all of our parents, teachers, and students to get systematic feedback; and on and on. All were developed with a steady and unwavering commitment to educating the students, not protecting the adults in the system.

Collectively, these programs and policies changed the New York City schools dramatically. Although they varied in approach, they were guided by a single core belief: find great school leaders, let them choose their teachers and the strategies that will enable their students to progress, and hold them accountable for results. No longer would the adults in the system prosper if they were unwilling or unable to do right by kids. This may sound like common sense, but, in public education in America, it was truly radical.

As a result of these changes, New York, like some other cities, made real progress, but not nearly enough. America now confronts a clear choice: we can continue on the path we've been following in public education, hoping that more money and small, incremental changes will fix it, or we can get behind the kind of fundamental restructuring that this book envisions. For too long, too many with wealth and power have tolerated a broken monopoly, perhaps because it didn't directly affect their own kids, who were able to find better options. But as inequality continues to bedevil our nation, other people's kids will have an increasing impact on the kind of country we become. When discussing education and America's economic future on Fareed Zakaria's Sunday television show in December 2013, Thomas Friedman, the *New York Times* columnist, said, "I don't worry about America, I worry about Americans." He's right in his concern, but wrong in his conclusion: if we end up worrying about an increasing number of Americans because they are poorly educated and lack the skills required by the contemporary jobs market, we'll soon be worrying about America. The lessons we learned in New York can help us reverse this unsustainable course.

LESSONS OF HOPE

1

Before

I was a city kid, born in the Bronx but raised first in Brooklyn then in Queens. The home I shared with my parents and sister in Bensonhurst was an apartment across the street from the home of my grandfather Abe and my grandmother Rose. In 1953, after I turned seven, my father announced that he could no longer live near his in-laws, and our family moved to a sprawling public-housing complex in Woodside, Queens, where more than a thousand families crowded into twenty large apartment buildings.

My childhood was turbulent. My father, a postman, was unhappy with his job and frustrated by his circumstances. At unpredictable moments, but with alarming frequency, he would begin to complain; his voice would fill with anger and suddenly he was shouting about his miserable job, lack of money, our terrible apartment, his awful marriage, and how he should just leave and never come back. My parents had few friends, and my father fought with those they had, always feeling slighted by what they said or did. My mother tried to be a peacemaker, but she was afraid of my father's temper.

The tension was constant. Our family discussions were perfunctory: "How was school?" "Fine." We never read together or talked about books, and we hardly spoke about my parents' lives. I knew virtually nothing about my ancestors in Hungary and Russia, my parents' child-hoods, or my father's service in World War II, where he was wounded and was awarded the Bronze Star. I had started college before learning that my mother had been married briefly before meeting my father.

In my father's eyes, I was the vehicle for my family's progress. He was loving with me, but constantly reminded me to think big when imagining my future. We spent lots of time together, just the two of us. Since his only real interest was sports—mostly the Yankees—that became the glue that bound us. In the first seven years of my life, the team of DiMaggio, Rizzuto, Ford, Berra, and Mantle won six World Series. In the next seven years, they would capture four more. On the days when my father took me to the stadium, or during the countless hours we played ball together, I forgot about how he pressured me and treated my mom.

His expectations for me felt heavy and ever present. I knew that I was expected to achieve in ways that would redeem a life he regretted as he struggled to provide for us. Sometimes he took his frustrations out on me. The beatings, while rare, were severe and left an indelible mark. Scoldings were more frequent; though I was basically a well-behaved kid, I felt as though I was always doing something wrong. It's not easy for a child to understand how someone who gives so much love can also inflict so much pain. School—orderly and predictable—became a haven for me.

My first school, P.S. 205, occupied half a block on Twentieth Avenue in Bensonhurst and educated mainly working-class Jewish, Italian American, and Irish American kids. The groups warred against each other and often the others teamed up against the Jews. After the move to Woodside, I went to P.S. 151 in Astoria and then to neighboring Junior High School 10. During these years, I was busy looking for, and finding, adult support away from the turmoil at home. One pillar was my grandfather Abe. I spent lots of time with him, especially during summer vacations, talking about the world beyond my corner of Queens. A patient, wise man, he was a marvelous storyteller. I also found refuge at a little storefront synagogue in Astoria, where Rabbi Aryeh Jacobs taught me in Hebrew school and frequently invited me to dinners with his family. The rabbi showed me how a man could be smart, generous, and loving—and the way a family could be a place of mutual support rather than constant discord.

Just before high school, my family moved again, this time to a second-floor apartment on a busy shopping street called Sutphin Boulevard in a gritty part of Queens known as Jamaica. Buses ran up and down the boulevard on the way to a sprawling Long Island Railroad station where eight tracks converged. The LIRR is the busiest commuter railroad in the country, and more than a hundred trains passed through the Jamaica station every day. In the 1950s and '60s, most were powered by diesel and spewed a greasy smoke that coated the neighborhood with a black film. My bedroom faced the boulevard, where the buses ran all night. I can still hear them.

Because I wanted to be with the kids I knew from elementary and junior high school, I got a variance that allowed me to attend Bryant High School in Astoria, Queens. I commuted by subway, joining a community of four thousand students and teachers housed in a massive four-story block of brick and concrete. My life at Bryant was truly joyful. I earned mostly A's and joined the math and chemistry clubs, played sports, wrote for the student newspaper, and was elected president of the student union. It was there that I fell in love for the first time.

Bryant's teachers were generally good, and I remember most to this day. They inspired me to love learning, saw that I thrived on new and increasingly difficult challenges, and gave me lots of personalized attention. My physics class was taught by an extraordinary man named

Sydney Harris, who couldn't stand wasted potential. "You have so much more ability than you think you do," he told me. "I'd like to make a deal. Spend a couple afternoons a week after school with me, and I'll teach you Einstein's theory of relativity. I think you can handle it, and more."

I took the deal, and Harris turned out to be right. Einstein was followed by a National Science Foundation scholarship to a summer program at Mount Hermon, a private boarding school in rural Massachusetts. There, I entered an entirely new universe, inhabited mostly by kids from prep schools who were more worldly than people I'd previously known. I managed the academic work, doing well in a physics course and reading everything by Hemingway on my own. But I was socially uncomfortable and missed my chance at romance because I felt too intimidated by classical music to join the others on Saturday nights at nearby Tanglewood, where they socialized while listening to the Boston Symphony. I had never been to a concert; my only real cultural outings had involved a couple of school visits to museums. Even so, the summer changed me: I gained some confidence from knowing I could compete with the best academically, and I made some new friends.

In my senior year at Bryant, Sydney Harris advised me to look beyond Queens College, which my father had chosen for me because there was no tuition and I could commute from home. With Mr. Harris's encouragement, I applied to Columbia. When the thick acceptance letter arrived in April 1963, it informed me that I had won the Joseph Pulitzer scholarship, which would cover four years of tuition and require me to live on campus. The scholarship answered a prayer so precious it had never been spoken aloud. My father immediately tried to nix the idea, saying that Columbia would still be too expensive because the scholarship didn't fully cover the cost of room and board. I was nevertheless determined to go—because it was Columbia and because I had to get away from home. I would work part-time to cover any shortfall. Starting as a newspaper-delivery boy in my freshman year, I wound up a bank teller by senior year and always earned enough to get by.

MY EXPERIENCE AT COLUMBIA WAS MIXED, THOUGH IT IMPROVED as time passed. In my first year, I took a physics course with the Nobel Prize–winning professor Polykarp Kusch, who announced that any student who got all thirty-five final exam questions right could have dinner with him. Noting the lukewarm response to his challenge, he added, "You don't know what two hours of a Nobel Prize winner's time is worth." He then said that no one had aced his exam since he started teaching at Columbia in 1937. I studied as hard as I could and came one answer shy of winning dinner. This near miss reinforced my feeling that, whatever my background, I could achieve academically.

But I remained socially uncomfortable. Most of my classmates came from greater wealth and privilege and had grown up frequenting museums, attending theater and concerts, traveling, and reading the great books. Many had gone to private schools like Andover, Exeter, Choate, and St. Paul's. I had read *some* of the classics, but didn't know a Picasso from a Renoir. My classmates dressed in classic preppie clothes. I dressed like a kid from Queens, with gold pants and purple sweaters. They spoke with tight-jawed, patrician accents and laughed as they said, "Dere goes Klein. He's goin' ta da moobies."

After I was rejected by two leadership clubs—Blue Key and Van Am—I thought maybe my father was right: I should have gone to Queens College. I considered transferring but, fortunately, pulled myself together. I decided to apply to a fraternity—Alpha Epsilon Pi—and when I was accepted, several of the older members befriended me. Still, I never felt fully at home. Between working hard in my courses

and earning money in part-time jobs, I didn't have much time for social events, and I found that I didn't make many friends in college—
though a handful became close and remain so to this day. Unlike most
of my classmates, I was too intimidated to date girls from Barnard,
thinking we wouldn't have much in common.

Despite my success in Professor Kusch's class, physics couldn't compete with the promise of the law. In television programs like *Perry Mason*,
movies like *Anatomy of a Murder*, and great books like *To Kill a Mocking-
bird*, I saw inspiring advocates at work. I wanted to have an impact, to
help make society fairer and better, and the law seemed to provide a
way to do that. I also suspect that the invisible hand of my father, who
wanted me to be a lawyer and had occasionally taken me to see trials in
lower Manhattan, played a role in my decision to apply to law school.

I was accepted by several law schools and chose Harvard because it
was Harvard. Harvard would also give my father something to brag
about at the post office, even though, as it later turned out, his cowork-
ers thought I had been admitted to "Harper Law School" (Harper was
a part of the state university in New York, and it didn't have a law
school).

Harvard educated me in countless ways. I studied with legendary
teachers like Paul Bator, who taught me to think harder than I had
imagined possible, and found most classes exciting and challenging. I
became good friends with professors like Alan Stone, a psychoanalyst
who taught interdisciplinary courses, and Alan Dershowitz, the great
criminal lawyer, both of whom would have a profound impact on my
values and life.

Harvard in the late 1960s and early '70s was a place focused on ur-
gent national events, especially the war in Vietnam and the growing
disconnect between the government and its young citizens. This was a
turbulent time, one when many students became radicalized and occu-

pied or even shut down university buildings and programs. My alma mater, Columbia, was probably most heavily affected, while Harvard followed close behind.

Although I was not involved in radical groups, I went through my own time of turmoil. I took time off and decided to try my hand at teaching. I enrolled in education courses at New York University and then taught mathematics to sixth graders in Astoria, Queens, not far from where I had grown up. I loved teaching, but after being called into the army reserves, I decided to return to law school after my service. Still, those memories of teaching remain: the kids were smart and funny, the parents were engaged, and I felt challenged by preparing for class every day. Many of the kids were from immigrant families. It was the era of so-called new math. Several parents unable to help their children asked me for advice, and I suggested we meet as a group one night each week. When I asked for permission to hold these meetings, my principal told me not to do it—even though I expected no extra salary and the school was already open for evening events. The principal explained, "If you do it, the parents will expect the other teachers to do it, and they won't want to, so they will resent you." So it didn't happen. This was my first real experience with low expectations in a school and the damage they can do.

After completing my army reserve training at Fort Dix, I returned to Harvard and finished my studies. Upon graduation in June 1971, I spent a year with an extraordinary group of scholars at the Center for Advanced Study in the Behavioral Sciences at Stanford University. Before graduation, I had worked for my law professor, Alan Dershowitz, who had been selected for the Stanford program and didn't know he wasn't permitted to bring along a research assistant. Luckily, I was welcomed to stay.

Among the scholars in attendance that year was the famous Bruno

Bettelheim, a Holocaust survivor, who was one of America's most prominent psychologists and a popular writer whose work ranged from a concentration camp memoir, *The Informed Heart*, to a book about kids in an Israeli kibbutz, *The Children of the Dream*. Some of Bettelheim's ideas, especially those about autism, would eventually be discredited, but he was a profound thinker and writer whose works on the nature of childhood, the meaning of love, and other aspects of the human condition were insightful and accessible. We hit it off surprisingly well and often discussed intellectual matters—psychology, politics, history, law—as well as personal concerns. Bettelheim made two observations that affected me deeply and stayed with me forever. One was, "Most people want security—they want to make sure tomorrow is just like yesterday. You're not like that. You only want to look ahead." He said this approvingly, and it made me feel good. But he also said, "You do so well with other people, but you have to learn to do well with yourself."

Bettelheim's second statement described my tendency to look outside myself for inspiration, direction, and reassurance. Although I didn't know it at the time, the insecurity of my childhood had led me to focus my attention on others and had taught me how to meet and even exceed their expectations. Years—and a lengthy psychoanalysis— would pass before I truly understood what this meant, but Bettelheim had detected something very real. In my pursuit of success, I was almost always focused on experiences and achievements that would satisfy my father, whose demands had become internalized as my own, without my really knowing it. Had Bettelheim not helped me find my inner anchor, I wouldn't have been able to do many of the things I subsequently did in life.

After my year at Stanford, I spent the next eight months traveling throughout most of Europe and Africa funded by a fellowship awarded by Harvard. I returned to the United States in May 1973 to start my legal career, beginning with a clerkship for Chief Judge David Bazelon of the U.S. Court of Appeals in Washington, D.C. Highly respected, Bazelon was intensely focused on the rights of individuals, and he issued many important rulings in favor of the mentally ill and criminal defendants. It was Bazelon who greatly broadened the "insanity defense" and also first ruled that people placed in the care of state mental institutions had a right to treatment for their illnesses, not just custodial care.

After my clerkship with Judge Bazelon, I worked over the summer at the Mental Health Law Project, a public interest law firm advocating on behalf of the mentally disabled. Next I clerked for Supreme Court Justice Lewis Powell, a genteel and thoughtful jurist. Powell, appointed by President Nixon, was a conservative. At the time, my own politics were quite liberal. But despite our differences, I was thoroughly won over by his humility, intelligence, love of country, and sense of public service. I learned how a jurist could begin consideration of a case with his core principles, listen to arguments on all sides, think through what he believed to be right, and then work with colleagues to reach a just conclusion. Powell was a truly rare individual; as I would later say at his memorial service, "Unlike most people in Washington, D.C., when Lewis Powell danced with you, he looked in your eye, not over your shoulder to see if there was someone more important to dance with."

My only brush with conflict came as the court considered *O'Connor v. Donaldson*, a case in which a Florida man, Kenneth Donaldson, claimed the state had improperly deprived him of the right to liberty by confining him to a mental hospital without treatment, even though he was not a danger to himself or others. Having clerked for Judge Bazelon and worked at the Mental Health Law Project, I knew this kind of case well and understood that tens, if not hundreds, of thousands of people were, like Donaldson, then being unnecessarily confined in similarly harsh conditions.

Mr. Donaldson was a sympathetic figure, and the legal issues seemed clear to me. I compiled a stack of previous court rulings, medical research, and relevant academic papers, and made sure they circulated among my co-clerks. I knew, of course, that Chief Justice Warren Burger—previously Bazelon's nemesis on the court of appeals—disagreed with the lower court rulings favoring Donaldson and the right to treatment initially declared by Bazelon. Burger was eager to reverse them.

As has previously been reported, the chief justice chose to write the opinion himself and circulated a draft that would have scuttled any notion of a right to treatment. Quietly, I gathered support for Donaldson among the clerks and watched as the justices slowly lined up against the chief. Donaldson ultimately prevailed, and Bazelon's earlier right-to-treatment ruling remained as a precedent for future cases. Chief Justice Burger wrote a blistering opinion, attacking the notion of a right to treatment, but none of the other justices joined him.

The Brethren, a major book on the Supreme Court written by Bob Woodward and Scott Armstrong, dissected the Donaldson case. Knowing I was involved, Woodward interrogated me, revealing in the course of our interview that he had been misinformed on some details. Faced with allowing him to publish incorrect information, I became a source, a decision that I suspected would not please my boss, Justice Powell. I fessed up over a pleasant lunch after which Powell—a patrician, soft-spoken man—said he appreciated my candor before informing me that there were two things in life that could get a man in serious trouble: "a stiff prick and talking to the press."

AFTER THE CLERKSHIP I WENT INTO PRIVATE LAW PRACTICE
and eventually helped found two Washington law firms. The second,
originally named Onek, Klein and Farr, was started by three former
Supreme Court clerks, and our practice was devoted largely to cases on
appeal. Although we had a small firm, we were fortunate and became
enormously successful. We ended up arguing three to four cases a year
before the Supreme Court and many more before the courts of appeals
throughout the country. Our won-lost record was extraordinary; I won
nine of the eleven cases I argued before the high court. The press was
full of praise, dubbing us "The Little Firm That Could." In the late
1980s, I started teaching again, combining classes at the Georgetown
University Law Center with my caseload at the firm.

I might have remained an appellate lawyer and law professor, but a
call from the White House led me to a meeting with President Clinton's
legal counsel, with whom I subsequently served first as consultant and
then, from 1993 to 1995, as deputy counsel to President Clinton. What a
sharp contrast this was to the cerebral, academic law practice I was used
to. In the White House everything happened quickly, and politics and
the press were always shadowing policies and programs. My first lesson
came from a former White House counsel who advised me to begin
leaking information to reporters who would value me as a source and—
should the need present itself—rise to defend me. Many use this tech-
nique with real success but, as a newcomer embroiled in highly sensitive
legal and policy matters, I hesitated. Justice Powell's admonition, about
the ways a man might get in trouble, had obviously left an impression.

The White House was a swift introduction to real-world politics—a
constant mix of strategy, hardball negotiation, and insider backbiting,
all wrapped in the daily press frenzy. Looking back, I realize how the

tumult of that job prepared me for the job of schools chancellor. In White House, I worked on issues like affirmative action and CIA-FBI relations, both of which raised difficult policy and legal questions, and I was heavily involved in President Clinton's decisions to appoint Ruth Bader Ginsburg and Stephen Breyer, two distinguished jurists, to the U.S. Supreme Court. But it was the so-called Whitewater controversy, centered around a failed Arkansas real estate development company, that occupied a lot of my time. Clinton was accused of exerting undue pressure as Arkansas's governor to secure a loan for a project the Clintons had invested in. Driven in large measure by partisan politics, the controversy dragged on for years. The Clintons were never charged with wrongdoing, but the endless investigations produced tons of work, constant distraction, and frequent negative press coverage. Suffice it to say, this was a very demanding assignment, and I was ready, in the spring of 1995, to move over to the Department of Justice—something of a homecoming for me given my appellate-law background—where I started as principal deputy to Assistant Attorney General for Antitrust Anne Bingaman, and then succeeded her in that role when she left in 1996.

Charged with monitoring corporate America to prevent monopoly abuses and other anticompetitive practices, the antitrust division had the potential to make waves by challenging businesses hoping to have things their way. Bingaman attempted to revitalize the office by filing some high-visibility cases. When the president named me to head the office, many observers, including the *New York Times*, predicted that I wouldn't be aggressive enough. A *Times* editorial urged Clinton to withdraw my nomination. In fact, I did think it appropriate to recognize the legitimate needs of businesses, believing both that we should reward innovation and also evaluate practices based on real-world market considerations rather than hypothetical concerns about "bigness." But I also initiated several major cases, making clear that the Department of Justice wasn't afraid to take on powerful adversaries. By the time I left in 2000, no one—not even the *Times*—was saying we weren't tough enough. We had blocked or modified almost two hundred mergers, imprisoned fifty-two executives, collected more than $2 billion in fines, and successfully challenged many anticompetitive practices in court.

Our boldest move was against Microsoft, which dominated the marketplace for computer operating systems and programs. We charged the company with abusing its monopoly power in operating systems by bundling in separate products—in this instance, a browser—and thereby foreclosing competition for these other products. Microsoft fought back hard, mustering a huge legal team and public relations campaign. We selected a team from among our 340 attorneys, got further support from twenty state attorneys general, and brought in outside help, including David Boies, a world-class litigator.

As the biggest antitrust case in generations, the Microsoft prosecution would require an entire volume to explain. The trial, argued before Judge Thomas Penfield Jackson in Washington, D.C., was scrutinized daily by all the major media. We put on a strong case with testimony from industry witnesses, and Boies was remarkably effective in cross-examining the Microsoft witnesses. The long and arduous trial ended in autumn 1999, with the judge finding in our favor. In 2000, following our recommendation, Judge Jackson proposed to remedy the violation by breaking the company into two parts—an operating-systems company and an applications company. Ultimately, the appeals court agreed with us on the legal analysis and upheld the finding that Microsoft had abused its monopoly power, but the court rejected the break-up proposal. I would leave office as George W. Bush and the Republican Party won the White House, and others would manage the continuation of the case until it settled in late 2002.

Approaching age fifty-five, I was at the height of my career as an attorney when I left the government in October 2000. My years in the Clinton administration, especially as antitrust chief, had helped me gain some prominence in both legal and political circles. The experience had been exhilarating but challenging, and I was gratified that *The Economist* called me a "disarming revolutionary" and a "skilled politician." I was enormously grateful to President Clinton for having given me the opportunities.

While I had lots of generous offers from law firms eager to have me lead their antitrust practices, I decided this was a time for new beginnings. I was not only leaving government service after seven years, but had gone through a painful divorce, was the father of a sixteen-year-old daughter, and was about to marry Nicole Seligman, a Washington lawyer who had represented President Clinton in Whitewater and during his impeachment trial. Although I knew I wanted something different, I never could have imagined the call that would set me on a new course and plunge me into the center of a tremendous struggle—one where the stakes were and continue to be so high for all of us.

2

Everybody Deserves
a Good Education

Before the 2001 mayoral election season, Mike Bloomberg was just another very rich guy who happened to speak with a Boston accent. This should have disqualified him as a candidate for public office in New York, but in the mid-1990s, Bloomberg quietly began to show that he was more than a checkbook as he started to focus on urban issues. Taking note of the dismal state of the city schools, he began to think seriously about the challenge of fixing them. He brought the acumen of a successful businessman to the task, conducting his own research, consulting experts, and reading whatever he could get his hands on. He decided that only a strong mayor with control of the system could get the job done. "I want to fix public education," Bloomberg told Ester Fuchs, a Barnard professor who had worked in Mayor David Dinkins's administration. He added, "Everybody deserves a good education." A product of the public schools in middle-class Medford, Massachusetts, Bloomberg—like so many others—believed that one of the stones in the foundation of his own success had been a good public education.

When he decided to run for mayor in 2001, Bloomberg—a lifelong Democrat—switched parties, without abandoning his support for

Democrats like Hillary Clinton and for traditional liberal ideals like gay rights and gun control. This move startled Republican insiders. How, they thought, could Bloomberg get the GOP nomination without embracing the party platform? Republicans would never view him as one of their own. And even if he did secure the Republican spot on the ballot, how could he win a general election when the Democrats in New York City outnumbered Republicans five to one? Rudy Giuliani had ascended to the mayor's chair as a Republican, but he had long been committed to his party, and his success fighting crime as a prosecutor broadened his appeal.

Although conventional wisdom may have discounted Bloomberg's approach, he had built his reputation on being able to analyze challenges and devise unexpected solutions to problems. He was prepared to spend a lot of his own money to introduce himself to the voters, and believed he could win the GOP spot on the ballot and then pivot to offer all New Yorkers a chance to elect a centrist mayor beholden to no one and capable of building a less-corrupt and more-effective government. He stumbled a few times early in the campaign but soon demonstrated competence and optimism, which many New Yorkers found attractive. On primary day he seemed headed for the GOP nomination when the voting was disrupted by the Al Qaeda terror attacks of 9/11.

New York was physically scarred and psychically devastated by the death and destruction. I was in Germany when it happened, in a kind of shock. I needed to be with my family and friends in my city but, as no one could return to the States for several days, I remained in Europe. The city's residents came together in profound ways, manifesting a quiet resolve not to be defeated. In the last months of his tenure, then-mayor Giuliani won over even his harshest critics with his postattack leadership, becoming known as "America's mayor." Across the nation, but especially in the city, people began to feel and express a new kind of care and concern for one another and the place they called home. Most of all, they yearned to do something to help the 9/11 recovery.

When the city primary election was held on September 25, Bloomberg defeated his lone opponent by a margin of more than two to one. In the general election, Bloomberg spent more money than any candidate not seeking the presidency, making himself known and promoting his plan for businesslike efficiency for city services and sweeping improvement for the city's schools. Repeated polls showed that schools were the number one voter concern. Bloomberg's message was a winning one.

Bloomberg's election was a far more transformative moment than most people could have imagined. Rejecting the notion that New York City and its government were too big and unwieldy to be managed or improved, the new mayor began building his team with accomplished people from both the public and private sectors who would reject traditional political gamesmanship and work hard to improve things.

Assessing the schools and drawing on his previous studies, Bloomberg saw a fantastically complex system where power and authority were so splintered and irrational that it seemed to have been designed for the sole purpose of maximizing benefits for well-connected adults— politicians, unions, bureaucrats, and their friends—and blocking improvements for kids. To fix this, the new mayor first had to wrest control of the system from the thirty-two separately elected community school boards, created in 1969 in a spasm of decentralization. He would also have to get rid of the seven-member central Board of Education. Appointed by six different elected officials, the board's main duty was to select, or fire, a chancellor who, in any event, had little power over the system. Bloomberg was willing to be held accountable for the schools, but only if he could run them with his own people, in his own way.

Others had identified the kinds of problems Bloomberg saw standing between the city's children and better schools. Indeed, in the years after a 1983 federal report on education problems called A *Nation at Risk*, the entire country had engaged in a ferocious debate about underperforming schools, in which productivity and creativity had lapsed, crime was increasing, social services were failing, and, worst of all, children were losing the chance to become educated workers, partners, parents, and citizens. Bloomberg took in a system that was a tragedy both for individual children and the nation whose well-being was threatened by the situation. The middle-class core that made our country stable and supported our growth could not survive without good schools.

Among America's public school systems, New York City's ranked well below the middle when Bloomberg came into office. Only 42 percent of the city's grade-school students were proficient in reading, and just 31 percent were up to par in math. The numbers were much worse for students who were black, or Latino, or poor. These metrics were based largely on the city's own standards and, as bad as they were, were probably elevated by the political necessity of grade inflation. Not surprisingly, given how many kids fell behind each year, fewer than half graduated in four years, a number that hadn't moved in a decade.

Sadly, even basic safety was lacking; two thousand violent crimes occurred in the schools in the year before Bloomberg took office. Then there was the problem of teacher competence. Overall, 16 percent of the city's roughly eighty thousand teachers were without certification as teachers even under the truly minimal requirements that applied. Nine percent of math teachers had failed four times or more to get a passing score of 60 percent on a math certification test. In addition, lots of teachers, especially in math and science, were teaching subjects that they weren't licensed or expert in.

The physical and technological infrastructure of the schools was no better. Many of the buildings were run-down and had safety hazards: 41 percent reported major plumbing problems, and half didn't have Internet access. The school construction process was enormously cumbersome and inefficient, leading to huge cost overruns and lengthy delays before new school buildings were completed. A quarter of middle schools and high schools lacked adequate supplies or textbooks. Predictably, these problems were worse in minority and poor neighborhoods.

Who was to blame for the mess? Many of the adults in charge, including the teachers and the people who staffed the bureaucracy, liked to point to poverty and disengaged parents, and to the many social problems kids brought to school, as the reasons for low performance. The professionals in the system also tended to resist the more aggressive ideas that were then being proposed by reformers across the nation for fixing schools, like holding educators accountable for student progress and offering meaningful choices among schools for students.

Bloomberg refused to accept that any of the city's problems defied solution, and this was doubly true where the schools were concerned. In his brief inaugural speech, on January 1, 2002, delivered outdoors on a bright but freezing day, school reform was the first major item mentioned by the new mayor after his nods to dignitaries and declarations about recovering from the 9/11 attacks. He asked state and local officials, as well as the teachers union president, Randi Weingarten, to help bring the system under mayoral control. Weingarten, who had opposed the idea of mayoral control of the schools for many years, backed Bloomberg. So did many local politicians, including members of the state legislature's Black, Puerto Rican, and Hispanic caucuses, whom he lobbied personally. Though they would likely lose access to patronage jobs and overall political influence, they could see that the schools needed fixing and appreciated Bloomberg's personal commitment.

By mid-May 2002, less than six months after Bloomberg took office, the mayor had taken control. Under the new system approved by state lawmakers, local school boards were eliminated, and their powers consolidated in the hands of the mayor, who now had the authority to hire (and fire) and empower a chancellor in charge of the schools. The old central Board of Education was replaced by a new Panel for Educational Policy, which would function as an advisory group with limited power. Eight of the board's thirteen members would be appointed by the mayor, with the rest named by the city's five borough presidents. Since the mayor could dismiss his appointees and replace them with new members as he pleased, this structure gave him control of the panel. Coupled with a new contract with the teachers, which traded big pay increases for one hundred minutes more work per week, this new system of governance set the stage for the kind of reform Bloomberg hoped to achieve. All he needed to start work in earnest was his own education team.

I BECAME FRIENDS WITH THE VETERAN REPORTER MARGARET Carlson in the late 1990s, when she was working for *Time* and I was at the Department of Justice. By 2002, we knew each other well, and she believed I would be a good candidate for chancellor. She knew I had the passion and commitment to tackle thorny political and policy issues and that public education was important to me. She had seen me in action in the Clinton administration and could vouch for my credentials as a fighter, unafraid to take on big, established interests. Margaret was close to Bloomberg and asked me if I'd like her to put forward my name. Without hesitation, I said yes.

I'm the type of person who is willing to consider almost anything. However, until the moment Margaret and I spoke, my only involvement in education policy had been as a member of an informal group advising Mayor Anthony Williams on the District of Columbia's much-troubled school system. I didn't imagine myself as qualified for the top education job in New York City. Besides, I wasn't exactly available. Only eighteen months before, I had signed a five-year contract with the international media group Bertelsmann AG to serve as chairman and chief executive officer of its American corporate operations. It was a big job, and I was committed to it.

Toward the end of May 2002, shortly after he won control of the schools, Mayor Bloomberg called my office and said, "We're looking for someone to run the schools. Would you have any interest?" I told him I would be glad to talk, but I wasn't sure my background was what he needed. "I'm not a career educator," I said. "I know that," said Bloomberg with his you-think-I'm-an-idiot? voice. Then he asked if we could meet right away.

When we talked, Bloomberg stressed the once-in-a-generation opportunity made possible by mayoral control of the schools. The job of chancellor would be among the most important appointments he would make; the voters cared deeply about education and would judge him on whether he fulfilled his promise to fix the schools.

If I had been advising Mayor Bloomberg, I would have told him to leave me out of it. But I probably would also have discouraged him from taking on the problems of the schools so actively in the first place. I thought Bloomberg was a smart guy who had done a stupid thing by making himself accountable for public education. No urban school system in modern memory had come close to success—test scores and high-school graduation rates were all appallingly low—and the resistance to major change was deeply entrenched. Why would New York, the largest and in many ways most politically complex of America's cities, be able to succeed when all these others hadn't?

The meeting with the mayor, which took place at his home on Seventy-Ninth Street in Manhattan, included deputy mayors Dennis Walcott, Patti Harris, and Marc Shaw, along with Nat Leventhal, who chaired the mayor's committee on appointments. Dennis was the former head of the New York Urban League. Patti had served in Mayor Ed Koch's administration and went to work for Bloomberg in 1994. A constant presence in his work life, she had overseen his philanthropy and served, in effect, as his chief of staff. Shaw was an expert in governmental operations with deep connections in state and local government. Leventhal, an attorney, had a career in politics, serving elected officials and community groups, and had run Lincoln Center for the Performing Arts for seventeen years. Smart and focused, the mayor's people quizzed me on how I would pursue his agenda for the schools. Having studied the problem some, I drew on my reading and my own experiences in running organizations to outline what was, for lack of a better term, a philosophy of change.

I said that when it came to public education, New Yorkers, like people everywhere, cared most about their neighborhood schools. They didn't identify with the system as a whole, which was comprised of more than a thousand schools. The system was as remote to them as any big bureaucracy, but their children and their neighbors' children were dependent on local teachers, administrators, and staff to keep them safe, teach them what they needed to know, and help them grow into productive citizens. A good local school casts a glow on the surrounding community, becoming a source of pride, social energy, and even economic stability. A bad school casts a shadow, making a neighborhood less desirable for families and frustrating kids who need a good education.

Fixing New York's schools would require a new system that would hold everyone—from students, teachers, the chancellor, right up to the mayor—fully accountable. But logic and experience suggested that the central players in this new game would be those in charge of the individual schools—the school principals. Without a great leader, a school—like any other organization—doesn't work well. To make schools efficient and effective, principals needed to be empowered and supported from above to get classroom teachers up to snuff and get rid of those who couldn't hack it.

I knew enough to know that increased accountability and empowerment would be shifts likely to shock the 130,000 or so people then working in the city's schools. Long controlled by the political patronage practiced by state lawmakers, City Council members, and borough presidents, administrators within the system were accustomed to playing insider games that kept them safe in their jobs. Teachers enjoyed the protection of an extraordinarily powerful union that too often spent its time defending the worst among them. Any attempt to wipe away the old power structure would meet massive resistance because it would make everyone feel vulnerable and uncertain. But it would be necessary if the schools were going to serve the needs of children, rather than the needs of the adults who worked in or depended on them. I suspected Bloomberg knew all this, but I wanted to impress on his team that, if they didn't want to change the status quo profoundly, I wasn't their man.

There was also discussion about the wisdom of appointing a total outsider like me to fill the chancellor role. Everyone appeared to know the risks: the press could have a field day with my lack of experience and, whenever anything went wrong or disagreements flared, the mayor's critics would bring up my qualifications. I quickly acknowledged that these were real concerns but suggested there were other, potentially more important, considerations. I said they needed someone with the right experience and perspective. My guess was that the existing crop of leaders, talented educators perhaps, had become accustomed to the system—and the politics that tend to drive it. They were not likely to break the status quo. Unlike the careerists, I was willing to take on those who resisted change because I wasn't looking to stay in the field and wasn't worried about my next job. I would surround myself with a strong team, including career educators, whose skills and experience could supplement what I brought to the table.

Although Bloomberg and his team seemed generally to agree with my views, I left the meeting thinking that nothing would come of it. I had heard that some big names in education were under consideration for the job, including former Chicago schools chief Paul Vallas and Barbara Byrd-Bennett, who was a veteran of the New York system and then headed Cleveland's city schools. I figured that even if Bloomberg was prepared to take a risk, cooler heads would convince him not to. So slim did I think my chances were that, after the meeting, I called my wife, Nicole, to tell her we should move forward with a deal for an apartment based on my Bertelsmann salary.

Nicole had come to respect my gut reactions and assumed there would be no offer. Except for my daughter, Julia, no one has as good a sense of me as my wife does, and I had felt this way from the moment we started dating in Washington. I met Nicole when Margaret Carlson invited me to the White House Correspondents' Dinner in April 2000. We were married in November 2000, and ever since she has been my best source of support, wise counsel, and love. Like me, Nicole is a realist; she understands how politics works. As an attorney at the fabled Williams & Connolly firm, she had represented Oliver North, Bill and Hillary Clinton, Richard Trumka, and many prominent media clients. In 2001, she became chief counsel at Sony in New York. Experience in the upper echelons of power led her to conclude that I was a long shot for the schools job. And like me, she almost forgot about the possibility.

As spring turned to summer, Bertelsmann's business kept me on the move, and I found myself at a company meeting in Berlin during the middle of July. While still in Europe, I got a call from Deputy Mayor Dennis Walcott that surprised me. He said, "The boss is serious." I was excited because I knew I wanted the job. Bloomberg had the vision to create a new kind of system for the city and I wanted to be a part of it. I returned to New York to wait it out. Later I learned that the mayor had settled on me almost immediately after my interview. "He was serious about 'No more business as usual,'" Patty Harris recalled. "He didn't care whether someone was from inside the education establishment. What he wanted was someone who would be a fighter and work with the mandate to do bold and controversial things."

On Thursday, July 25, Bloomberg called. "Can I buy you a cup of coffee?" he asked. We met around the corner from Bertelsmann, in a restaurant on Forty-Fourth Street off Broadway. The mayor got right to the point.

"Would you like to do this?" he asked.

I told him I wanted the job. I confessed I was a bit concerned about taking a big pay cut as I left the executive suite for public service, having just bought a new apartment. I asked if I would be eligible for the $10,000-per-month housing allowance my predecessor, Harold Levy, had received. The mayor said, as only he could, "Forget it—it will look bad, and it's not a lot of money, in any event."

The money in truth wasn't an issue, but I was under contract with Bertelsmann, and I needed to talk to my boss Thomas Middelhoff before accepting the city job. When we spoke, the conversation was strained. "You and I are going to transform Bertelsmann," he said. "You can't leave me now. If you do, it will be a betrayal."

Middelhoff was about to travel to Mallorca, where he had been summoned to meet with the company's owners, with whom he had had

some heated disagreement, some of which spilled into the public domain. I suspected they were going to ask for his resignation. If so, my
departure would not be a betrayal but rather an appropriate response to
changing conditions. I was Middelhoff's man in America and his successor would likely want to replace me. The next morning Middelhoff
called to say he would be resigning. Although I still had three-plus
years left on my Bertelsmann contract, with a guaranteed salary of
more than $2 million per year, I accepted the mayor's offer without a
moment's hesitation.

THE MAYOR CHOSE TO ANNOUNCE MY APPOINTMENT ON MON-
day, July 29, 2002, at the old New York County Courthouse, known as
Tweed, which had just been renovated so that it could house a new
school administration office. Rudy Giuliani had redone the building
with the intention of making it a museum, but Bloomberg switched
gears to show his personal commitment to the newly established Department of Education by making this glorious building its headquarters. The old headquarters, at 110 Livingston Street in Brooklyn, was
Kremlin-like in appearance and had come to symbolize all that was
considered wrong with the school system. Bloomberg moved us to the
courthouse and put 110 Livingston Street up for sale.

The Tweed Courthouse took its name from the notoriously corrupt
nineteenth-century political boss William Tweed. Fewer than fifty
steps from City Hall, the location made it easy for my team to consult
with the mayor's. At the announcement, Bloomberg said we would "deliver to this city what we promised—a quality education for all of our
children." For my part, I thanked my own teachers for helping to make
this day possible and committed to do "all that I can to give each child
in the city of New York a first-rate education." In the questioning that

followed, a reporter asked me, "Who are your heroes?" I hadn't prepared for such a question, but immediately responded, "Lewis Powell, for whom I served as a law clerk, and Sydney Harris, my high-school physics teacher."

No one in the media, or education circles, expected my appointment. Some thought the mayor had chosen *Joe* Klein, famous as the author of *Primary Colors*, a roman à clef about Bill Clinton's first campaign for president. One professor at Columbia University's Teachers College told the *New York Times* that I would have to prove that I was a friend of the schools, not an enemy. "He has no history with the education people," said Ruth Vinz. "He doesn't even know the rhetoric."

Others thought that my outsider status wasn't such a bad idea. Non-educators had enjoyed some recent success running schools. Former federal prosecutor Alan Bersin, for instance, was doing quite well in San Diego. The *New York Times'* education writer Anemona Hartocollis noted my experience attacking monopolies at the Justice Department and asked if there was a bigger monopoly than the public school system. "It is a government-regulated system," she wrote. "It controls everything from bus contracts to teachers." The mayor's people let it be known that he appreciated my experience tackling difficult problems that seemed to defy solution.

Overall, the press coverage of my appointment was positive, and it left me feeling as if I was going to get a fair shot. Even the United Federation of Teachers president Randi Weingarten seemed to support me as she told the press, "Let the guy get his bearings."

WITH LITTLE MORE THAN A MONTH BEFORE SCHOOL WAS TO begin, I shifted into high gear. I needed to meet with a wide array of people who wanted to brief the new chancellor and I had to assemble a core team to hit the ground running in September. This latter piece was especially difficult: it's one thing to put together a team in a field where you've worked and know the players; it's a very different thing to do it when you're entirely new to an area.

Fortunately, the mayor had already assigned Deputy Mayor Dennis Walcott to work with me. Dennis quickly became a real partner and, ultimately, a de facto member of my team. This wasn't inevitable. City Hall oversight is always a tricky business, and relationships between agency heads and deputy mayors can be tense. It's natural for people in a mayor's immediate circle to look out for his interests and to want to make sure that they keep a tight rein on what's going on. Deputy mayors can have their own priorities and can be aggressive in pursuing them. They also may think, perhaps correctly, that agency heads are not sufficiently attuned to the political issues that the mayor and his deputies have to manage.

I worked closely with Dennis for my entire tenure, and none of these kinds of frictions ever materialized. A deeply caring and thoughtful man, Dennis was impossible to rattle. Even when Bloomberg got angry, as sometimes happened when we screwed things up, Walcott remained calm. As a former head of the Urban League, who had been heavily involved in city politics and was experienced in dealing with sensitive racial issues, Dennis knew the key players—public and private—in the city and the state. The mayor trusted him completely, and I quickly learned to value his wisdom and loyalty.

Beyond Dennis, I was lucky to immediately find two young people who were eager to join my team: David Yarkin, a talented communications professional from Bertelsmann whom I had met through Margaret Carlson, and Matt Onek, the son of my former law partner and a recent Yale Law School graduate. I got additional help from John Doerr, the famous venture capitalist, whom I had met during my antitrust days. He called to say he was sponsoring a school-reform investment group called the New Schools Venture Fund, which had a summer associate from Stanford named Kristen Kane, who knew education and was as sharp as they come. John said Kristen would be willing to spend the rest of the summer helping me get organized. As it turned out, both Matt and Kristen stayed for years, rose up the ranks, and contributed much to our effort. Kristen became my most reliable internal operations person, coordinating almost all of our key initiatives. Matt oversaw the external work, including public relations and our communications with City Hall and other government agencies. Kristen and Matt got married in 2007, something we always list as among our administration's great achievements.

As I pulled together a senior team, I was mindful of the legendary CEO Jack Welch's advice to "hire slowly and fire quickly." Although this normally makes sense, I didn't have the luxury of time: schools were opening soon; the mayor and city would want to know we were staffed up and ready. I decided I needed a five-member senior team to start: three deputies—one for teaching and learning, one for finance and administration, one for operations and planning—a chief of staff, and a senior policy adviser. The most important hire, in terms of public perception as well as the scope of the position, would be the teaching and learning deputy. This was the person who would be responsible for academic issues—curriculum, classroom practice, principal and teacher support, and professional development. He or she would have direct supervisory authority for running the schools.

Without question, this was the hardest job to fill. In the end, I choose Diana Lam, who was then superintendent in Providence, Rhode Island, and had previously run several other school districts, including San Antonio, where she had gotten good results. Diana, an immigrant from Lima, Peru, was a tough, no-nonsense educator who wasn't afraid to take on powerful interests when necessary. Although I could tell she wasn't very trusting of others—in our discussions, she had kept her cards close to the vest—I admired her persistence and commitment to children. She contributed significantly to our work, but it became clear over time that the fit wasn't right.

I rounded out the rest of the team by selecting Michele Cahill as senior adviser, Kathleen Grimm as deputy for finance and administration, Tony Shorris as deputy for operations and planning, and Marcelite Harris as my chief of staff. Cahill was then running educational philanthropy for the Carnegie Foundation and had long been a major player in the education reform movement in New York City. She knew policy and I learned an enormous amount from her about education. Kathleen Grimm was working for state comptroller Carl McCall when I met her. She had a long history inside the complex budget and finance worlds of New York government and knew how to navigate the bureaucracy. Cool and effective, Kathleen stayed for the full twelve years of the Bloomberg administration and did a tough, unglamorous job with distinction. Tony Shorris, deputy chancellor for my predecessor, Harold Levy, enjoyed a reputation as a politically savvy operator who knew how to get things done. He served me well during the transition period, providing stability in the central organization while watching over day-to-day operations.

Marcy Harris was a former two-star general in the air force (the first African American woman ever to achieve that rank). Alan Bersin, the head of San Diego's schools, had recommended I hire someone with Marcy's credentials, advising that the military background would help bring much-needed discipline to a bureaucracy that was bound to resist the kinds of big changes we had in mind. In this instance, unfortunately, her inflexibility became her undoing, and she left soon after she began.

The mayor and I announced the team on August 28, 2002. The reaction in the media was generally favorable, although reporters were perplexed that we had accomplished it all in true Bloomberg fashion—without leaks to the press. I was elated: I had been on the job for less than a month, and a lot had been accomplished. In addition to assembling a team, I had consulted widely with political leaders, major players inside the school system—including most of the existing community superintendents—representatives from community and faith-based groups, and school-reform experts throughout the country. I had worked grueling, sixteen-hour days to get the job done, but the result was worth every second of it. School was about to open, and we were ready.

3

No One Knows
Anything

For some kids, the first day of the school year brings feelings of loss—a summer vacation is ending—and anxiety about the new teachers, classmates, and challenges that await. As a kid I never felt that way. For me, a return to the classroom had always meant the excitement of a new beginning. Needless to say, my first day of school as chancellor was a little different. Suddenly, I found myself responsible for the education of 1.1 million kids. I would be graded by millions of New Yorkers, not to mention interested parties across the country. And my boss, the mayor, was depending on me to begin an era of reform. His reelection and, more important, his place in history would depend in no small part on how well I did my job.

The magnitude of the challenge was hard to grasp. Not only is New York City the largest school district in the nation, outdistancing its closest rival, Los Angeles, by more than three hundred thousand students, but it was also one of the most complicated. Some of New York's communities are relatively wealthy and have strong, stable schools. Others are poor, often with more transient populations and poorly performing schools. Most of the kids who attend the city's schools are from families whose incomes are below or near the poverty level, and almost three quarters of them are black or Latino. Many Latino kids, along with a considerable portion of the Asian population, don't speak English. In fact, more than 150 different languages are spoken by the students and their families in the New York City schools. Just communicating with such a diverse population would be a daunting task.

In addition to its enormous complexity, the city school system was directly under the influence, if not control, of very strong forces. The unions, especially the United Federation of Teachers (UFT), were accustomed to getting their way. The UFT alone had almost two hundred thousand members, including close to eighty thousand full-time teachers plus another eighteen thousand paraprofessionals who served as classroom aides. With such a large membership, the UFT had lots of dues monies to spend on elections, publicity campaigns, and strategic advisers. Like the unions, the politicians—mostly Democrats—were also very influential. Not surprisingly, they invariably had strong ties to the unions as well as to the superintendents and other high-level officials who ran the school system before Bloomberg. These forces weren't about to disappear. Notwithstanding mayoral control, they would fight against any changes that threatened their interests.

Going in, I was determined that two core values—equity and excellence for all students—would guide our work. Equity, long missing from the public schools, was our first priority, but we were determined not to compromise excellence in pursuit of it. Although the chancellor's job came with a high level of visibility, including the kind of press attention that I had never experienced, I saw no reason to change the basic values I had brought to my work since my law school days. At Harvard I had taken courses dealing with the interplay of law and psychiatry taught by Professor Alan Stone, a psychiatrist/psychoanalyst. Stone favored, among other books, John Rawls's A *Theory of Justice*, which could be boiled down to two main concerns: equality and fairness. Inherent in Rawls's work are the notions that individuals expect equality of treatment and that society can function only when people believe it is essentially fair. Corruption and conflict arise amid inequality and also when people feel that a system—the New York City Department of Education, for example—is not fair.

This sense of unfairness permeated perceptions about the city's schools. For example, most everyone knew that getting into a good school often depended on having the right connections with someone inside the system (a superintendent or principal) or outside it (a politician). Some people, typically in the more affluent communities, were better able to pull strings. This was neither fair nor equal. More broadly, people in poorer communities believed that more resources, including better teachers and nicer buildings, were going to the schools in the wealthier communities. Tellingly, when middle-class communities became disenchanted with the public schools in the 1980s, the city had responded by creating a substantial number of magnet schools and programs for higher-performing kids. At the middle- and high-school levels, these schools and programs established demanding academic admissions requirements that most kids from the poorer communities couldn't meet. These so-called screened schools and programs provided higher-performing kids with attractive new choices that kept many of them in the public school system. But nothing comparable was done for struggling students in the poorer communities. For them, the only hope was their neighborhood school, period. This, too, was neither fair nor equal.

Not unsurprisingly, from day one, I came under pressure from politicians who wanted favors. An assemblyman took me aside after a hearing and said, "Protect this principal's job and I'll protect you politically." I told him, perhaps naively, that I didn't need protection. Another assemblyman demanded I move his daughter, a teacher, to a new school that she preferred. I told him I wouldn't. When a borough president couldn't get children placed in certain schools, he called to ask, "What happened to constituent services?" I jokingly replied, "We probably forgot about that in our reorganization." He said, "Fuck you, why can't we work together?" This was a new way of doing business, and the politicians weren't happy with it.

Given the scope of the changes we were contemplating, I knew I would have to devote a sizable portion of my time to explaining our approach to affected constituencies and the public in general. I would have to be a constant presence on television selling our message of reform. I would have to communicate effectively with the press, attend community and church functions, and respond personally to parents, principals, teachers, and others who e-mailed me. Everyone, it seemed, had my e-mail address.

Each day I awakened at 6 a.m. and answered e-mails for an hour. Then, typically, I would head to Tweed, where I spent at least another couple of hours answering more e-mails. People were amazed that I responded to hundreds and hundreds of e-mails each day, but I found that it kept me abreast of what was really going on in the field, and it built confidence, especially with parents, who felt that at least the chancellor was listening and responding to them. Every week I attended several community and school events, where I tried to connect with people. I would discuss our goals and values, explain how we expected our actions would affect them, and, I hoped, leave no doubt about our commitment to their kids.

To bring about the changes we planned, I knew we would have to be creative, flexible, and open-minded—and be prepared to take risks and fail. We would inevitably try some things that wouldn't work. Change entails risk, and it was likely that people would accuse us of "experimenting" on kids or, when things didn't work, focus on our failures. No successful large urban school system offered a model for success. We had to be prepared to try new approaches and quickly change course if they didn't work.

ONE KEY FACTOR OBVIOUSLY SLOWING CHANGE—VOLUMINOUS, complex, and confounding union work rules that micromanaged virtually everything that happened inside a school—remained a crucial concern, making positive changes on behalf of students more difficult than necessary. Like anyone who first encounters the teachers' contract in New York City, I had trouble believing that certain parts of it were real. For instance, fully half of all job openings in the schools could be claimed by veteran teachers solely on the basis of seniority. It didn't matter whether the principal or other faculty wanted to hire the teacher for the job. And it didn't matter that a particular teacher had bad evaluations at other schools or a string of complaints trailing him. If he wanted the job, and he had seniority, he got the job. The process was so ridiculous that, even midyear, after a terrific new teacher had been hired, she could be bumped out of her job by a more senior teacher in search of a placement. If the kids suffered as a result of the change, so be it.

Many senior teachers looking for spots had been "excessed" by other schools. An excessed teacher hadn't been fired. Instead, her job had been eliminated, ostensibly through no fault of her own, and she was therefore eligible to claim an opening elsewhere. Insiders talked about an annual ritual—called the dance of the lemons—in which unwanted instructors were "excessed" and shuffled around. Good teachers were never excessed and the young, inexperienced ones invariably were already in the toughest assignments where they suffered burnout at a shockingly high rate. Children who attended schools dominated by excessed and inexperienced teachers paid the price.

In September 2002, right after I started, the principal of a Manhattan high school recruited two new science teachers who had voluntarily participated in a two-week summer training program without being paid. They were eager to work at the school, and the principal was thrilled to have them. Several weeks into the new school year, however, the principal received a call from our human resources office and was told that the two new teachers were out and had to be replaced by two excessed teachers, one of whom had just received an unsatisfactory performance rating at another school. Hard as it is to believe, this kind of thing happened all the time.

In my second year, I met with three principals from high-performing schools on the East Side of Manhattan. I asked them, "What is the worst thing I've done so far?" They all said, "You sent us excessed teachers from another school." I replied, "I oppose that policy, but it's in the union contract, so we don't have a choice." To which they responded, "In the past, we never got excessed teachers, because everyone knew our community wouldn't tolerate them." I then asked, "Well, what should I do with them?" To which they replied, "That's your problem. Just don't send them to us." But the truth is, it wasn't just my problem; it was a problem for kids in poor neighborhoods who in the past had disproportionately gotten these excessed teachers whom no one wanted.

Worse than the lemons were teachers who had earned such serious complaints—including sexual abuse of students—that they were under disciplinary review. Because the union contract called for a Kafkaesque arbitration system, with dozens of steps and procedures that limited how quickly things could move, we couldn't legally fire, or stop paying, these teachers for years. To keep them away from students, school officials barred the worst from classroom assignments and required them to appear every morning at special reporting centers—euphemistically called rubber rooms—where they idled away their time. On any given day, hundreds of teachers dwelled in these places, doing nothing, in order to receive their pay and benefits. The problem of the rubber rooms was so outrageous that the press periodically checked in on the practice and reported with utter amazement that it was still going on. In 2000, before Bloomberg became mayor, the *Daily News* discovered that 372 teachers were reporting to rubber rooms, where they spent school days "watching Jerry Springer, playing jacks, counting ceiling tiles, whatever."

All of this insanity was made necessary by contract provisions, reinforced under state law, governing how and when a teacher can be terminated. To fire a single teacher took an average of almost two and a half years and cost the city over $300,000. Even after enduring this lengthy process, the city usually couldn't fire the teacher. The arbitrators who decided these cases had to be approved by the union, which had no interest in selecting people who would fire teachers. This made it virtually impossible to remove a teacher charged with incompetence. A recent study showed that, between 1997 and 2007, only twelve teachers were terminated for incompetence, or about one per year out of a workforce of more than seventy-five thousand. According to the author, who examined the record of every case, "Teachers who had years of 'unsatisfactory' ratings; who were proven over months of hearings to be grossly incompetent; who were verbally and physically abusive to children, parents, and colleagues, or who simply failed to come to work for days and weeks on end were returned to the classroom." The study concluded, "In practice, teachers are dismissed only if they are proved to have been grossly ineffective and 'incorrigible,' without even a remote possibility of improving."

(At Governor Cuomo's behest, the legislature in New York amended the law in 2012 to help speed up the process, but it still takes way too long, and, in the end, almost no teacher is removed for incompetence.)

The lemons and the denizens of the rubber rooms not only deprived students of the good teachers they deserved, but they also cost a fortune. Even at the low end of the pay scale, each year that one of these teachers remained on our payroll amounted to the equivalent of three thousand new textbooks or eight hundred classroom computers. We were dealing with well over a thousand of them annually.

The union contract controlled numerous other aspects of school life, including when principals can observe teachers in classrooms or review their lesson plans; which grade a teacher can be required to teach; who can be assigned to extra duties, including after-school programs; and so on. For example, if a principal wanted to select her best reading teacher to run a remedial program, she couldn't. She'd have to choose her most senior teacher, even if he was no good. The contract itself was more than two hundred pages and incorporated almost a thousand pages of addenda. The guiding principle was that rules, rather than trust, were the best way to run a school. The union dismissed out of hand the idea that a principal might observe a teacher or review a lesson plan in order to help the educator improve and instead held firm to the cynical belief that these were all adversarial moves designed to unfairly discipline the teacher.

But trust is essential to running any organization well, including schools. Tony Bryk, a well-known and distinguished education researcher, did a major study of the Chicago schools in the 1990s and concluded that trust among the adults was the defining characteristic in determining whether a school made academic gains for its students. This is hardly surprising news but is still largely ignored in most schools where rules, grievances, and due process proceedings are the operational hallmarks under the union contracts that govern them.

Even the principals, who should hold operational power in a school, were constrained by politics and union rules. I was amazed to learn that they weren't allowed to pick their own assistant principals. Those jobs were controlled by the district superintendents. Between the work rules protecting teachers, the fact that principals couldn't hire or fire even their own assistants, and the constant top-down management from the bureaucrats, the principals were actually the weakest players in the whole system. In addition, although principals functioned as managers of their schools, they were still required to belong to a union. Remarkably, they were put in the same union as the assistant principals, who outnumbered them by almost three to one. The union brass, who could do the arithmetic, generally made sure to prioritize the interests of the assistants. For example, if a principal wanted to fire an assistant principal, the union could make that nearly impossible.

The trouble that public unions could potentially cause for citizens was one reason that President Franklin Delano Roosevelt, hero of Democrats and union organizers alike, opposed them for government workers. Republican Fiorello La Guardia, a great mayor of New York, opposed them, too. Unlike in the private sector, where unions were a needed counterweight to strong management, in the public sector unions had a big say in selecting management through the election process. As a result, they had a lot of power on both sides of the labor-management negotiating process. Roosevelt and La Guardia thus feared that, when government officials and unions battled over power, citizens could lose out.

For decades this is what had happened in New York when mayors sought to please both the teachers union and taxpayers with hidden goodies that allowed them to get a contract without granting a big pay raise. In one case, a mayor who preceded Bloomberg gave the teachers an extra week off, with pay, in February. He could say he saved tax money by withholding wage increases, but families suddenly had to find child care during that week, and kids missed a week of schooling that most of them sorely needed. In another negotiation, a different mayor gave teachers the option of investing retirement funds in an account guaranteed to pay 8.25 percent interest. It didn't matter if the market rate was half, or a quarter, of this amount. The city just guaranteed the return and pushed the price of paying it off into the future. These kinds of actions repeated over the years, along with crippling pension commitments, fewer workdays, and job security protections like tenure and seniority, were the legacy of the mutual back-scratching that took place between the unions and the politicians.

These bizarre and often paralyzing rules and practices were everywhere, and the more I learned about them, the more I began to appreciate how difficult it would be to turn the system around. Looking to buck myself up, I was eager to hear some news about an urban district where things were getting better. I took a field trip to San Diego to see Alan Bersin, who had made great strides in four years as superintendent of the nation's eighth-largest school district. Like me, Alan was a lawyer by training and a former prosecutor who had been hired because he had experience dealing with extremely difficult and complex problems. He wisely brought in a thoughtful and talented New Yorker, Anthony Alvarado, who had transformed one of New York's local school districts before serving briefly as chancellor, to work as his number two.

In San Diego, Bersin and Alvarado had moved fast in pursuit of results. Instead of the gradual change Alvarado had introduced in New York with cooperation from the union, they instituted a sweeping program of teacher training and quickly fired more than a dozen principals. A new, comprehensive curriculum that emphasized reading was installed, and teaching coaches were added at every school. Bersin and Alvarado also expanded charter and alternative school opportunities for students. Amid protests by some teachers and community leaders, student test scores began to improve.

I left San Diego with not only a better understanding of the problems faced by reformers, but also of the particular difficulties encountered by the rapid pace set by Bersin and Alvarado. They were under pressure to produce immediate results because they enjoyed the support of just three of the five members of their district's elected school board. If one switched sides, or was ousted in an election by a reform opponent, they would likely lose their jobs. In contrast, my position was secure for as long as the mayor was satisfied, and he had been elected to a four-year term. That meant I could afford to be even more aggressive than Bersin and Alvarado. In a city where, despite very low requirements, fewer than half the kids in the third grade can read at grade level and fewer than half ultimately graduate from high school in four years, I had to be.

RETURNING FROM SAN DIEGO WITH EXCITEMENT AND OPTIMISM, I was now ready to fix my sights on the immediate challenge before us—opening more than twelve hundred schools. I selected Kristen Kane, the young woman whom John Doerr had sent my way, to serve as point person for this assignment. Kristen had become fascinated by the challenges in education when she was in college. But unlike many others, she didn't go into teaching. Instead, she immersed herself in the world of finance, hoping to find new ideas for funding innovations that, if proven effective, might be deployed across the education landscape.

I could see that Kristen was astonished by the obstacles we faced. The district superintendents all ran large field offices, each of which operated according to its own procedures, and the organizational structures and quality of the personnel varied widely. In some places, competent managers took pride in their work and managed operations quite efficiently. In others, the phones went unanswered, and no one ever took responsibility for anything. These were, in essence, mini-fiefdoms run by the superintendents with little, if any, interference from the chancellor's office.

Many of the people who survived in this system tended to soldier on in a state of resignation and defensiveness. Frustrated and powerless, they nevertheless hoped to hold on to their jobs, and their paychecks, until they reached retirement age and a good lifetime pension. In order to do this, they sought to avoid notice and accountability. This wasn't so much a conscious approach as a matter of adaptation. Put enough time in, and you learn to shift problems to someone else, while forming protective alliances with fellow workers. The system of scattered districts overlaid by duplicative functions at the central office made the bureaucracy so diffuse that it was almost impossible to discover who was responsible for anything.

Just as school was about to start, I gave my first formal address to some thirty-five hundred new teachers—about half the number of new teachers who were set to begin work in the city schools. Gathered at the Theater at Madison Square Garden, they were mostly young, recent college graduates. Thanks to the new contract the mayor had negotiated with the UFT, which had raised starting salaries to almost $40,000, nearly all of our new hires had passed the state test to be certified as teachers, though many were still not licensed to teach the subjects they would be assigned to teach. Nevertheless, having almost all certified teachers was a first for the city.

I began my remarks by telling these new teachers they were an incredible and talented group ready for the job that awaited them. "I use the word *job*, but it is not a job," I added. "It's truly a mission, because the education of young people is one of the greatest challenges and responsibilities we as a nation and you as an individual teacher face."

After I talked, the teachers heard from Randi Weingarten, who was president of their union, the United Federation of Teachers. The UFT was the largest teachers bargaining unit in the country, and Weingarten, whose mother had been a teacher, was one of the most visible labor leaders in the country. She and her two predecessors, Albert Shanker and Sandra Feldman, were primarily responsible for the labor contract that controlled so much of what we could and could not do in the schools. In her address, Randi told the teachers that they were the most gifted class of newcomers ever recruited to serve the city schools. She then sounded a few notes of warning, which seemed to encourage them to be wary of the year ahead. "Don't lose your soul, don't lose your common sense, and don't lose your love of yourself and your job."

I wished Randi had sounded more encouraging, but I understood where she was coming from. Having grown up as the son of a postal worker's union member, and then gone on to serve as a lawyer for the union that represented employees in southern textile mills, I knew that many workers harbored feelings of mistrust toward their employers and counted on their union to be there to protect them against an imperious boss. Still, I found it a little jarring when I heard this kind of thinking applied to a profession like teaching.

Soon after the Garden event, Randi and I sat down for our first lunch. After exchanging pleasantries, I asked her, "What's your view of the appropriate pace of change for reform?" She immediately replied, "Sustainable and incremental change." As Randi would later recall, I cringed and said, "No, no, it must be radical reform." I don't know about cringing, but I was indeed looking for "radical" reform: the system was unquestionably broken. "Incremental" sounded to me like code for keeping the status quo largely intact, meaning the results wouldn't change much, either.

But we were just at the beginning, and, although I was disappointed by her view, I was determined not to reach any quick conclusions. I liked Randi personally—she was whip smart and uncharacteristically blunt for someone in the public school power structure—and I was being told that she was someone we could work with. She had already supported mayoral control, a gutsy move for a union leader who might see her own power—and, derivatively, that of her members— diminish as a result. So I decided not to take her comment too seriously and instead to wait to see what she would do when we made concrete proposals.

THE SCHOOLS OPENED IN SEPTEMBER 2002 WITH NARY A HITCH. This was due in part to the care and diligence of Kristen and her team, but I also suspected the district superintendents had gone above and beyond, each hoping to impress the new chancellor. I was now free to focus with my team on our reorganization and reform priorities. I had a brief honeymoon period and would have to act quickly. Bloomberg favored fast and dramatic action over long-term deliberations and incremental moves. With this in mind, we immediately sought and received a $4 million grant from the Eli and Edythe Broad and Julian Robertson Foundations to hire experts in education policy and finance, along with the consulting firm of McKinsey & Company, to help us understand the day-to-day operational challenges we faced. McKinsey sent more than a hundred investigators to schools and offices across the city to find out what was actually going on.

We also used the money to fund a massive community outreach program. During the fall and early winter of 2002, we met with families and interested citizens in every community in the city. We saw hundreds, if not thousands, of people at a time, and found them eager to tell us their views about what needed to be fixed in the public schools. All told, we heard from some fifty thousand people, mostly parents of kids. Not surprisingly, they didn't focus on systemic issues like the role of the bureaucrats, politicians, or unions, but on practical things like more choices, better buildings, more supplies, smaller classes, and new programs. Nothing on this scale had previously been tried in the city, and the fact that we were reaching out so broadly bought us goodwill with families and communities.

During the day, when we were not digesting parental input, we were reviewing what McKinsey was learning in the field. The McKinsey researchers had been shocked to discover that the schools were managed with the same types of paper-based reporting and information systems that were common in the 1950s and '60s. E-mails were still considered unusual inside the system, and very few administrators used up-to-date budgeting and cost-control software. It took six months to collect data on how many kids ate school lunch on a given day. It seemed no one in the system really knew anything for certain.

This dearth of data explained, to a large degree, why so many education problems were being ignored. In New York, and many other places, basic information—like individual student test scores—was not even shared with teachers and principals in time for them to be used as a guide for classroom assignments at the start of the next school year. Worse, lots of pertinent information was never shared at all by the city, state, and federal officials who collected it to track a district's compliance with guidelines for grants and other monies. The flow of data was almost all one way—up and out—rather than being used to help specific kids and teachers. Many adults in the system were happy with this situation. They had no desire to obtain data on school, teacher, and student performance because they feared being compared with their peers and being held accountable.

I personally encountered the data problem during my early days when I tracked down the person in charge of information collection and analysis. Lori Mei, who ran the office of accountability, was a good data analyst, but she was also a realist. When I told her I wanted to run some numbers to find out which teachers were getting the best results in high-poverty schools, she said, "I can't do that." When I asked her what the problem was, she added, "The union doesn't let us do things like that."

We forged ahead nevertheless, getting what data and information we could from McKinsey, while pressing the bureaucracy as hard as possible for the information it had. Based on all of this work, we co-alesced around an initial set of reforms that we would pursue. Because we wanted people to know we planned, always, to prioritize the needs of students, we chose to call our agenda Children First. We said our aim was "not a great school system, but a system comprised of great schools," and we made clear that the individual school would be the key link in our organizational structure. We would focus on principal recruitment and training because, without good leadership, we couldn't have good schools. We also knew that we had to take operating control away from the district superintendents and to bring coherence to the chaotic mishmash of academic standards and curricula throughout the city. Those moves were necessary to disrupt the established, balkan-ized, and still too politically driven order, and they would also provide the organizational control needed to implement the next changes that we were contemplating. Finally, we had to figure out how to get parents more involved in their children's education. These would be our first major initiatives.

4

A System of
Great Schools

*An Italianate landmark restored to be both beautiful and func-*tional, the Tweed building in Manhattan was so vastly superior to the old Education Department building on Livingston Street in Brooklyn that the resistance put up by those who were asked to move seemed, at first, completely irrational. Tweed featured marble-and-glass-tile floors and brightly lit spaces. Our offices would be organized around the "bullpen" model favored by Mayor Bloomberg, which meant that top officials would work in big open spaces divided by low walls. The idea was to foster teamwork and conversation. Naturally, long-tenured bureaucrats accustomed to the secrecy and intrigue at the 110 Livingston labyrinth would be unnerved by the bullpens at Tweed. They felt they'd be observed and monitored. However, the core group of deputies and special assistants whom I had hired to work with me would thrive. We had a mission to pursue and shared a common sense of purpose. In the bullpen we could learn from one another in a way that would be impossible if we were separated into small, enclosed offices with doors that could be shut, and even locked.

The openness at Tweed was a terrific antidote to the bureaucratic blockades that had long shielded school officials from the public. A great illustration of how the old way worked against solving problems arose during the two weeks I had spent at 110 Livingston, when, literally on my very first day in office, I looked at my phone and saw a light blinking to indicate a caller on hold. After a few minutes I finally asked one of the staff assistants, who was a holdover from the previous administration, about the caller. "Oh, ignore that," I was told. "It's just an angry parent. If we leave it on hold long enough she'll go away."

As it turned out, the most exciting thing about being housed in Tweed was the mayor's decision to put a school right there, on the ground floor. It was a bolt of genius. He said he wanted all the adults who worked there to enter the building through the school "so they would be reminded daily that they were there to serve the kids, and for no other purpose." The school was designed for elementary students, grades K–5. It was majestic, with seven large, brightly lit classrooms plus a lunchroom and direct access to City Hall Park, which became a playground for the kids. My favorite classroom had a huge map of the city painted on the floor that kids eagerly used to show off where they and their friends lived. I spent many hours visiting those classrooms, watching lessons, and talking with kids and teachers. But I must confess, my favorite times were when I joined the kids in the park and played ball or jumped rope with them. I kept a picture on my desk of several kids, mouths agape, clearly astonished that the chancellor would—much less could—jump rope.

Beyond Tweed, I would frequently encounter numerous other students during school visits, and they wouldn't hesitate to tell me what worked and what didn't. Many wanted more extracurricular activities and off-site visits, quite a few complained about their teachers, and almost none liked school lunches. One of my favorite memories is from a class I

visited with the mayor where the kids were learning the difference between opinion and fact. I asked whether the statement "Bloomberg is a
great mayor" is an opinion or a fact. When the student correctly said,
"An opinion," I jokingly added, "The mayor likes to think it's a fact."
Everyone cracked up, and I suspect those kids will always remember
the difference between an opinion and a fact. In another class, I noticed a high-school student focused on his iPhone with earbuds plugged
in. I asked him what he was doing, and he responded, "I'm listening to
an online course at MIT. This class sucks." From the mouths of babes!

I also received more formal student input from a group called the
Chancellor's Student Advisory Committee, which was made up of
about twenty-five student leaders from high schools throughout the
city. These tended to be very bright and motivated students, who were
invariably candid and informative. We met monthly for wide-ranging
discussions—How well are you being prepared for college? How do you
learn what college opportunities might be available to you? How many
of your teachers are good? Are there active gangs in your school?—and
I learned a lot. Most were seniors, and I was always sad to see them
leave at the end of the year, though I'm pleased that I still get e-mails
from some of them telling me what's happening in college.

IN THE EARLY DAYS OF OUR ADMINISTRATION, I RELIED HEAVILY
on my senior policy adviser, Michele Cahill. Few people had been
more involved in helping poor kids in American cities than Michele.
With undergraduate and graduate degrees in urban affairs, she had
created a policy studies program for nontraditional students at St. Peter's College in Jersey City. Her work in education reform included the
hugely successful Beacon Schools program in New York and innovation experiments in more than twenty U.S. cities for the Washington-

based Academy for Education Development. Immediately before joining us, she had been working for the Carnegie Foundation, overseeing $30 million in grants, a third of which had already been awarded to a group called New Visions for Public Schools to help the city replace eight large, failing high schools with new, smaller schools.

Days after I was announced as the new chancellor, Michele called to offer her help. I didn't then know enough about the new landscape I occupied to understand her place in it, but I quickly came to realize that she viewed things from a valuable perspective. She had spent decades working on ways to enhance the quality of life in cities by improving the lot of their youngest citizens. She had lived through the expansion of services delivered in the schools—health care, counseling, antiviolence programs—and come out the other end clear that more wasn't always better. Rather, she believed that young people need targeted supports and opportunities that build their competencies and foster positive identities, including academic ones. She had coauthored one of the first critiques of this multiservice approach in the early 1990s, warning, "The myriad of add-on programs that compete for space in the school day, the school building, and the school budget have led to the now common cry that schools cannot do it all."

In trying to do it all, educators had acted with enormous empathy and concern for kids and a sense of alarm about problems like drugs, AIDS, poverty, and crime, which were destroying lives and entire communities. Teachers and school administrators were most keenly aware of the way children were victimized by the problems of adults who sent them to school hungry, stressed, ill clothed, and generally unprepared. Teaching these kids was a big challenge. And with good reason, many educators came to believe that their best efforts were thwarted by the impoverishment of their students' lives outside the school.

To their credit, many of the people who made this poverty argument tried to attack the problem directly. They opened schools early and closed them late so they could provide everything from job training and literacy classes for parents to dental care for the kids. Some teachers became part-time social workers, visiting families, often on their own time, and struggling to help parents navigate the welfare and social service bureaucracies. Many community agencies tried to make up for poor-quality schools but lacked the resources to have much effect.

The extra programs helped certain people, but, as Cahill noted in her paper, the approach was deficit-oriented, reflecting a "fix-then-teach philosophy" that put education in second place. Time and energy were poured into addressing social problems, but their impact was limited because they didn't affect the classroom experience or the quality of the instruction. Tutoring and after-school enrichment in drama, chess, or music, while good, were no substitute for the core academic education that kids weren't being provided during the school day. One ironic outcome of all this effort is a child who receives the social support he needs to start dreaming of a better future yet never develops the academic skills and knowledge base needed to succeed.

A child's early school success can come in academic areas like math or reading, in the arts, in sports, or even in the social realms of friendships and group activities, where leadership traits emerge. A child's first experience with competence and success breeds the kind of genuine confidence that foreshadows more competence and success. On the other hand, repeated failure, especially at an early age, is highly corrosive to a child's spirit and sets her up for more failure. This is doubly true for the kid who has been told, by well-intended adults, "You are special" and "You are wonderful," only to discover, in the cold reality of a report card, that he or she is not even average.

Somehow, in the latter decades of the twentieth century, building self-esteem in children had become such a major concern for adults that significant numbers of parents, teachers, coaches, and others began devoting lots of time and energy to activities intended to make kids feel good about themselves. Some schools even adopted an "I Love Me" program that required children to recite self-affirming statements every day. Self-esteem-building slogans were posted in hallways. Motivational speakers appeared at school assemblies. By the mid-1990s, schools were filled with an entire generation of kids nurtured on the mantras of self-esteem.

Efforts to raise a child's self-image of course are not bad, per se, but as experts and experience slowly confirmed, they work only when a kid gets a chance to do something that is truly admirable. The ribbon awarded to the kid who wins the race does build self-esteem. The ones handed out to everyone who participates do not. This truth began to circulate in the late 1990s as Case Western Reserve University psychologist Roy Baumeister and others published studies showing that self-esteem programs didn't work as hoped when it came to improving behavior, raising attendance, or reducing drug use. On the other hand, the research did seem to show a positive correlation between good grades and reductions in social problems.

While Michele helped me understand this basic point, a former colleague from the Clinton administration, Larry Summers, then president of Harvard, drove it home when we appeared together on a panel. He said one of the key problems with K–12 education in America is that the education schools all push out the notion that "a kid needs self-esteem to achieve," while Larry was sure it was the other way around. "A kid needs to achieve in order to build self-esteem," he said. Good performance also contributes to greater success for adults. This was a notion we were determined to build into the culture of the entire school system.

THE FACTS THUS ARGUED IN FAVOR OF SCHOOLS STAFFED BY teachers who could help children reach serious academic goals. However, this kind of work is more difficult than the cheerleading that is prescribed by the self-esteem movement, which brought me to one of the essential truths that emerged in my early effort to understand the problems of the city schools. To put it bluntly: many of the people who had entered the teaching profession were not sufficiently skilled, and too often they lacked real expertise in their subject areas. Most of these people care deeply about the children they are responsible for, and many work hard to try to learn the subject matter they teach, but the truth is they often come unprepared, and, even if they try to catch up, they usually don't.

In the 1990s, college graduates who became elementary-school teachers in America averaged below 1,000 points, out of a total of 1,600, on the math and verbal Scholastic Aptitude Tests (SAT) given to high-school seniors; in New York City, when we began, the citywide average for all teachers was about 970. Unfortunately, low SAT scores were just the beginning. As several leaders in the field had begun to note in the late 1990s, grade inflation was becoming a problem in schools of education. They weren't alone. High grades for average work were a problem in many departments, even at elite colleges. But for administrators tasked with hiring new teachers, grade inflation meant that even graduates from prestigious institutions may not have been especially well prepared for their jobs.

Perhaps the most surprising description of teacher preparedness came from Albert Shanker, who headed the UFT during its formative years, from 1964 to 1985, and also ran the national union, the American Federation of Teachers (AFT), from 1974 until he died in 1997. In a 1993 speech at the Pew Forum, he said: "In our system, we have a large number of teachers who have not reached even very low levels of literacy and numeracy. Some of our professional development programs are designed to get teachers to understand fractions or how to read; some other programs teach what tenth graders should know. You would not even be admitted to a college in these other countries, let alone get a job as a teacher, unless you knew those things." When I first read this, I was shocked. As America's leading education union leader, Shanker had no reason to exaggerate the poor state of the teaching profession, but he was clearly alarmed.

Shanker's successor, Sandra Feldman, who also had run the UFT before becoming head of the national union, echoed the same theme in 2003 (soon after I started in New York). Noting that teachers who were then retiring were "very smart people," she lamented, "We're not getting in now the same kinds of people. It's disastrous. We've been saying for years now that we're attracting from the bottom third." Similarly, in early 2014, soon after New York City's new mayor, Bill de Blasio, who had opposed many of Bloomberg's policies, appointed long-time educator Carmen Fariña as his schools chancellor, she emphasized the same problem in her very first interview with the *New York Times*. Commenting on her years as principal of P.S. 6 in the 1990s, she said that she had had to get rid of 80 percent of the teachers because they weren't up to snuff. That's an extraordinary revelation: P.S. 6 is on the Upper East Side and serves the richest community in the city. If 80 percent of its teachers were unqualified, just imagine what it was like in the South Bronx, where poor kids go to school. In fact, I'm sure many of those whom Fariña got rid of ended up teaching in poor communities—that's the way the lemons dance.

Teacher quality is a deeply sensitive and long-developing problem that isn't easy to fix. Many teachers are terrific, but many others simply don't have the knowledge and skills, even if they have the heart, to be effective instructors. That basic recognition necessarily limits what you can do in turning around a school system like New York's, especially when the UFT is hell-bent on protecting even the least qualified of its members.

Of course, as with anything in education, every issue could be considered from a myriad of perspectives, and the minute you start talking about the quality of the people entering the teaching profession, you immediately hear about low pay, declining respect, and worsening conditions. It was easy to grant that these factors, which combined to make teaching less desirable to many bright young people, were important. But at least two other elements of the problem were rarely acknowledged: the shift in the workforce after World War II, followed by the rising equality of women in the workplace.

After the Great Depression of the early 1930s, teaching became a highly desirable career choice precisely because it provided lifetime job security. Many families had been greatly hurt by the Depression, and they often encouraged even their most talented and accomplished children to pursue the economic security provided by a public job subject to civil service protections. My own father, who didn't have the qualifications to teach, chose a job as a postal worker for just this reason, and he remained there until retirement even though he hated the work. Economic certainty for his family, even if at a modest level, came first.

Many others, who might have pursued different callings had they not come of age in the shadow of the Depression, chose teaching and likewise stayed through retirement. Although this practice changed significantly during the 1950s, when a new optimism infused the country after World War II, its impact endured through the 1960s when most of these so-called Depression children, who were a terrific source of teaching talent, retired.

More significantly, the discrimination that barred women from most jobs until the start of the feminist revolution of the 1960s had been an enormous boon to schools. For the previous century, give or take a decade or so, college-educated women with the ambition to work were funneled into teaching in great numbers. In every community, from rural one-room schoolhouses to inner-city high schools, these capable women were a ready source of high-quality labor willing to work for relatively low wages because they had few good options. As civil rights legislation and changing social expectations opened more university programs and professions to women, teaching lost its nearly exclusive claim on the very best.

Of course brilliant and talented women, as well as men, continued to become teachers, but the profession no longer drew nearly as many of the top-ranked female college graduates because those women had many more options. No one would want America's women to abandon the opportunities they have found in the world since the 1970s, but their gain has been education's loss.

The net result of all the trends that have eroded the teacher corps could be seen in the city schools I visited. One of the first was a high school serving more than three thousand students in the Bronx community of Williamsbridge. Evander Childs High School was opened in 1930, a year when almost 90 percent of the city's high-school seniors passed their state Regents exams and the school board president credited elementary schools for the fact that the system "has never been in better shape." (My mother attended Evander Childs for a year in the early 1940s.) The high school, which filled an entire block on Gun Hill Road, was named for a son of old New York who had spent fifty years working as a teacher and administrator in the city schools. At age seventy-two, Evander Childs had died at the principal's desk in P.S. 10, on Eagle Avenue in the Bronx.

Long considered a good school that prepared graduates to enter college or the workforce, Evander Childs High School had become, by 1980, a place where more and more kids were dropping out and failing to graduate. Many of the better students in the district opted for private schools or applied to attend one of the special high schools that accepted students on a competitive basis. As both the school and the surrounding community suffered from violent incidents, Evander Childs was one of the first city high schools to install metal detectors at its entrances. By the end of the 1990s, fewer than 30 percent of the school's students scored well enough on the Regents exams to be deemed proficient in English.

When I visited Evander Childs in the fall of 2002, I asked a student what he was reading. He showed me a page in a book, but he couldn't tell me what it said. He was in ninth grade, and he couldn't read. In another classroom I saw a very energetic young teacher who put a few math problems on the blackboard. About three or four of the kids had real trouble with them, so she spent quite a bit of time helping those kids after the others had finished. I asked those who were waiting, "What do you do now?" They said, "We talk to each other until they are caught up." I asked them if they wanted to do more problems. They were happy to, so I gave them some more, and we solved them together. I didn't do this to show up the teacher, and she didn't take it that way. Instead, after the bell rang, we talked about how little advice she had received in her short time on the job, and how much she craved it.

My experience at Evander Childs was hardly unusual. In our first months at Tweed, members of my team came back from the field to report that they had seen plenty of high schoolers who couldn't read and teachers who struggled in isolation. After one planned stop, where the staff took me on a well-choreographed tour of a school that seemed to be on alert for the visiting chancellor, I talked to Jesse, my city-assigned security officer, about finding another school where we might just drop in, unannounced. He suggested a middle school that his son had attended. As we got there, the bell rang to signal the end of the period.

As classroom doors swung open, the hallway was suddenly filled with kids screaming and pushing, shoving and punching one another. Out of the din I could hear "motherfucker" and "asshole" flung from one student to the next. Not one teacher emerged from a classroom to take a stand for order and safety, and as Jesse and I stood our ground we came to understand why. For the first and, as it turned out, only time in my eight-plus years as chancellor I felt afraid for my safety. No single adult, no matter how big and strong, would be able to affect the jostling mob. Only a coordinated effort by every adult in the building would work.

By the next time the bell rang, word had obviously spread that I was in the building. Students didn't explode out of classroom doors. Instead, teachers stepped into the hallway followed by single-file lines of young men and women who moved quietly and deliberately. I heard a few teachers call out reminders for kids to behave themselves and lower their voices, but except for these commands the scene was almost tranquil. The principal, who by this time was glued to my side, seemed delighted until I asked him, "If you are able to create this kind of order for me when I stop in, why do you ever tolerate all that dangerous craziness?"

"You know, I'm not sure," he answered.

I should have fired him right then and there, but I was still new to the job and chose to let my leadership team look into his performance. In any event, had I tried to remove him, he probably would have won his case because, at the time, the teachers union contract prevented principals from insisting that teachers do hallway duty. It may seem hard to believe that kids' safety and overall orderliness could be sacrificed by such silly rules, but that's the way it was.

The good news for that particular school is that, while I didn't fire him, the principal got the message and soon volunteered to leave the job. He was replaced by a much more effective and consistent leader. The experience reinforced my own strongly held view that the principal was the most important piece in the education puzzle. A principal could lead a school toward order and excellence or allow it to descend into dysfunction and worse.

The New York Department of Education employed roughly twelve hundred principals, and, lacking data, we had no easy way in the beginning to determine which ones were effective and which ones weren't. However, in the course of working as chancellor I inevitably discovered good principals quietly doing excellent work. For example, in a visit to my alma mater, Bryant High School in Queens, I discovered a terrific principal named Bernadette Kriftcher. Big like Evander Childs, Bryant under Kriftcher was nevertheless a safe and orderly place where the Regents exam success rate had improved considerably.

Although I was personally able to discover some great principals, others made it their business to track me down and introduce themselves. Early in my career as chancellor I started receiving e-mails and phone calls from a principal named Anthony Lombardi, who ran an elementary school in Queens with almost five hundred students from mixed backgrounds, including many from poorer, immigrant families. A big, stocky guy who had played football as a kid and had lost an eye while doing so, Tony was a former teacher who dreamed of actually leading his school in the way that a coach leads a winning team, with high standards and strict discipline. Unfortunately, he was tied down by the union contract that made it impossible for him to pick his players (teachers) or assign them to their positions.

After I invited Tony to dinner, and we began a friendship that continues to this day, he started sending me reports on the many ways the work rules had undermined his efforts. For example, while he couldn't assign a teacher to lunchroom duty, a teacher with the right level of seniority could insist on getting assigned to lunch duty *for summer school*, which meant he or she got paid a little something extra to show up for a couple of hours each day of the summer session. If Lombardi wanted the same teacher to do instructional work, he couldn't make that happen. Tony dealt with this precise issue when an especially effective math teacher said she was happy to work, but only as a lunchroom monitor. She got the spot and received her full pay while the kids who came for summer school were denied her expertise as a math teacher.

In his determination to improve his school, Tony devoted much of his time to observing teachers and offering them feedback. Those who engaged students in a stimulating way and attended to every child won his praise. Others, who seemed unable to engage their students or allowed some of them to avoid participating, got suggestions for improving. Lombardi used the procedures that were available to him to keep pressing teachers to improve, even if he made a pest out of himself.

Tony didn't like the idea of constantly observing teachers, but since he lacked the authority to get rid of anyone unless he or she committed gross violations of the rules, his only choice was to monitor and mentor the subpar teachers until they did better work or sought transfers themselves. On occasion, the standoffs devolved into open conflict. In one case, Tony had to deal with a male teacher who refused to communicate, except to make threatening gestures and glare at him during staff meetings. When eventually brought to disciplinary proceedings, the man, whom Tony had begun to fear a little bit, simply disappeared.

As Tony tried to get control of his school, and his frustrations led him to speak out about the absurdity of the work rules in the UFT contract, he eventually caught the eye of the union, which would have none of it. A union official wrote to other union leaders in Queens, saying, "Lombardi has not learned the lesson that was taught to Al D'Amato [a former New York senator whom the union helped to defeat]: an attack on our union is an attack on our teachers." He encouraged them to have their teachers "express their outrage to Mr. Lombardi." This kind of thuggish behavior would have intimidated many principals. But Lombardi is tough. He held firm, and the good news is that, despite the UFT's repeated attempts to topple him, the teachers and parents at his school just loved him.

As someone who believes that strong leadership is essential for good schools—or to run any effective organization, for that matter—I found Lombardi's powerlessness to be absurd in the extreme. We moved immediately to provide principals with more authority and support. Over howls of protest from the district superintendents, I gave the principals the power to hire their own assistant principals. The superintendents literally told me, "Most principals wouldn't know how to select an assistant principal." I responded, "If we have principals who don't know how to pick their assistants, we'd better get rid of them immediately. Any leader who can't assemble a team can't lead."

I next began to develop plans for a principals Leadership Academy that would select and train newcomers to be part of our team. The existing process for selecting principals was badly broken, and, while it produced some good leaders like Kriftcher and Lombardi, far too many were chosen either because they had political connections or they knew how to play ball with the superintendents and unions. We would look for people who weren't afraid to challenge the status quo and then provide them with the kind of training that would enable them to do just that.

Fortunately, I was able to turn to Caroline Kennedy for help. Aiming as high as we could, I had persuaded Kennedy to serve as the head of our Office of Strategic Partnership, where her role was to work with business, philanthropic, and not-for-profit groups to develop public-private partnerships that would help secure support and funding for our initiatives. The symbolic, as well as substantive, value of Caroline's commitment to the city's public schools is hard to overstate. I still remember the tears in the eyes of teachers and administrators when she walked into a school. But public education in New York is always controversial, and despite Caroline's extraordinary work, she was still criticized for sending her own children to private school.

Caroline's first big success for us would be a $15 million grant to support the principals' Leadership Academy from the Wallace–Reader's Digest Fund. Soon we would get millions more from corporations in the city that were being solicited by the Partnership for New York City, which was, in effect, the city's chamber of commerce. The partnership's leader, Kathryn Wylde, was committed to the public schools and knew that leadership training would appeal to the corporate CEOs she represented. We also got support from the big foundations, including our second major grant from the Broad Foundation, which had a special interest in education and was increasingly donating to organizations that sought to improve America's big-city schools through better management and greater accountability.

A FORMALIZED TRAINING PROGRAM FOR PRINCIPALS WAS NOT an entirely new concept in New York City. In the summer before I took over as chancellor, about four hundred of them had gone through a program run by a former principal named Mary Butz, who had worked in the city schools for more than three decades. Butz organized semi-

nars and lectures, provided mentors, and brought in visionaries to inspire the principals. I first learned about her early in my time as
chancellor when I consulted one of the leading voices in American
education, the influential academic and writer Diane Ravitch.

Ravitch played as big a part as anyone in calling America's school
reform movement into existence by prominently articulating the core
ideals—accountability, choice, and innovation—that animated it. But
despite having been a strong supporter of Bloomberg and the programs
we were pushing, soon into my tenure she became the reform movement's and my fiercest critic. People often commented that the inten-
sity and persistence of her attacks made it seem personal.

What caused this complete turnaround? Only Ravitch can know
for sure. But, at least as I see it, one possible source might have been a
personnel decision we made. Here's the way it happened.

Ravitch became a well-known education reformer when she served
as a high-level official in the Department of Education under the first
President Bush. After that, she became a prodigious opinion writer in
scholarly and popular journals on education reform. She had advocated
abolishing New York City's local school boards in 1995, which Bloomberg eventually did, and she had been a leading proponent of accountability, calling for reports on student performance that would let parents
compare one school with another. In 1998 Ravitch published an article
called "Put Teachers to the Test," which noted, with dismay, that more
than 25 percent of teachers were tasked with teaching subjects that they
had not studied much themselves, and this problem was "particularly
acute in [high-poverty] schools where . . . nearly half the teaching staff
was teaching 'out of field.'" In this vein, she attacked urban districts for
acting like "job programs for adults at the expense of the children they
are supposed to serve." This commentary came as she made a big push
in favor of charter schools in New York City, which would allow new

partners into the system. She also supported using vouchers to allow students to attend private or religious schools, explaining in a 2002 *New Republic* article, "We must do whatever we can to end the awful cycle of wasted lives—which includes giving vouchers a chance, and thereby giving poor kids a chance to escape the schools that are cruelly not educating them."

Ravitch had little tolerance for those who made excuses for bad schools. She wrote in a 1995 *Washington Post* column that "the low socioeconomic status of . . . students" should not be used to "rationalize poor performance." Those who argued otherwise, she said, were incorrectly "implying that poverty equals destiny and so no one is to blame for failure." Nor did she pull her punches when describing how bad our inner-city schools were. In 1998, at the Brookings Institute, she said: "By any measure, student performance in the nation's urban schools is low. In urban schools that enroll high proportions of poor students, performance is appallingly low."

Mayor Bloomberg urged me to meet with Ravitch, who, he said, had been helpful advising him on education during his mayoral campaign. I quickly studied up on some of her work on New York and was impressed to see she had written that "New York City's public school system needs to be reinvented from the ground up. Organized a century ago and never seriously revamped since then, it has become a bureaucratic monster that wastes vast sums that should be spent on instruction. But what is worse than wasting money is wasting lives." She also had a good sense of the system's politics: "The power of the union is unparalleled. Union leaders like to think that the union is in the vanguard of reform. When confronted with proposals that threaten to reduce their power, positions, or long-held prerogatives, however, they bring their full influence to bear on public officials."

Although she talked tough and supported reforms that many teachers found threatening, Ravitch commanded great respect because she was a serious scholar and a savvy operator. She maintained close ties with union leaders and politicians, and the power of her intellect made her a formidable force, whether or not you agreed with her. Bloomberg was smart to get her on his side; no one else in New York had the depth of experience and scholarship or the credibility that she had. I was eager to meet her.

As it turned out, Ravitch was spending summer weekends on Long Island, as was I. We agreed to meet in August 2002 on Shelter Island, which sits between the North and South Forks of what's known as the East End. I found her to be intelligent, forceful, and formidable. In short, she was a big mind, and I sensed that she liked being regarded as a big mind. As is her wont, Diane got right to the point:

"Why do you think you can succeed when no one else has?" she asked.

"I don't know if I can succeed," I answered. And then I went on to say, in essence: "But the existence of mayoral control gives us operating room that no one else has had. Also, I think there's an advantage in the fact that this is not my career. I am willing to take the heat because I'm not looking to move from New York City to another higher position in the education field. I'm in this because there's nothing more important, no other mission that matters more. I also know that I'm working for a mayor who will fund us and will have my back politically. Given all this, I like my chances."

Although I may have sounded a bit idealistic, even preachy, I *really did* believe that nothing mattered more than education, especially the public education offered to poorer kids in New York and across the country. Diane herself had repeatedly talked about these issues, and many economists and others had begun to sound alarms about the future of the American middle class in the coming era of global competition and rapidly changing technology. In the 1950s workers could achieve a middle-class lifestyle with a high-school education, or less. Even as recently as 1970, 30 percent of all jobs were open to people without a high-school diploma. However, by the twenty-first century, over 90 percent of all jobs required a high-school diploma or more. The small number of jobs to be had by the undereducated paid low wages, and the competition for these jobs could be fierce, as recent immigrants flocked to them in great numbers.

Ravitch keenly understood these core issues about education in America, but, like me, she was most concerned with the immediate task of fixing what was wrong in New York. She had published a piece in the *New York Times* right after Bloomberg's election in 2001 urging him to "insist on new working arrangements to ensure that principals have the authority to make decisions." This would require, she explained, changes in both the teachers' and principals' contracts that, among other things would "guarantee that both teachers and principals will receive the professional training they need to meet their responsibilities." When our conversation turned to those issues, Ravitch urged me to talk with Mary Butz who, she told me, was her longtime partner. Ravitch explained that Butz had received a federal grant to run a principals training program. She urged me to learn more about Butz's initiative and to give it more prominence by having Butz report directly to me.

Since I was interested both in the principal's role and in establishing a leadership-training program, I immediately met with Butz and asked her about her training program. I told her I had plans to expand in this area. Butz was clearly experienced, and she cared deeply about the principal's role and the training necessary for the job. I decided to ask her to write me a memo, describing how she thought a much-expanded leadership-training program should operate. She got back to me soon thereafter, and I asked my deputy, Diana Lam, and my senior policy adviser, Michele Cahill, to review the memo.

At this time, there was a lot of academic and practical attention being devoted to the role of the principal and proper leadership training. This reflected a recent shift in focus, borrowed in part from the corporate world, where strong leadership was seen as essential for running a successful operation. Schools weren't corporations, of course, but that didn't mean they couldn't learn from this basic organizational principle. Richard Elmore at Harvard and Marc Tucker and Judy Codding at the National Center on Education and the Economy had been writing extensively on this subject, and school districts were beginning to pay attention. And Jon Schnur, a visionary, young education reformer, had recently started a nationally recognized organization called New Leaders for New Schools, which had established a demanding yearlong program to train principals throughout the country. Viewing Butz's proposal through the lens of this literature and existing practice, Diana and Michele concluded that it was not sufficiently comprehensive to meet our needs. From my perspective, it didn't adequately come to grips with the questions of how to select the right people for this role or how to train them to be the change agents that we wanted them to be.

AS AUTUMN TURNED TO WINTER WE SIGNALED TO EVERYONE who had a stake in the schools that we would start our reform efforts with a plan to improve leadership—through a combination of support and accountability. On December 11, 2002, we announced that we were prepared to pay top-performing veteran principals $75,000 in bonuses if they agreed to transfer to troubled schools and serve for three years, during which they would train their own replacements. But this simple proposal had to be negotiated with the principals union, and it took us until 2008 to agree to terms with them. We were amazed that the union balked at such an obviously sensible idea, one that applied only to principals who volunteered and would get paid extra for it, but that's how hidebound the lockstep pay system was. On the same day we also warned that we expected to fire the fifty worst-performing principals in the system within a year's time, which then amounted to about 4 percent of the total group. This we could do without the union's agreement. The number was modest, we thought, given the number of failing schools, but the announcement so rattled the system that we were flooded with calls from anxiety-stricken administrators and their union. We promised to conduct a fair dismissal process, but we also reminded everyone that we were authorized, under a 1999 city regulation, to dismiss any principal with a record of "persistent educational failure." It didn't matter to us that the Department of Education had never actually used this authority to fire someone. We were going to use it.

No other enterprise would have accepted persistent failure for so many years, but the city schools had endured it under the old system of splintered control. Too often the local superintendents felt they couldn't dismiss a principal who had political connections, especially one whom they themselves had appointed. And many, if not most, principals had political connections. In our newly consolidated system we weren't blocked in the same way. The principals union was not as strong as the teachers union, and the information and data we could assemble to support a dismissal would be hard to refute. In some of our elementary and middle schools, fewer than 20 percent of the students were passing their state exams, and in some of our high schools, only 25 percent of the kids were graduating in four years, even though the state exams and high-school graduation requirements were weak. No one, we thought, could defend this level of failure.

Considering the breadth of the changes we wanted to make, I decided to give several press interviews and even met with the editorial board of the *New York Times*. Remembering that six years earlier, the editorial board had published an attack on my nomination to head the antitrust division of the Justice Department, I approached the meeting with some trepidation. But this time was different. The editors were receptive to my ideas and soon the paper was supporting our proposal for a leadership academy to train principals, calling it "admirable."

After the *Times* backed us, Ravitch contacted the editorial page editor, Gail Collins, to say that our academy wasn't really needed because the Department of Education already had a training program. Ravitch described Butz's program in detail and told Collins, "Mary organized a Principals University during the summer with about sixty different courses that covered practical problems encountered by principals." She added, "I just want to be sure that you and those who write about New York City educational matters are aware that there is already a national model in place in this city for training principals. Those who have struggled to make it happen deserve recognition for their successes; today's editorial suggests that they don't even exist."

Ravitch e-mailed me a copy of her letter to Gail Collins, emphasizing that what Butz was doing had already been recognized as "a national model," and telling me that "if you talked about what the department is presently doing to help inexperienced principals, more people in the press would know about it." Two weeks later, Ravitch e-mailed again, saying, "My pal Mary Butz is trying to figure whether you or Diana Lam want her to stay on or not." She asked, "Does she figure in your plans? . . . If not, please give her a chance to plan accordingly."

Knowing the importance of this issue, I discussed Butz's role in our new Leadership Academy with my team. We agreed that she was a smart and experienced person who understood that the principal is the key player in every school. But we concluded that her approach didn't emphasize the kind of transformative leadership that we thought necessary. In contrast to Butz's program, we were looking to provide much more hands-on training, over a significantly longer time, and sought to teach principals how to fight through the enormous resistance that they would encounter in being change agents in schools staffed by people who would strongly resist change. We were also looking to recruit new, and different, people to the principal's role, hoping to find those who would be willing to advance the aggressive reform agenda we would be pushing. This meant that the selection process itself would be critical.

To lead a training program that sets out to do these kinds of things requires skills and experience that longtime veterans of the school system rarely have, since they typically learn to operate within the change-resistant culture that has long prevailed. We wanted to send a message that this was a new day and, starting with the Leadership Academy, we would be making clear that new people—with a new approach and a different sense of what was possible—would be leading the way for us. We even decided to set the academy up as a separate nonprofit organization so that it wouldn't be captured by the bureaucrats at our department who might want to undermine it. To head this kind of program, we expected we would need to bring together two people with complementary skills—someone from outside the education world who had major change-management experience and someone who was deeply steeped in school operations and who understood the practical, as well as the academic, dimensions of principal training.

Because Ravitch was a high-profile person who had supported the mayor, however, I made sure Bloomberg knew what was brewing. If he backed me, as I chose someone to run the academy who wasn't Ravitch's favorite, it would reinforce my belief that he wasn't just another politician. He said, "Do what's right for your department."

After Butz was told that she wouldn't be leading the new academy, Ravitch wrote me an e-mail saying, "I was shocked to learn that Mary Butz was told to leave. If you don't have room on your team for a person as knowledgeable, as committed, as experienced and as energetic as she, I despair for your initiatives." She also suggested that we might lose a $3.4 million federal grant that she had previously helped Butz to secure, telling me that "[s]ince the award was premised on her program, the feds might not pay out the money for an entirely different program that was not part of the original proposal." I immediately responded that "we made the decision based on our sense of what was needed for the new institute. I regret the pain it has caused to Mary and you."

The right choices for the Leadership Academy started with Robert Knowling, who became the CEO. Knowling was a successful African American businessman who had extensive leadership-training and change-management experience in the private sector. Working at several of the regional Bell telephone companies, he had developed an expertise in turnaround leadership as the Bells moved from monopolies to competitive businesses after the breakup of AT&T. Sandra Stein, an education professor at Baruch College, where she was teaching leadership as well as training principals, agreed to be academic dean. After she and Knowling partnered for a few years, Sandra became sole head of the academy and did a terrific job.

To bolster this executive team, we created a small advisory board, again mixing corporate and education expertise. We chose John F. "Jack" Welch, the hard-driving manager who led the hugely successful turnaround of General Electric, to head the board. He was joined by Richard Parsons, then CEO of AOL–Time Warner, and Tony Alvarado, the former New York City schools chancellor who was then working with Alan Bersin in San Diego. Welch himself was iconic. One of his more controversial policies called for dismissing employees who ranked in

the bottom 10 percent after managers thoroughly reviewed their performance. But he was not ruthless. He advocated setting goals, providing
support and feedback, and measuring results carefully.

By involving Welch and the other advisers in our academy, we
demonstrated that we were serious about making schools run well. At
the press conference on January 13, 2003, where his appointment was
announced, Jack promised to challenge principals in the same way that
he challenged managers in industry. He told reporters, "This is no B.S.
We have a chance to take a swing at something and make it sensa-
tional." With Welch, Parsons, Alvarado, Knowling, and Stein we knew
we had a team that would enjoy instant credibility and visibility. Knowling and Stein took advantage of Butz's experience by bringing her into
the new academy, where she spent a year assisting them in getting
started and training our first class. Though she then retired, Butz
wanted to stay on as a paid consultant for the academy, but Knowling
declined the offer.

In the meantime, Ravitch became increasingly critical of Mayor
Bloomberg and our policies. In March 2004, she teamed up with union
president Randi Weingarten to call for rolling back the mayor's authority
over the schools. A direct contradiction of her earlier stands, the proposal
they made in the pages of the *Times* included a call for a new school
board to stand between the mayor and reforms. In the same piece, they
took a few swipes at me, saying that I suffered from a "lack of experience"
and had made "controversial" appointments. Over the years, Ravitch
would go on to write numerous pieces attacking our policies (most of
which she had previously forcefully advocated) and our performance,
often presenting what we believed was an incomplete, or misleading,
picture of what was going on or what we were accomplishing.

Several years later, I invited Ravitch to lunch, hoping to rebuild our
relationship. The lunch was pleasant, focusing largely on her concerns

about our curriculum. She knew a lot about this area, and I was genuinely eager to learn from her. We also discussed what had happened with Butz, and Ravitch disputed the suggestion that she had turned against us because we hadn't hired Butz to run the Leadership Academy.

Although the lunch seemed to have gone well, Ravitch followed it with a series of e-mails, insisting that Butz had nothing to do with her attacks on our programs and performance. At the same time, she was adamant that we had mistreated Butz. She wrote, "Mary is eminently more competent than Bob Knowling and vastly more respected by the city's best principals" and, she told me, "It is not too late for you to invite her to serve on a task force or advisory committee. Anyone who noticed would reach the conclusion that you are doing the right thing by someone that you wronged." Thereafter, Ravitch's attacks on us were frequent, harsh, and, in my view, totally unfair.

More broadly, as she distanced herself from her earlier positions, Ravitch seemingly turned her apparent antipathy toward anyone and everyone associated with the school reform movement, publishing multiple blog posts each day, and writing lengthy articles and two books on the subject. Some of her critiques were especially barbed and personal. At one point, she went so far as to write, "There is a special place in hell for everyone who administers and funds this revolting [school reform] organization."

For obvious reasons, I have thought long and hard about what happened between Ravitch and me. I had so much respect for her insights about New York City's and the nation's education problems and her creative and aggressive solutions. Finally, we were putting in place much of what she had advocated, and it was working. Yet she not only was no longer on board, she was now leading the effort to tear it all down, much to my great sadness and regret. And given Ravitch's prominence and prodigious output, there's no question that she affected the media and, ultimately, public opinion, thus making the work of school reform more difficult.

I am sure I didn't handle this as well as I could have. I likely should have given Butz credit during my first meeting with the *Times* editorial board in 2002 for having started on the principal leadership path. But I never fully grasped why this got so out of hand, and why the attacks became so bitter and personal. What was clear is that Ravitch radically changed her positions on virtually every issue in education. Scholars, of course, have every right to alter their thinking. And anyone has the right to criticize me and the policies we adopted. Indeed, with hindsight, some of Ravitch's criticisms about our curriculum seem fair. But when someone this influential experiences this kind of sea change in thinking, it is important for her to be specific about which facts have changed, or why her interpretation of those facts was so wrong for so long. In this instance, Ravitch's conversion seems to have been absolute, sudden, and largely unexplained.

5

Children First

The man standing in the shadows of a cold December evening on the steps of the Tweed building looked as if he'd been there for a while and was waiting for someone. When he called out, "Hey, Chancellor Klein," I stopped to talk.

A big African American man, he told me that his daughter had been lucky enough to be admitted to a good, out-of-district school, which accepted students from other communities. Proudly, he said that she was thriving. His son had not been so fortunate. He attended a neighborhood school with a much worse reputation, where he was not being well educated. I was moved and impressed when, rather than ask me to intercede for his son, he simply encouraged me to push for change as hard as I could. Children like his son needed better options. Before we parted, he expressed gratitude for his daughter's school. "You know what?" he added. "She's teaching me to read."

To this day I tear up when I think about that wonderful man. He wouldn't tell me his name, so I was never able to follow up with him. But he served as a constant, gut-wrenching reminder that, for many families, the schools weren't getting the job done. The families themselves couldn't always fill the void: you can't read to your kid if you don't know how to read yourself or get him a tutor if you can't afford one. For families like that man's, there was no Plan B, only the hope of public schools.

I kept fathers (and mothers) like this in my mind—and there were many over the years—as we raced to finish our plan of action. The Leadership Academy for principals was a done deal. We had begun the process of enrolling some ninety new trainees to start yearlong training in the summer of 2003. But we had to address structural issues that made it so difficult to turn around certain schools. Our research showed that at least 10 percent of the total, or almost 130 schools, were chronically underperforming. Some of the worst problems occurred at the larger high schools, where too many students dropped out and too few—perhaps one in four—graduated. These schools were all located in the city's poorer communities and were overwhelmingly attended by black and Latino students, many of whom started high school way behind and were never able to catch up.

We began to target the most troubled schools for closure. Our plan was to phase out dozens of these failing high schools, eliminating a grade per year. Between four and six new smaller schools would replace each of the ones phased out, and these would be ramped up one grade at a time. This enabled the new schools to grow their faculties carefully—five or six teachers would be added every year—and to start with ninth graders in year one so they would have the full four years to work with the students they admitted. All of these schools were to be "choice" schools, meaning that students would have to apply, rather than "zoned" facilities that they were forced to attend. As "choice" schools, the new schools would have to earn their students by offering good programs and increasing student performance. They would still be traditional public schools, subject to union and other regulatory rules, but because they would open with only ninth graders and grow one year at a time, the principals had wide latitude in choosing their teachers and other staff.

By including high schools in our first wave of reform, we would buck the national trend, which typically saw reforms applied to elementary schools first. Theoretically, younger kids benefit more from reform efforts, and high-school students are too old to adapt and grow in new conditions. However, as my policy adviser Michele Cahill argued at the time, older students in failing high schools needed us to act on their behalf immediately, because they would soon age out of the public schools and face the challenges of adult life. In today's world, you can't even join the military without a high-school diploma, and almost every entry-level job requires basic literacy. Yet thousands of New York high schoolers were attending big, dysfunctional schools, veritable dropout factories where good teachers felt overwhelmed and bad ones marked time until retirement. From the outset, Michele insisted, and I agreed, we could not look away.

The most troubled of these high schools—Evander Childs, Erasmus Hall, Bushwick, and many others—often functioned as dumping grounds for students who had fallen many grades behind and for teachers whom other schools had excessed. Good teachers faced insurmountable odds in these places. Imagine starting a job as a ninth-grade teacher with five sections of freshman biology, in which half the students cannot read the textbook. These children—not closely monitored by guidance counselors for behavioral or other nonacademic issues—rarely have access to remedial reading programs. You, the biology teacher, have neither the time nor the mandate to teach them how to read. In the end you might conclude that the illiterate students are beyond help and thus abandon them in favor of the others, with whom you'd at least have a fighting chance. The abandoned students become disconnected, or, worse, defiant and oppositional. At the end of the year everyone feels less competent, less happy, and less hopeful. As soon as they can, the students who cannot read drop out and you seek a transfer.

We wanted to chart a very different course in the new schools. The hope was that the increased personal attention along with strong community group supports would bolster the schools and foster, as Michele Cahill put it, "groups of adults who would be totally committed to success for smaller groups of students." This was not a revolutionary idea. Experiments along these lines had already achieved strong results in schools opened in the city over previous decades. In some new facilities in the Bronx, a nonprofit group called New Visions for Public Schools provided support, professional development, and other program enhancements and was beginning to see results, helping kids accumulate more course credits and reducing dropout rates.

But school systems rarely attempted to close big high schools because they knew they were bound to meet intense opposition from alumni, community leaders, and unions. High schools are the object of more nostalgia and ongoing loyalty than elementary and middle schools, even when they fail to provide adequately for current students. Those with fond memories of their high-school days protest closings. Joined with community boosters, who may cherish a high school as a symbol of pride and continuity, alumni can bring intense political pressure to bear against closures. The unions also oppose closings to protect administrators and teachers in the threatened schools. I was always amazed at the resistance we encountered when we tried to replace bad schools with better ones.

Our choice agenda also called for more charter schools, especially for children in elementary- and middle-school grades. A successful model already existed in the Bronx in a Knowledge Is Power Program (KIPP) school, which operated first as a program within a traditional public school and then—after New York State passed a charter-authorizing law in 1998—as an independent charter school. Begun in

Houston by two young Teach for America (TFA) alums, KIPP garnered
national attention by operating schools throughout the country that
were serving largely poor and minority students. The program had substantially increased student achievement by hiring excellent principals
and teachers, training them constantly, lengthening the school day and
year, imposing strict discipline, and granting rewards for success that
included class trips and even merchandise for individual kids. The first
school in Houston posted phenomenal results in its first year. The nation's second KIPP school, the middle school in the Bronx, did nearly
as well. In 1995, only one third of fifth graders entering the Bronx KIPP
school had passed their tests. By eighth grade, three quarters of these
same students passed.

Although they operated as charter schools, the nonprofit KIPP
schools in New York and elsewhere were fully public, by any fair use of
that description. They were open to all applicants and, if oversubscribed, used a lottery to select their students. The money to run them
came from the taxpayers, via the Department of Education, based on
total enrollment. Organizers sometimes supplemented these funds
with grants from other sources, which were usually used to help defray
start-up costs. KIPP principals wielded far more power than their colleagues in regular public schools. They hired teachers willing to work
longer days (three hours more than teachers worked at regular public
schools) and shoulder greater responsibilities in exchange for high levels of support and the excitement of being part of a school succeeding
with kids previously doomed to fail. If a KIPP or any other charter
school didn't perform well, it was required by law to be shut down.

Most of the teachers at KIPP and other charter schools were much
younger than their counterparts at regular city schools. A good number
came from the Teach for America program, which recruited dedicated
college graduates who lacked the usual teacher's education and creden-

tials. TFA trained them and gave them the chance to teach. Although many TFA teachers moved on after a few years, principals, students, and communities accepted the higher turnover in exchange for the extraordinary energy and devotion of these teachers who seemed happy to burn themselves out in the effort to help children.

At the Bronx KIPP school, a student's day started at 7:30 a.m. and ended at 5 p.m. Music lessons were mandatory, as were Saturday programs. A significant number of KIPP's eighth-grade graduates went on to win scholarships to prestigious private schools. We wanted more KIPPs and KIPP-like elementary and middle schools, to feed better-prepared students into the smaller high schools that we hoped would soon be ready for them.

I SPOKE WITH DEPUTY MAYOR WALCOTT ALMOST DAILY, AND the two of us met with Bloomberg every week. We got together in the bullpen at City Hall, sometimes joined by others from the mayor's team or mine. The mayor invariably got right to the point: What were we focused on? Were we moving fast enough? What were the challenges? How could he or his people help? When we presented specific proposals, he drilled down carefully. Would we have the capacity to open all of these new schools? How confident were we that they would be better than the ones we replaced? If we were proposing to reorganize operations, were we sure we were doing so in a way that would minimize ongoing political influence in favor of effective managerial oversight and accountability?

These weekly meetings—sometimes supplemented by lengthier ones—were fundamental to the way Bloomberg operated. He gave a lot of discretion to his appointees but insisted on being fully informed. He never hesitated to push back against something he thought was unsound.

If he felt strongly about matters, he let us know in no uncertain terms. For example, he thought the policy of social promotion—moving a kid onto the next grade even though he had failed the current one—was harming students, and although he knew that changing the policy would be controversial, he kept returning to the issue in our meetings. Similarly, when we proposed that we reorganize the existing geographically based school districts into regions, he wanted to ensure that the regions spanned more than one borough so they would be less amenable to political control by local politicians.

The meetings that I remember best were those that focused on our performance. The mayor understood and devoured data. Where others' eyes might glaze over at the numbers on a page, Bloomberg eagerly pored over charts with test scores, crime data, attendance, summer school results, and anything else that would indicate how we were doing. Sometimes, when we were reviewing information that we would present to the public, he would redo a chart right there at the meeting, insisting that his changes would make the information clearer and easier to understand. Whenever anyone asked me what meeting with Bloomberg was like, I'd always respond, "I'll tell you one thing: you'd better make sure your numbers are bulletproof."

BY THE BEGINNING OF 2003, THE BLOOMBERG/KLEIN SCHOOL reform agenda had also begun to focus on developing new ways to empower school leaders while holding them accountable for progress in their students' performance. The more we emphasized accountability and school choice, the more pushback we expected. Special interests, especially the unions, would oppose us every step of the way because we were aiming at the heart of the status quo they wanted to preserve.

Few people really appreciate how all-powerful the teachers union has been. In the decades before Bloomberg, the United Federation of Teachers had been able to control almost any decision that pertained to it. The union drew from dues payments automatically deducted from members' paychecks to influence city and state elections. Some of this money was donated directly to candidates; some was used to pay for advertising, PR and political consultants, and get-out-the-vote efforts. With so much money, and thousands of members who might vote as a bloc, the UFT was perhaps the most formidable political player in the city and state.

The UFT also benefited from the fact that New York was a very Democratic, pro-union town. It enjoyed the support of the liberal establishment, including the *New York Times*, and the backing of other powerful labor organizations. Finally, the UFT had lots of troops on the ground. With chapter leaders in every school, the union could dig up dirt to feed to reporters. If we made mistakes, as surely we would, the union would use them to discredit us with the press and public. We knew we would have to steel ourselves for the inevitable attacks and be prepared to fight back in the court of public opinion.

In part for this reason, we realized we wouldn't be able to accomplish our goals without engaging everyone in the city, including many who had a tenuous connection to the city's schools, in the cause of better public education. We had to build support with community leaders, key religious figures, and politicians while drawing help and financial backing from wealthy and powerful figures whose children did not tend to be students in public schools. I thought it essential for these potential contributors to understand how bad things were for many kids, what we were trying to do, and the reasons for the political and labor opposition that we would face. Most were politically active Democrats and reliably pro-union. They provided lots of financial support to political candidates and carried large amounts of influence in a city where virtually every elected official was a Democrat. I wanted them on our side, even though public education had not typically been important to them.

These facts of life lay behind my decision to engage in a series of semi-confrontational talks with some of the city's most powerful and wealthy people. These gatherings, often held in apartments overlooking Central Park, were set up as dinner parties or receptions, and they continued throughout my tenure. Few of the invitees arrived expecting to have their consciences pricked, but that's what I always hoped to do. I tried my best to show them how citizens of all sorts—even those who could afford to send their children to private schools—would benefit from better public education.

Why should the rich and powerful care about the public schools? First, I would say, it was incumbent on all of us to help the country fulfill its commitments to those who weren't as fortunate. I reminded them that our laws—along with Supreme Court decisions like *Brown v. Board of Education*, which barred "separate but equal" schools—promised every kid "an equal educational opportunity." "We haven't remotely delivered on that promise," I continued. "We're two hundred and twenty years into our nation's history. It took us one hundred and sixty-five years to get to *Brown*. We can't afford to wait another hundred and sixty-five years to deliver on our promise."

Better schools, I argued, would also help create a safer, more economically vibrant New York where citizens had the means to make it into the middle class and the faith that the system can work for them. Wealthier people would also benefit through lower taxes: safe, functional cities do not require such big investments in prisons and other services necessary in communities that are falling apart. And they would be able to select from a better-prepared workforce in the future.

I often told people about two schools occupying the same building on the edge of East Harlem between East Ninety-Fifth and East Ninety-Sixth streets on Third Avenue. One half of the building, opened in 1959, housed P.S. 198, also known as the Isador and Ida Straus School. The other half was home to P.S. 77, the Lower Laboratory School for Gifted Education. Straus faced north toward Spanish Harlem and, because it served neighborhood kids from that community, was populated almost entirely by black and Latino children from poor and working-class families. Lower Lab, as it was called, faced south toward the fashionable Upper East Side and accepted only children who scored very high on special "gifted and talented" tests administered to four-year-olds. Its students were almost all white and Asian and typically came from better-off families. I described these two schools as "a tale of two cities within a single building."

When I visited, I had noticed the kids entered the two schools through separate doors. The same segregation governed the entire day, as staggered activities assured that the two schools stayed separate. Facilities in the schools were starkly different. The Lab School enjoyed the best of everything, thanks to donations from a wealthy parent organization. Straus was adequately equipped but without extras. Straus teachers spent their own money to buy supplies for special, off-budget projects. The "extras" at the Lab School were paid for by the parents organization.

Although they were normally separated, the students in these two schools occasionally bumped into one another in the schoolyard. When I asked some fourth graders at Lower Lab about these encounters, one of the boys offered a startling report. "We don't like those kids," he said. "They tell us, 'When we get older, we're going to buy your school and throw you out.'"

These seemingly aggressive expressions increased the concerns of the parents whose kids attended the Lab School. They weren't thrilled that their kids had to share a building with others who were unfriendly, but, because they loved Lab, they accepted it. But what they feared most was that someone like me would try, in the name of equity, to merge the two schools. That, they made clear, would not be tolerated.

It would have been easy to dismiss the worries of the Lab School parents as class- or race-based fears, but there were real human concerns at work. I had no doubt that these parents were ardent supporters of equal opportunity and civil rights. What they feared was that, if the schools were combined, their children—innocent and deserving—would lose access to an excellent school in the name of a social experiment. That's too much to ask. After all, our goal was to create more good schools, not to destabilize those that were performing well.

"But if you lend a sympathetic ear to the Lab parents and their kids," I would say, "you must also consider the Straus School community in the same way." No child should have to enter school via the back door, whether we're speaking literally or metaphorically. "Let's be honest," I would add, "while some of you might consider sending your kids to Lower Lab, you would never let them go to Strauss or probably 90 percent of the other schools in the public school system. Whose kids go to those schools? Kids in families that had no choice, could not move to a better neighborhood, and certainly couldn't afford private schools. In other words, the kids with the greatest needs get the schools none of you would ever tolerate.

"That is wrong," I would conclude, "and I'm going to need your help and support as we try to make big changes to a system that is broken but has many strong defenders nevertheless."

IN JANUARY 2003, AFTER WE HAD COMPLETED EXHAUSTIVE INTERnal analyses and extensive community outreach, the mayor announced our administration's sweeping education reform agenda with the most carefully crafted public address of his time in office. The speech covered the actions required to wrest operating control from the balkanized school districts and to standardize the education system citywide. Although the mayor had gained control by eliminating the thirty-two elected school boards, community superintendents still ran those districts and wielded a lot of power. Because the community superintendents controlled only the elementary and middle schools, the city had created five borough-wide high-school superintendents, as well two specialized superintendents, one for schools servings students with severe disabilities and one for schools serving troubled children, including those in prison. We had decided to eliminate all but the two specialized superintendents.

This would be seen as a centralized power grab, but the mayor was ready for the battle. He had carefully reviewed the proposals, agreed with their rationale, was excited about the scope and breadth of what we were doing, and looked forward to the announcement.

He chose to make the speech on an auspicious date—Martin Luther King Jr.'s birthday—and in a symbolic setting, the Schomburg Center for Research in Black Culture in Harlem. Many luminaries were present, and the audience bristled with anticipation as the mayor took the stage. One attendee was Geoffrey Canada, who had been doing innovative work on behalf of poor, mostly black, children in Harlem through an organization called the Harlem Children's Zone. HCZ operated a preschool and workshops for young parents and offered support for every child who lived within its catchment area. Canada's strategy for saving kids from poverty depended on providing intensive services to families and children who were closely monitored for signs of academic trouble. Those whose attendance slipped or grades declined were contacted and helped before problems could worsen. No child within the zone was permitted to fall through the cracks and suffer out of sight.

Bloomberg looked at Canada when he called for a "new movement" to save the city's neediest children, who happened to come disproportionately from minority communities. To do this, he added, "We must have the courage to stand up to the apologists, to the entrenched self-serving special interests, to the self-promoters, and doubters, and the apathetic." This language was fair warning for the challenge to the status quo he was about to announce.

Under the plan the mayor then described, the district superintendents' offices would be disbanded, and the newly centralized school system would be run by administrators at Tweed, supported by ten regional superintendents who would operate relatively small regional offices. The ten regional superintendents would each have ten so-called "local instructional superintendents" reporting to them who, in turn, would supervise approximately ten schools each. The main responsibility of these new instructional superintendents would be to help their schools implement a single, new curriculum—standardized across the city—that would emphasize reading and math skills and replace the dozens of different programs then in use. The very best schools, according to their test scores (about 20 percent of the total), would be allowed greater flexibility in choosing their curriculum, but if their performance declined, they would come under the common curriculum system. The mayor also announced that our schools would end the social promotion policy that allowed children to move from grade to grade despite academic deficiencies in order to maintain their self-esteem by staying with their classmates—even if they couldn't keep up with the work.

Some teachers and principals would resent being told what and how to teach, but we expected to get even more pushback on our decision to eliminate the district superintendents' offices. Those superintendents and their offices had long been the operational backbone of the city's school system. Their positions would now be gone and their power removed. In addition, more than six thousand people worked in these offices. Some would be able to find spots in the new regional offices, but many would be dismissed or, in effect, forced to retire. Among them would be a significant number of once important men and women who would be hard-pressed to find jobs, salaries, and benefits that matched those they enjoyed as patronage appointees. However, their departure would free up hundreds of millions of dollars each year, which we could now spend on students. It would also open up enough building space to create new schools for eight thousand students.

The mayor ended his speech on a high note, explaining that we were creating a new position—called a parent coordinator—for every school. These coordinators would reach out to parents to try to get more of them involved in school activities and to help resolve problems that might arise between a parent and the school. We meant this to be a parent-friendly initiative that would be popular and well worth the cost, as it turned out to be. Nevertheless, we were criticized by parent-activists, who wanted the coordinators to report to the parent associations, not to the principals. But we didn't want to do anything that would undermine principals, whom we were determined to empower, and we believed that truly independent parent coordinators could wind up challenging principals for authority. We also rejected the UFT's request that the coordinators be members of its union. We didn't want the teachers to control the parent coordinators, which they would be able to do if they all were part of the same union. They wound up in the school aides' union, which made the UFT unhappy with us, because it meant a loss of potential union members and dues that would otherwise have accrued to them.

A few days after Mayor Bloomberg's big speech, I followed up with a set of more specific curriculum and teacher-support initiatives. I announced which literacy and math curricula we would use, explaining that we were seeking to "bring coherence and academic excellence to a school system that heretofore has offered a grab bag of curricula with only small pockets of success." I also announced that we would be providing extensive professional development and support to our teachers, including hiring full-time math and literacy coaches for all of our schools. This was a major commitment—the coaches alone would cost more than $200 million—but we could find the money in the savings we secured by dismantling the district superintendents' offices.

The immediate response to the mayor's address and my specific proposals was quite favorable. The press said we were acting boldly on a wide range of ideas, and Randi Weingarten expressed her approval, noting, "This is a good first step. We now have a unified school system." She called Children First—the name we gave to the package of reforms—"breathtakingly possible."

Unfortunately, this initial wave of enthusiasm was short-lived. Soon, a politician in Albany, upset that we had eliminated the patronage practices of the district superintendents' offices, sued us in state court. Worse, our choices of literacy and math curricula turned out to be more controversial than I would have anticipated. The English language arts program, in particular, called balanced literacy and fashioned after a program at Columbia's Teachers College, led us smack into a fight with the U.S. Department of Education in Washington.

Curriculum was not my area of expertise, and I learned only after my announcement that we had stumbled into a long-running dispute known as the reading wars. One side in this conflict was occupied by self-described progressives who favored "whole language" instruction based on stories and books intended to incite a passion for reading. On the other side stood more tradition-minded educators who preferred a highly structured method called phonics, which encourages children to recognize the sounds represented by letters and combinations of letters. Most baby boomers learned to read with phonics. Many of their children learned with whole language instruction. By the start of the twenty-first century, several studies had concluded that phonics was more effective, especially in providing a strong base for future reading. Nevertheless, the argument continued and became politicized, with liberals generally leaning toward whole language and conservatives embracing phonics.

On a national level, the Bush administration had come down firmly in favor of phonics, making it a requirement for so-called Reading First grants under the No Child Left Behind initiative. Soon after our curriculum was announced, Reid Lyon, a high-level federal official, called to tell me that the city was in danger of losing $38 million in aid because our reading program didn't comply with Washington's standards. Evidently, our "balanced literacy" approach wasn't all that balanced after all. We scrambled to beef-up the phonics component with a program called Voyager, of which the Bush administration approved. This move didn't fully satisfy anyone in the trenches of the reading wars, but it averted a financial crisis and, in fact, brought a somewhat better balance to our reading instruction.

Our math program, based on a textbook titled *Everyday Math*, was also controversial and stoked a conflict between educators who favor traditional computational math and those who prefer a newer, more intuitive approach called constructivist math, which generally relies on applied learning experiences that seek to engage a student more deeply in mathematical concepts. Although this dispute didn't affect federal dollars, our preference for a constructivist approach fed the notion in some quarters that we were not being rigorous in our curriculum selection. I thought this was an unfair knock—later on our math textbook was found by the federal government's researchers to be one of the very few that improved results for students—but it hurt us with many educators and advocates who might otherwise have been supportive of the kinds of reforms we were proposing.

The cross fire I experienced left me feeling let down by my teaching and learning team. They were the people who were supposed to have my back when it came to these kinds of curriculum issues, but I felt that they had not adequately prepared me for the controversy I was walking into. Many years later the national debate would shift again, in favor of a so-called Common Core set of learning standards that was more demanding than what most school districts and we had been following. More than forty states, including New York, would end up embracing Common Core. As those events unfolded and I became more immersed in curriculum issues, I realized that we should have insisted on a reading curriculum that was based more on the acquisition and mastery of knowledge than ours was. At the time of our announcement in 2003, however, the changes we made were at least a step forward given the generally weak and chaotic programs they would replace.

As we reviewed the rollout of our initial Children First reforms, despite a few tense moments, my team felt good about the substance and much of the reaction, especially the support from Randi Weingarten. We knew we were taking the first steps needed to dislodge a deeply complacent, bureaucratic school system. And while we had made some unnecessary missteps, the basic thrust of our efforts remained firmly intact. At the same time, bold as it all was, we knew it was only a small first step. The mayor had purposely not focused on high-school choice and charter schools in his Martin Luther King Day speech. This decision was not so much a matter of strategy as it was an acknowledgment that there were limits to the number of issues that could be covered in a single address and then be implemented effectively. Both the city and we had to be able to digest these changes before facing others. At Tweed, in particular, we realized that we would need to get control of the system through centralization, and bring some efficiency and academic coherence to it, before we could move forward on the more fundamental changes we were planning.

Of course, we also knew that, if we stopped with the reforms we had announced, significant as they were, we would fall way short of what we needed to do. The school system required more radical change, and we knew we would face strong and angry resistance and pushback from many quarters. As Bruno Bettelheim had told me, "Most people want to make sure tomorrow is just like yesterday." Toward this end, they fear change and fight it. And did they ever.

6

Dollars and Sense

Although children should stand at the center of every debate about education, it's often money that matters most to the adults in the system. Financial security—for individual educators and for their memberships as a whole—is the first priority of the labor unions. No one should blame them for this. Unions exist to make sure members get the greatest compensation and other benefits. UFT president Randi Weingarten had said as much, noting that the members of the union were always her first priority. When she withdrew her support for us in a scorching speech at the union's spring 2003 conference, she certainly drove home this point.

On May 10, 2003, a mere four months after she enthusiastically endorsed our first major set of Children First reforms, Weingarten changed course, labeling our efforts "P.R. gimmicks" that would accomplish little for our children. Using a bobblehead doll as a prop, she described the mayor's educational policy advisory board (the Panel on Education Policy) as a rubber stamp body and tried to rally taxpayers by complaining about the cost of our programs. Left unsaid was the fact that the teachers' contract was set to expire in three weeks, and that Weingarten was looking to capture tax dollars for her members. She was also upset that the mayor had imposed a budget cut, even though, reflecting his prioritization of education, he cut us by only 4.5 percent while cutting all the other agencies by 7.5 percent.

Weingarten was following a strategy from the same old playbook that had created New York schools crises in the past. Traditionally, union leaders accelerate attacks as negotiations approach, trying to win over the public by painting government officials as out of touch, power mad, or worse. Randi had already made an inflammatory, heavy-handed move the week before her speech, filing a lawsuit charging us with racial discrimination as we planned to lay off some eight hundred (out of a total of seventeen thousand) paraprofessionals who served as classroom aides to help deal with the mayor's budget cut. The paras were primarily black and Latino, and so, the argument went, we were acting in a racist way. The suit would never go anywhere, but the complaint could create the impression—especially among minority communities whose trust we needed—that we were the bad guys.

In addition, two days before Randi's speech, the powerful head of the State Assembly's Education Committee, Steve Sanders, along with sixteen other lawmakers and the principals' union, joined what, until then, had been a rogue lawsuit challenging our elimination of the district superintendents. Lawsuits are always unpredictable things, and this one had some legal basis; the thirty-two district superintendents had a defined role under state law. According to Sanders's argument, we might be able to limit the superintendents' authority and hiring practices but could not remove them altogether. The timing of this highly political lawsuit was no coincidence—we were facing a well-coordinated and sophisticated attack orchestrated by the UFT.

Had Bloomberg been the same old kind of politician, with one eye on campaign donors and another on public opinion, he probably would have started backpedaling on policy to quiet things down. But the mayor was not beholden to political contributors, and while he cared about reelection, he cared more about changing things. He felt confident that he would be able to communicate well enough with voters when the next election season rolled around and we had produced positive results.

In the meantime, the mayor wanted us to do the right thing for the city's kids. It's difficult to overstate how important this mandate was to our relationship and how, time and again, he stood firm when the politically expedient thing would have been to cave. Perhaps to underscore this point, whenever Randi publicly said I should be fired, Bloomberg would call me and jokingly say, "I'm really upset. Randi just said you should be fired. Now I can't fire you even if I want to." This was vintage Bloomberg: fiercely loyal and always there for his people when someone was gunning for them.

Despite the noise generated by the coordinated attack on our reforms, the mayor told me to push ahead with additional reforms, while he told his press secretary, Ed Skyler, to push back against Weingarten. Skyler issued a statement saying, "Like a lame politician Randi has flip-flopped, and, under the circumstances, one has to wonder what her motivations are. Her actions are getting more and more bizarre and irrational. The mayor is not going to engage in what should be a serious discussion about the education of our children when she performs a circus act with bobblehead dolls and personal attacks." The war had begun. It would ebb and flow over the course of Bloomberg's mayoralty, but peace would never again be fully at hand.

I was genuinely surprised at Randi's moves. Sure, she didn't like budget cuts, and her job required her to fight layoffs and build public support for her members during a contract dispute. But the nature of her wholesale attack on our entire agenda seemed disproportionate. It felt as if she wanted to teach the new kids—Bloomberg and me—a lesson: the union runs the school system, like it or not, and a governance change like mayoral control wasn't going to shift the fundamental balance of power. I was especially taken aback by her decision to file a lawsuit playing the race card, which is always a dangerous move. For this, she was roundly criticized in the local press, most memorably by the well-respected journalist Wayne Barrett, writing in the *Village Voice*, who expressed real dismay at what he termed "Weingarten's War."

I liked Randi personally and also admired the political sophistication with which she exercised her power. She was a consummate professional and knew how to play the game as well as anyone I had met. If she wanted to do a deal, she would get it done and wouldn't let prior estrangements get in the way. Over the course of our six years together, in fact, we did several good deals. Although she didn't shy away from personal attacks, she had a fundamental sense of decency. When the mayor announced my resignation in 2010, for example, her spokesperson, unbeknownst to her, put out a statement accusing me of "vilifying" teachers. Randi later found out about the quote and made him withdraw it, e-mailing me that "[I] was surprised and angered by the quote . . . I really am sorry." That took class.

On the other hand, I increasingly came to realize that Randi would never become a full partner in school reform. As she had told me during our first lunch meeting, she was looking for incremental change and wouldn't support radical reform. This realization informed everything we subsequently did, not only in labor-contract negotiations but also in deciding which reform strategies to adopt. We knew we would have to find areas where the union didn't have the legal authority to block us.

Although the UFT's attacks made for a hectic and intense final month of the school year, we ended on something of a high note. On June 10, 2003, we settled the lawsuit with the legislators who had challenged our reorganization. We agreed to appoint a superintendent for each of the thirty-two community school districts and provide each with a small two-person office located within the district. While unfortunate, this change didn't significantly impact the overall reorganization plan. The power would remain with the ten regional superintendents; these district offices would be largely relegated to dealing with technical and compliance issues.

Still, even as we celebrated the legal victory, we knew the new school year would be challenging. We would be implementing big organizational changes with the union looking to criticize us at every turn. This made for an exhausting summer as I pushed my team hard to make sure we were managing the transition well and would be ready for stormy seas.

IN THE FALL OF 2003, MY OPENING-DAY OPTIMISM WAS TEM-pered. For all their problems, the superintendents' offices had helped to open schools in previous years. Now, we wouldn't have their assistance. In addition, tens of thousands of teachers were being asked to adopt the new curricula for math and English, which would clearly be challenging. We also knew that thousands of students would be moving to new schools. Some moved under the transfer provision of the federal No Child Left Behind law, which provided parents of kids in failing schools the opportunity to go elsewhere. Others were relocated to the sixteen new small high schools opening that year. Some of these, operating under our New Beginnings programs, were designed for students identified as troubled, though not violent, and in need of extra attention.

On the Sunday before school was to begin, I attended the Bridge Street African Wesleyan Methodist Episcopal Church service in Brooklyn, where I asked the congregation to pray for the schools, the children, and me. They responded warmly, in part no doubt because so few top school officials had ever reached out to them. I enjoyed church visits like this and found them to be a good way to recharge my batteries while connecting with different communities and explaining what we were doing and why. I attempted to show how committed we were to their kids and communities. In my years as chancellor I am sure I spent more time in churches than had any Jewish man before me in New York City. Overall, the experiences were positive, and most pastors, especially in the poorer communities, were generally supportive: they knew their kids weren't getting what they needed and came to believe we were prepared to fight for them.

After leaving the Bridge Street Church, I headed to P.S. 87 on the Upper West Side of Manhattan. I had been urged to stop at a pre-opening get-together by Judy Horne, a parent who had taken to e-mailing me, on a frequent basis, to share her thoughts and concerns. As it turned out, the fourth-grade class I visited included the daughter of the writer and cartoonist Jules Feiffer. Feiffer was there with the other parents and read from his book *Some Things Are Scary* before sketching out a fast caricature of me with a big bald head, glasses, and a worried look on my face. He said, "Being Chancellor Klein on the first day of school is scary." I thought at the time that Feiffer was quite insightful, since I anticipated things were about to get noisy for us.

I wasn't wrong. On the first day of school, with the press in tow, I visited one school in each of the city's five boroughs, heralding our changes and hoping to generate excitement. We soon heard reports that some parents were showing up at schools and demanding to register their children because they had heard the No Child Left Behind law entitled them to withdraw from underperforming schools and enroll elsewhere. This was technically true. However, parents had been given the opportunity to make transfers in the spring, in anticipation of the new school year. As they learned in September, they couldn't simply walk in on the first day of the new school year and expect to find a spot. This was heartbreaking and reinforced our belief that we had to move fast and fight hard to open schools that would give them what they wanted and deserved for their kids.

The first-day commotion also included buses that failed to show up for grade schoolers and some chaos at a few high schools where hundreds of unexpected students, including a great many new ninth graders, lined up to be admitted. It turned out that enrollment projections generated the previous spring by the old school district offices had been extremely inaccurate. (I couldn't help but wonder whether this was a deliberate act of sabotage by people in the offices that we were in the process of closing down.)

Some parents complained quite loudly about the changes they saw as the new school year began. In Carroll Gardens, Brooklyn, where middle- and upper-middle-class parents had worked hard to improve a middle school, one mother told the press that she was worried that adding forty-one transfer students under the federal No Child law would depress test scores and deprive teachers of the right to opt out of the new math and English curricula. This occurred at the Brooklyn School for Collaborative Studies. Parent Amy Sumner told the *New York Times*, "We created that school to be small in terms of the number of classes in each grade, and in terms of the number of kids in each class." I understood and even sympathized but believed that the transfer opportunities for families whose kids were in failing schools took priority.

I had no sympathy at all for a bit of political grandstanding by Betsy Gotbaum, the city's elected public advocate. New York is one of the few places in the country with such an elected ombudsman whose office can be a stepping-stone for the politically ambitious. Gotbaum's predecessor, Mark Green, had been Bloomberg's opponent in the 2001 mayoral race, and everyone expected that Gotbaum would have similar ambitions of her own. In September 2003, on the first day of school, she issued a report claiming that we had postponed important repairs on fifty-three schools, and that in eight instances these delays had permitted "life safety" or "hazardous" conditions to persist. "Anecdotally," she told the press, "there are problems all over the place."

For the photographers and reporters scouring the city for first-day-of-school stories, Gotbaum was a godsend. We were initially caught off guard by her report, but, as we checked her numbers, we realized it was from data that was at least a year old. Among the more dangerous problems she had cited were cracks in the facades of buildings and missing hardware on doors. Our crews had actually addressed the most serious issues and were moving forward on the rest. But Gotbaum apparently never called to find out what had changed in the many months between the identification of the repair needs and her news conference.

On the same day that Gotbaum tried to score points, we also heard that parents were arriving at schools with two different city guides published to help them navigate a school system in transition. One came from us at the Department of Education; the other was issued by the Office of the Public Advocate, putting Betsy Gotbaum's name in the hands of lots of parents and voters. Gotbaum claimed there had been some mix-up—she was only trying to provide a public service and had no knowledge that we were putting out a guide. But a member of the nonprofit groups that helped prepare our guide publicly confirmed that she had participated in conversations about our guide before it was issued. As it turned out, the wording in Gotbaum's guide was almost identical to ours, leading me to think that her guide was either intentionally designed to sow confusion, or her office was trying to take credit for our work.

Although the press accounts went against us on opening day—the *New York Times* pronounced it, "Back to Class, with Chaos Beyond"—we recovered quickly. We managed to calm parents and kids at the buildings swamped with new students and made sure that the missing buses were found and the drivers got their routes straightened out. The media fires created by Betsy Gotbaum's report on so-called neglected repairs were quickly doused, and though the dueling guides for parents caused complaints about government waste and confusion, they didn't create any problems for families since they were virtually identical.

As soon as our 1.1 million kids were settled into a routine, we began preparing to announce some of our initiatives regarding high-school choice and charter schools. We also started to step up our fund-raising efforts, which would be critical to support some of these new initiatives. We didn't want to use public monies for such controversial moves because our critics would have argued that we were short-changing other priorities, such as reducing class sizes, for example.

At the time, we were seeing encouraging interest from a variety of potential partners, including Geoffrey Canada, who wanted to open a charter school as part of the Harlem Children's Zone. Given Canada's reputation in the African American community, and the city more broadly, his announcement that he would run a charter school had great symbolic importance for us. I had also reached out to lots of other successful charter operators, like Dave Levin, Dacia Toll, and Norm Atkins, who were eager to open or expand in New York. Surprisingly, even Randi Weingarten said she wanted to have the UFT open a charter school to show what great teachers could achieve without bureaucratic oversight and regulation by the likes of those of us at Tweed. It was a backhanded form of encouragement, but we were thrilled that the union might do this: at a minimum, it would make it harder for them or others to criticize our charter school plans.

WE DECIDED TO MOVE FIRST ON THE HIGH-SCHOOL REPLACE-
ment strategy. We knew this would be controversial, even though the
closing of perpetually underperforming schools made sense. But we
suspected it would spark less of an uproar than the charter schools because the new, smaller replacement schools would be traditional public
schools staffed by union teachers. This was an expensive initiative.
Each small start-up would cost about $1 million, and we wanted
to do hundreds. To help pay this cost, we began looking for private
funding.

In the year before I had started as chancellor, three major philanthropic foundations—Gates, Carnegie, and Soros—had contributed
$10 million each to jump-start a new small-schools program in New
York City. The city had opened twenty of them as of September 2003.
The Gates Foundation, which had enormous resources, was especially
eager to support a major, small-high-school initiative. We could certainly use their help.

Unfortunately, Gates posed a problem, one that was whispered
about when others at Tweed hoped I couldn't hear. Its founder was Bill
Gates, whose company, Microsoft, I had sued under the antitrust laws
when I was with the Justice Department. It had been an ugly case, and
everyone knew Bill had taken it personally, believing that the government was off base in challenging a great and innovative American company like Microsoft. How would we ever convince him to continue
funding the high-school initiative now that I was running the show?

Michele Cahill, always the can-do optimist, decided to make it
happen. She knew the people at the Gates Foundation well from her
previous work at Carnegie, and she personally assured them that we
would be pursuing their small-school agenda with unmatched scope

and commitment. Whatever people might have thought about my past, she added, on this matter I could be fully trusted. With Michele's leadership and Caroline Kennedy's help, Gates decided to let bygones be bygones. I was later told, by people who claimed to know, that, despite our disagreement over the lawsuit, Gates knew me to be fearless and determined, and if his foundation wanted to support meaningful school reform, I was a good person to bet on.

The Gates Foundation decided to give us $51 million to support our small-school efforts, and on September 17, 2003, Gates came to the former Morris High School in the Bronx to announce the grant. Built in 1897, Morris had educated some illustrious New Yorkers, including Armand Hammer and Colin Powell. By 2002, it was a failing school, and the city had already begun the process of closing it and using the building for five smaller schools.

On the day of Gates's visit, I was extremely nervous. I admired Bill enormously for backing us but worried what the day would be like. Our past encounters had been tense. As it turned out, Gates couldn't have been more gracious. We visited some classrooms together, talked to students, and chatted about some of the exciting things we saw. When Mayor Bloomberg spoke at the press conference, he joked a bit about the awkwardness of the moment. Gates replied, "I'm glad to be working on the same team." A little later Gates added, "There is one fact about my past that I am glad Mr. Klein didn't mention. Of course what I mean is that, despite my commitment to education, I am a college dropout." Everyone laughed at Gates's remark, knowing that, in fact, he really was referring to the antitrust case. When the program ended, as I finally started to relax while walking off the stage, a principal in the audience tugged at my sleeve and said: "Chancellor, $51 million is a good day's work. But imagine what Gates would have given you if you hadn't sued him."

Kidding aside, this was a remarkable day. We now had the financial support and momentum to move aggressively on our high-school-replacement strategy. Over the years, we would open hundreds of these schools. The Gates Foundation ended up giving us much more than $51 million, and years later, when assessing their small-school strategy, Bill said New York City was the only place where it had succeeded. But even then, the humor remained front and center. As part of this event, Bill invited everyone to his home for cocktails. When I arrived at the door, the man who opened it asked, "Are you who I think you are?" I responded, "I suspect I am." He then looked over my shoulder and said, "You're a brave man to show up without a taster." Bill's wife, Melinda, whom I had come to know over the years, then greeted me and took me downstairs to show me what she called the "Joel Klein pinball machine," a present she had bought Bill to relieve his stress during the lawsuit.

Bill Gates was, and is, many things, and my respect for him grew immeasurably as I came to know him over the years. The one thing he wasn't, of course, was your typical dropout. Gates was a genius who left Harvard to start his own computer company. A billionaire while still in his thirties, he became the stuff of legend as Microsoft grew to be one of the largest and most important companies in the world. From his position as a global leader, Gates realized that technology would rapidly displace low-skilled workers and that education would be essential to success for both individuals and nations, including the United States.

This education imperative was so powerful that few issues other than terrorism mattered as much to the public. In the 2000 presidential race it was the number one issue, according to an early *New York Times* poll, and it stayed high in voters' minds throughout the race. After Bush was elected, one of his first moves was to secure passage of the No Child Left Behind Act. Prior to the Bush years, the United States' commitment to local control of education had defeated many attempts to forge a serious national response to the problems of schools. In the vacuum, a host of private efforts had arisen. Profit-making ventures like Edison Schools attracted skeptical attention from those who were wary of the private sector. But the real innovations were being accomplished by nonprofits like Teach for America, New Leaders for New Schools, and the New Teacher Project, which together had brought thousands of highly educated and highly motivated new teachers and principals into the schools each year, and by funders like the foundations created by Gates, Eli Broad, Julian Robertson, and the Walton family. We would rely extensively and gratefully on all of these groups as we moved our initiatives forward.

But like the for-profit school operators, the big names and big fortunes behind education reform attracted critics who feared they would enjoy too much influence over schools that were, traditionally, a public trust. We sought to minimize these fears by directing their funding to nonprofit organizations like New Visions, Urban Assembly, Good Shepherd Services, and many other long-standing and well-respected community groups eager to partner with us as we adopted our reforms. We benefitted enormously from their involvement.

New Visions, in particular, was a lynchpin in our new-schools strategy, taking the lead in opening and supporting close to one hundred schools, while Urban Assembly added more than twenty others. These organizations set very high standards—for example, New Visions committed to 93 percent attendance and 80 percent graduation rates when the numbers at the schools they helped to replace were much lower. To this day, these groups are doing some of the best work with high-poverty students anywhere in the country.

I asked Michele Cahill to develop a plan that would make sure the new replacement schools wouldn't replicate the failures of those we were closing. Just making them smaller wouldn't get the job done. Under Michele's leadership, we set up a competitive process that allowed principals, teachers, universities, community groups, and others to apply for grants that would support them opening the new schools. Those applying had to submit a proposal satisfying more than a dozen research-based school-design criteria, including things like strong leadership, committed teachers, a rigorous curriculum, and accountability metrics against which to measure success.

The other thing we did was to set up a separate office—called the Office of New Schools—to administer this competitive process and then follow up with the schools once they were open to make sure they were progressing. This upset our ten regional superintendents, who wanted to control all the schools, including the new ones, but I knew that if we let them run the process, they would stifle it through micromanagement and bureaucratic overreach. Instead, I chose Kristen Kane, a committed reformer and excellent manager, to head this office, and, working with Michele, she implemented and ran the process in a thorough and demanding way. Thousands of applicants—many of them prominent nonprofit groups—sought to open new schools. All were subjected to an extensive review of their plans and personnel to assure they could meet and execute the design criteria we had established. Nothing like this had ever happened in public education, where individuals and groups could open new public schools through a competitive process. The schools remained subject to our management and control, and their teachers and administrators were all union members, but, in reality, considerable day-to-day operational responsibility was being devolved to the groups that were partnering with us.

The outpouring of new talent that this attracted to the school system was amazing. In addition to New Visions and Urban Assembly, Outward Bound, the College Board, the Asia Society, City University, and many other groups and individuals opened schools in the city. While not every school worked out as planned, overwhelmingly they succeeded in creating good options for kids in communities where the only previous choice had been a single, large, failing high school.

Over the years, I visited dozens and dozens of these new small schools and spoke at many of their graduation ceremonies. These were exciting places that were run—and often founded—by extremely talented principals, quite a few of whom were trained at our Leadership Academy. In many ways these schools had the look and feel and work ethic of the best charter schools like KIPP. The positive spirit was palpable, and you could see it in the eyes of the teachers. These people were committed to changing the world for kids who, in the past, would have fallen through the cracks at a large school like Evander Childs.

One of my early visits was to a small school in the old Evander Childs building, called Bronx Lab. It was headed by a young Teach for America alum, Marc Sternberg, who had subsequently gone to Harvard to get a joint degree in business and education and then worked his TFA network to find teachers to staff Bronx Lab. When I visited, I could tell he had succeeded. In a school made up almost entirely of poor black and Latino students, Marc was able to get 96 percent of his first class to graduate. Almost all of them went on to college. I spoke at the school's first graduation, and the pride that the teachers, students, and families felt brought tears to the eyes of everyone there.

Marc went on to be a White House fellow during the Obama administration, where he worked for Secretary of Education Arne Duncan. I then hired him to be my deputy chancellor, a position he held until the end of Bloomberg's third term. After that, he was chosen to run the Walton Family Foundation's education portfolio, which gives away hundreds of millions of dollars each year for education reform. That's quite a résumé for a man in his early forties. And yet, I'd bet that

no matter what he does, the work Marc did at Bronx Lab will always
hold a special place in his heart. It does in mine.

THE ANNOUNCEMENT OF THE GATES FOUNDATION SUPPORT
for our new small schools was generally well received and garnered lots
of media attention because of my history with Bill. We followed up by
immediately announcing a new high-school admissions policy that we
had been working on with Alvin Roth, a Harvard Business School professor who was an expert in this area. We set up a matching system,
modeled on the medical school residency admissions program, under
which each student would list his or her rank-order preferences for up
to twelve schools. The schools in turn would rank students based on
their admissions criteria—from grades, to geographic preferences, to
random lotteries. A computer would then match them all up in a way
that, as Roth set out to do, maximized the total good across the entire
student population. This replaced a system that had offered very limited choice, with most kids ending up at their neighborhood school.
Although those who knew how to work the system under the old approach might not be helped by the change, overall our approach was
much more equitable. For the first time, the city would use an objec-
tively fair process to place students, and knowing someone important
would no longer make a difference.

This kind of student choice was novel in public education. Not surprisingly, some families complained about the change, claiming that it
was too complex or that their kid didn't get his first choice. Learning
about and ranking up to a dozen schools could be a challenge for some
students and their families. But even if everyone didn't get his or her
first choice, the system turned out to work well in practice, which
largely quieted the critics. Over the years, almost half the kids got their

first choice and three quarters got one of their top three. Years later, we were pleased when many positive articles were written about our approach, and Roth received the Nobel Prize for the analytical work that provided the basis for our program, all of which helped to validate what we had done.

A few weeks after announcing the funding for our new small schools and this high-school admissions program, we launched our charter school initiative. Whatever the tumult so far, we knew this would be the most controversial thing we had done. The idea that a public school system would support and develop new charters to compete directly with its own noncharter schools was unorthodox at the time and remains so today. Typically, school districts resist competition and, at best, wait for outsiders—both for-profit and nonprofit—to raise money, develop plans, and seek approval for charters. That process could take years. But we believed New York City's kids couldn't afford to wait for better options.

Although we knew from the outset that charter schools would serve only a relatively small part of our overall population—probably less than 10 percent—we expected they would have a significant impact nonetheless. They would be concentrated in high-poverty communities, serving mostly black and Latino students, where the need was greatest. Over time, some communities, like Harlem, became real choice meccas, where more than a third of the kids in elementary and middle schools ended up in charter schools. Once that happened, it was impossible for the community not to notice whose kids were getting the best instruction, and for other parents to begin to demand more of the same.

I also wanted to encourage an all-hands-on-deck approach to school improvement. Just as we needed New Visions and Urban Assembly to help us start our new small high schools and add talent and program support to them, we wanted KIPP and Achievement First and Uncommon Schools—the biggest and best charter operators on the East Coast—to bring their talents and commitment to support our efforts. We thought that competition, pure and simple, would be good for the traditional public schools and certainly for those families that would suddenly have a choice. And, most important, to the extent the charter schools did well, and we believed in our bones many would, they would put pressure on the public schools to stop making excuses about why they weren't successfully educating kids from poor communities.

There was also another, more subtle reason we sought to bring high-performing charter schools to New York. The model under which they operated was one that appealed to us, and we hoped it would become a template for how we reorganized the traditional public schools. Charters had much more operational freedom than traditional schools because they weren't smothered by the micromanaging rules and regulations of the bureaucracy and union contract. They were, instead, pretty much free to determine their own course so long as they got good results for their kids. In short, charter schools were built on a model of empowerment and accountability, which made great organizational sense.

Personally, I couldn't help but be struck by the fact that the people who operated these charter schools are generally among the most politically progressive people I knew. Yet they did everything in their power to avoid unionization—at least in its current form. That spoke volumes about their view that, when it came to running their schools, a traditional unionized workforce was unlikely to be as successful.

Charters weren't an entirely new idea, but they had never really gotten off the ground in New York City. As we studied this problem we discovered that money had been a huge hurdle. Operating costs were higher in New York than anywhere else, but this didn't matter much because the state paid a reasonable, if not generous, amount to educate each child enrolled in a charter. The real reason that most plans for charter schools foundered was because no one could find a proper location. Real estate was both scarce and expensive in many parts of the city. Empty parcels were almost never available, and buildings ripe for demolition or renovation were snapped up by developers who could invest huge sums in construction and then rent or sell space to those who could pay top dollar. Even in poor neighborhoods, where you might find a site, construction was very expensive, due to New York labor costs and building code requirements.

The perfect fix for the real estate problem was to make existing classroom space available to charters, and this is exactly what we decided to do. We could start with the space that we had freed up by shutting down the massive superintendent offices. In addition to those former office quarters, we could also let the charters use classrooms in buildings occupied by traditional schools. Teachers and administrators in those buildings might not want to lose the space, or have their work compared with the efforts of a charter school in the same building, but we believed the space belonged to the kids, not the schools, and if the kids wanted to choose a charter school, they should command their share of the space as well.

To this day the fight continues to rage over our decision to colocate charter schools in public school space. In part, this conflict grew out of the concerns of teachers and administrators in traditional schools who didn't want to lose the space and didn't like the competition. But this battle was also a surrogate for opposition to charters more generally. Simply as a practical matter, without the real estate, there would be very few charters.

Of course, the proper conditions for a crop of new charters would include far more than just real estate. We also had to reverse a widespread perception and make clear to the charter community that our school district would welcome them. I did this by meeting personally with most of the major operators, giving them my assurance that I would be in their corner, while making a highly publicized speech announcing that we were determined to turn New York City into "the Silicon Valley for charter schools." Having invoked this comparison, I was signaling that our charter initiative would not be small or limited. We wanted all the good charter organizations to come to New York and expand. By encouraging this kind of growth, we knew that the charters would feel safe and that they could live in an environment that enabled them to learn from one another.

A robust charter community would also need support in navigating the practical and political challenges that it would face. We didn't want the public school bureaucracy to smother this nascent (and seemingly threatening) movement, so we ultimately decided to create a private nonprofit organization, called the Center for Charter Excellence, that would become the hub for charter school support and advocacy. As the name implied, we wanted the center to help ensure that our charter schools were indeed excellent; we weren't supporting charters for their own sake. This initiative mattered only if it resulted in more good schools for our kids. To get the center established, we raised more than $40 million from several large donors—the Robin Hood Foundation and philanthropists Julian Robertson and Joe and Carol Reich—all of whom remained strong, dedicated, and generous charter school backers, and each designated a representative to serve on the new center's board.

On October 30, 2003, the mayor and I went to Renaissance Charter School in Jackson Heights, Queens. In addition to announcing the Center for Charter Excellence, we committed to opening at least fifty new charter schools in the next five years. We also said we would push for changes in state law that would be conducive to charter development and expansion, including raising the existing cap on the number of charter schools that could exist statewide, something the unions had insisted on limiting in order to make sure charters didn't grow too quickly.

This announcement was widely perceived to be big news. The message to prospective charter operators—as well as to the rest of the city— was that we meant business. The huge financial backing signaled that we would have the wherewithal to attract new charter operators and give them the support they needed. The reaction from the unions, bureaucrats, politicians, and existing personnel at the public schools was predictably fierce. Aside from the fact that monopolists don't like competition, politicians don't like perceived threats to their community schools, where they invariably have strong ties and influence that they have built up over the years. Nor do they like explaining to constituents why some kids could get into a charter school but others couldn't because there wasn't enough space. Although it shouldn't have surprised me, one of the things I found most difficult to accept was the opposition to charter schools voiced by many legislators from minority communities, where the existing schools were failing and charter options were so desperately needed.

In fact, among the first schools to open under our charter initiative was an elementary school in Bedford-Stuyvesant, one of the most challenged neighborhoods in Brooklyn. With extraordinary financial support from the philanthropist Paul Tudor Jones, a successful charter group called Uncommon Schools opened the first all-boys school in the city, called Excellence Academy, converting a building that used to be a place where drug dealers and prostitutes operated into one of the most beautiful schools I've ever seen. The kids who attended were from the neighborhood, mostly black boys from low-income families. The principal, Jabali Sawicki, himself a young black man and a former teacher, enjoyed a reputation for leadership that far surpassed what you'd expect from someone in his early thirties. Sawicki himself had lived the American Dream, and he was determined to make it happen for as many other African American boys as he could.

Soon after Excellence opened, I paid a visit and arrived at the same moment that a young boy dressed in a neat school uniform showed up. He immediately said, "Good morning, Chancellor," which surprised me. As I had learned, most kids have no idea who the chancellor is or what he does. Sometimes, when I went to a school, especially if the media were around, a kid might say, "Who's that, the mayor?" But that's about as much recognition as I got. I could only guess that Excellence had taken the time to tell its students who I was and that I would be visiting that day.

When I asked the youngster his name, he replied, "Jamal." I asked, "What grade are you in?" And he said, "Kindergarten." I asked, "What do you do in kindergarten at Excellence?" He replied, "We start getting ready for college." I said, "Jamal, college is a long way away, why would you start getting ready now?" He replied, "Well, college is important, so it's never too early to start getting ready."

I never forgot that encounter. As I quickly learned, Jamal's thoughts were built into every aspect of the school culture at Excellence. Everyone was expected to go to college. Each classroom was named for a college, and the students visited colleges while in elementary school. The school insisted on high standards, its teachers went above and beyond, and its students prospered. Sawicki inspired his teachers and students, whom he treated as if each were his son. After graduating from Excellence at the end of eighth grade, Jamal went on to be an honor student at Bishop Loughlin, one of the best Catholic schools in New York. He hopes to go to college at Harvard or Morehouse and then work for Sawicki, who's now using his incredible teaching talent to design online interactive courses so he can reach—and teach—kids all over the world. I have often wondered what would have happened to Jamal if he had gone to one of the nearby failing neighborhood schools instead of Excellence.

Despite countless stories like Jamal's, in the end nothing—and I mean nothing—was more threatening to the education status quo in New York City than our charter school initiative. During Mayor Bloomberg's tenure, the city opened well over 150 new charters, and as they consistently outperformed the traditional public schools, the demand for them in high-poverty neighborhoods went through the roof. The waiting list in minority communities alone reached into the tens of thousands each year. Among the charters were two opened by the UFT, one on its own and one in partnership with Green Dot, a California-based charter group. Both of them shared space with other schools in our buildings. But these facts didn't matter. When it came to charter schools, all that mattered was that they competed with the traditional public schools, and, almost without exception, they weren't unionized. As a result, the unions, led by the UFT and supported by most Democratic politicians, opposed us at every step.

7

The Zombie
Bureaucracy

In most debates, people look for reliable information to establish, at the very least, some agreed-upon facts. In an enterprise like education, where tests are given routinely and grades are issued to track progress, you would think facts would be readily available. But you would be wrong. At the Department of Education, I discovered that solid data is a shockingly rare commodity. New York is not alone in this dark place of ignorance. At every level, American educators have failed to come up with coherent ways to measure school performance over time in a meaningful way. Socioeconomic factors and funding differences make it difficult to compare one cohort of children with another, and no one had come up with a formula to compensate for these differences.

Denied the kind of metrics and other information that guide decisions in most realms like business, or medicine, educators gravitate toward innovations that make intuitive sense or are supported by limited kinds of research. This is how, at one point, old-fashioned reading primers were replaced by phonics, which were supplanted by whole language, and then again phonics returned. Whether the subject is reading, math, science, or history, this trial-and-error exercise has been repeated in America's fourteen thousand school districts under the banner of local control, which keeps interference by big government at a minimum, but also makes it far more difficult for anyone to know what works and what doesn't.

More broadly, while there is some performance data available at the national and international levels, these numbers are essentially irrelevant to parents, teachers, and administrators who want to know how *their* schools are doing. The national exams—called the National Assessment of Educational Progress (NAEP)—provide state-by-state comparisons, and even some city-by-city comparisons, but they do not reveal individual school results. Similarly, educators and political leaders have struggled to understand whether America's schools are failing or succeeding in comparison with the schools of other nations. For the longest time no meaningful comparisons were even possible, because every country measured education in a different way. With the advent of the Program for International Student Assessment (PISA) in 1997, the experts began to address the problem through international comparisons, but PISA did little to help people in local communities, or even states, understand where they stood. The first PISA results put U.S. students near the bottom of twenty-one economically developed countries, but if you lived in a place with seemingly excellent schools, it was easy to dismiss this finding as relevant only to other people's schools and, therefore, other people's children.

The 2001 No Child Left Behind law was an attempt to break the data logjam in the pursuit of improvements in education nationwide. This was seen as a landmark in national education policy and one of the few successful pieces of bipartisan legislation to pass in recent memory. President George W. Bush, who ran on a school reform platform; Ted Kennedy, the liberal lion of the Senate; and George Miller, one of Speaker Nancy Pelosi's closest allies in the House, came together to get it done. It was the first federal effort to bring about school-based accountability and to provide some parental choice as part of the accountability process.

While No Child, as the law became known, was an important step forward, it was hampered from the beginning by the Republican insistence that education had to remain a state and local, not national, issue. Despite leadership by a Republican president, political realities made it impossible for those who drafted the law to create a set of national tests to measure student performance. Instead, the states were permitted to maintain their own standards and tests. Although this discretion created its own problems—some states would set the bar for passing at a much lower level than others—the mandatory annual reporting of information on every school's effectiveness, based on student performance in grades three through eight, was nevertheless revolutionary. Administrators would be required to improve results at failing schools or risk losing federal funds. Also, parents and students would be permitted to use the data about their school to get some sense of how they were doing. Those in failing schools (euphemistically referred to as "schools in need of improvement") could request transfers to better schools.

The notion of being able to transfer out of a failing school was encouraging in theory, but in reality the number of available seats in good schools in New York or other urban areas was small. Popular schools in New York, like P.S. 6 or P.S. 290 on the Upper East Side of Manhattan, or P.S. 321 in Park Slope, Brooklyn, were already overcrowded and, as a result, few if any transfers to these schools occurred under the law. Indeed, throughout the entire city, try as we might, given the space constraints in the more-desirable schools, we could accommodate only a relatively small number of transfers each year. This is what had caused such dismay when we opened schools in September 2003. From a high of several thousand applicants in 2003, the number seeking transfers declined to fewer than one thousand in 2004, a level that was maintained thereafter. The number of students who actually moved to different schools would be counted in the hundreds, but the decline probably stemmed from the fact that fewer and fewer actually sought transfers. As time passed, I also came to believe that the demand for transfers diminished because we were creating so many new good options and our schools were generally improving.

But despite the practical limits on transfers, the process created by No Child, thanks to the new data, allowed for an entirely different conversation about admission practices citywide. In the past, the lack of transparency masked all sorts of unfairness. For example, prior to mayoral control, when schools in more affluent neighborhoods had spaces open, they would handpick applicants from outside the catchment area they served. This happened quite frequently in some of the more sought-after schools on the Upper West Side of Manhattan, where the staff, and sometimes neighborhood parents, interviewed students and parents from nearby Harlem who were looking for better opportunities for their kids. The purpose of these interviews, I was told, was to find "the right kind" of minority students. The parents and educators in these communities proudly insisted that they were not prejudiced. As one explained it to me, "This isn't based on race, it's based on class." We dealt with class-based discrimination by outlawing it and requiring that, unless a school had established admissions requirements that we approved—like a gifted and talented program—all qualifying applicants from outside a school's catchment boundaries had to be accepted, and if there were more applicants than vacancies, a lottery had to be used.

Critics of No Child said that testing was too narrow a measure of a school's performance, and that it would lead many to teach to the test so that scores would be raised. As the psychologist Howard Gardner noted, "Test scores in themselves should not be the goal of schooling;

nor should practicing for the test be a primary activity for students." But with a little caution when it came to interpretation, the No Child data was still useful on multiple levels. In the very first year, for example, it confirmed troubling trends in the education of African American and Latino students and patterns of failure in big cities. In 2003, more than 8,000 U.S. schools were deemed failing under the law, with 366 of them in New York City. For all the criticism and limitations, the bottom line was that the impact of putting out data and identifying failing schools under No Child was undeniable. People were beginning to pay attention to kids—mostly from poor, predominantly minority neighborhoods—who had previously been invisible.

Somewhat surprisingly, even as we reported that many of our schools were underperforming under the No Child criteria, mid-2003 brought reports of a small improvement in student test scores in both math and English for grades four and eight. At the start of 2004, the state reported that the number of failing schools in New York City had declined by about 10 percent. Randi Weingarten said the teachers deserved credit for the good news, because the UFT had agreed to a small increase in instructional time as part of the 2002 contract with the mayor. Since these results came about before many of our reforms had taken effect, I was hardly ready to declare victory for anyone except the individual students and teachers who worked hard to improve. Instead, I told the press that we had a long way to go to reach our goal of making sure that every school was a school we'd all want our own children to attend. While the press always focused on one-year changes in test scores, at Tweed we understood that little, one-year upticks (or for that matter little downticks) were not especially meaningful. Tests would never be a perfect or totally consistent measure, and small year-to-year changes might say as much about the tests as they did about student performance.

During this time, we were dealing with several problems, including some caused by our reforms. For instance, a few of the better schools, which were in high demand, not only couldn't accept transfers, but also couldn't serve all the neighborhood kids. In some new schools, glitches in the bureaucracy had delayed paychecks for teachers, who were howling. Most seriously, the system for disciplining disruptive students was completely bogged down as a result of our reorganization. The delays understandably infuriated teachers and parents who wanted kids who threatened a school's peace and safety quickly suspended or thrown out altogether. This last problem became a big issue.

Shortly before Christmas 2003, admitting "we've screwed up," the mayor announced a new, beefed-up program that significantly improved the suspension process. The mayor's announcement astonished the city. No one could recall a public official taking responsibility for this kind of failure. But Bloomberg, in his typical fashion, said, "You cannot blame anybody else. . . . I wanted control [of the schools], and I got control. And I am going to do something about it."

I remember that Friday morning vividly. The mayor phoned me at 5:30 a.m. He was angry, and let me know how this kind of misstep could hurt our entire effort because, he emphasized, our critics would seize on it to paint us "as the gang who couldn't shoot straight." He made it clear that my team had better fix the problem quickly and make sure nothing comparable happened again. I felt awful. We had blown it, and the mayor had to take the hit.

At about the same time, we were also hearing complaints from teachers regarding the implementation of our new department-wide math and English curricula, some of which, frankly, struck me as being on target. The way the programs were being administered by our people in the field was often highly prescriptive. They would insist, for example, that kids had to sit in certain spots for particular activities and that so-called mini-lessons could last only ten minutes. Bureaucrats, as I was learning, loved to throw their weight around, and, believing they knew more about instruction than did the teachers, they would often insist on these kinds of silly rules, hoping to micromanage classroom teachers into success. Despite our best efforts, our bureaucrats, it turned out, weren't much different.

With all these changes and challenges, some school administrators bailed out on our effort, choosing to quit rather than learn new methods and endure a rough transition. Others kept the faith. I was personally heartened by the words of Dave Raubvogel, a principal at one of our New Beginnings schools, who likened the Children First reforms to changing a tire while the car is moving. Still, he maintained his optimism. Dave was just the kind of leader we were looking for. During his own years in high school in New York City, he was constantly in trouble. He eventually transferred from a neighborhood high school to one of the city's alternative, less-structured schools called City-As-School, which featured internship programs as part of its curriculum. City-As, as it was called, saved lots of kids who otherwise would have dropped out, proving once again that a one-size-fits-all approach doesn't work. We knew we needed much more diversity among our high schools.

Dave went on to become the principal of Richard Green High in lower Manhattan, a school that served almost all minority kids from low-income families who wanted to become teachers. He became famous for creating an environment where students actually wanted to go to the principal's office because they so enjoyed spending time with Dave. Like so many others who beat the odds and ran good schools in challenging circumstances, Dave and his boundless optimism were a constant inspiration for those of us who believed that strong principals would ultimately become the key to a successful transformation of the public schools.

Dave's reference to Children First being like changing a tire while the car is moving struck me as particularly apt and, frankly, comforting. I myself had used a similar analogy to describe our reforms, often saying, "We were redesigning the airplane while flying it." It would have been easier to focus on operations and slow down change, as many had urged us to do, but I knew we didn't have that option. We had to move quickly because each year without improvement would affect lots of kids forever.

Also, the resistance to change is so deeply entrenched in a massive bureaucratic system like the New York public schools that, if you slow down, backsliding is inevitable. I would constantly tell my team—especially when things got very noisy and contentious—that if we ever started to feel comfortable, then we weren't moving fast enough. But we knew that this speed meant there would be implementation errors, inevitable in any large-scale change effort, and more likely when many don't embrace the change. These mistakes would fuel the critics, who opposed change and would point to them as evidence that we didn't know what we were doing. These were painful moments and harmful to our efforts, even if inevitable at times. I tried to comfort myself by recalling Theodore Roosevelt's prescient lines from his legendary "Man in the Arena" speech—"There is no effort without error and shortcoming"—but it still drove me nuts when we screwed up an implementation. Besides, I wasn't eager to get any more wake-up calls at 5:30 in the morning from the mayor.

IN THE DAILY PRESS, OVERCROWDED SCHOOLS, SILLY RULES about where kids should sit on rugs, and delayed discipline for violent students got lots of attention, and deservedly so. Our critics on the City Council, notably Education Committee chair Eva Moskowitz, didn't hesitate to point out our mistakes. But we tried to remain focused on the big picture. While we responded to the immediate challenges of running the schools, we were looking for sustained improvements, especially in the schools serving poorer kids. As we sent our first graduates from our new principals academy into the field, we learned that change wasn't coming fast enough. Many of these new principals echoed what we were hearing from teachers about their classrooms. They said that the bureaucracy was still too powerful, despite the fact that we had eviscerated the community districts. Apparently the ten new regional offices we had created to support principals and their schools were often more likely to interfere with them. There were too many forms, too many rules, and too many meetings—*especially meetings*—all of which the bureaucrats loved.

Although I had hoped that the new structure and their redefined responsibilities would persuade the regional superintendents to support our agenda, that didn't happen often enough. At best, most didn't interfere with our initiatives, and sometimes some even tried to sabotage them. The regions, in short, largely turned out to be extensions of the old bureaucracy rather than agents for change.

If, like a zombie, the old bureaucracy refused to die, we would have to invent something new to compete with, and ultimately replace, it. This would be tricky. We had just dismantled the community districts and created a regional structure. If we started yet another organizational model, our critics would argue that the regional structure had failed. I saw it differently: I knew all along that the new regional structure would be transitional and that, after a few years, we would replace it with a different, more school-based, operating model.

From my first conversation about education with the mayor, our goal always had been to empower principals by giving them far greater operating discretion. As I later emphasized in a speech at New York University, the top-down regional management structure could facilitate needed improvements, but it couldn't provide the creativity and dynamism necessary for long-term success. Michael Barber, a leading British school reformer with whom I consulted often, explained it to me this way: "Your regional structure can help move the system from awful to adequate, but it could never move it from adequate to good, much less great." I knew he was right—that greatness cannot be mandated; it can only be unleashed.

We thus began the quiet but accelerated effort to design a multiyear transition away from the regions. Setting aside the traditional constructs that grouped schools together geographically, we imagined a kind of virtual school district, which we initially called the Autonomy Zone. Principals whose schools were admitted into the Zone would be excused from attending most Education Department meetings, as well as regional meetings, and freed from writing most of the routine reports that every other principal had to submit to higher-ups. At the same time, they would be given as much authority over their school operations as the law and union contracts would permit, including setting their own policies and standards for curriculum and instruction.

But this freedom would come with a price. Although we would give power and control to these principals, we would also insist on strict accountability based on measurable goals—mainly improvements in student performance—that would initially be set by them and approved by us. To ensure that the regional superintendents felt they were a part of the project, we asked them to nominate schools to be included in the Zone. For a moment, we worried that the superintendents, seeing a chance to improve the performance of their regions, would offer up the principals of schools with the lowest test scores and highest numbers of problems. But they seemed more interested in getting rid of the principals whom they found to be rebellious and annoying. Almost to a person, the nominees were outspoken and even a bit defiant. But they were also energetic, independent, and determined to do better by the kids in their schools. These qualities made them ready to agree to the kind of performance-based accountability that would have been impossible to impose more broadly at this point in our reforms. The accountability metrics we would use included test scores, but also attendance, safety measures, and, for high schools, graduation and college acceptance rates. We were beginning the process of importing to the public schools things that were working in good charter and private schools—like giving them greater authority over their own operations, while holding them accountable for outcomes.

Twenty-nine schools joined the Autonomy Zone in the fall of 2004, coming under the protective wing of a former principal named Eric Nadelstern, who was called not superintendent, but chief academic officer of the Autonomy Zone schools. A pioneer of reform in the 1980s, Nadelstern had founded the International High School (IHS) at LaGuardia Community College in Queens. Recent immigrants were given admission priority at IHS, and most students arrived with limited proficiency in English. Yet 90 percent of the students graduated and went on to college. Eric was uncharacteristically fearless for a principal, and he got these great results by breaking the template for school management. In the process he had learned a great deal about how principals can effectively navigate, or trick, the bureaucracy in order to solve everyday problems like building maintenance and student transportation and to achieve more long-term goals like developing a better faculty despite the byzantine hiring processes. He was eager to help others learn to do these things as well as he had done them.

As Eric would eventually tell me, he had always been a radical educator who was willing to try almost anything to help students succeed. The International High School had been born out of his frustration with working for micromanagers who lacked creativity and didn't ap-

- -

preciate it in others. He was also impatient with those who didn't recognize that human organizations, especially big bureaucracies like the
New York school system, inevitably become diverted from their initial
purposes as the people inside them seek status, power, advantages, and
comfort. People don't usually set out to destroy institutions in this way,
but if you don't do something to counteract this process, it will happen
even to the best.

To his credit, Eric was honest about certain aspects of his personality. He confessed that he was "pretty controlling" and had to fight his
instinct to issue orders and demand that things be done his way. He
knew he had to make a conscious effort to give others a chance to make
decisions and suffer setbacks on their way to an important goal. With
this purpose in mind, he gave the principals of Autonomy Zone schools
as much authority as he could, and he hoped that they in turn would
grant power and authority to the teachers in their buildings. "You cannot control what happens in more than seventy thousand classrooms
after the teachers close the doors," he would say. "But the principals can
create the conditions where they will do their best."

Each year, the normal attrition rate for principals allowed us to install new leaders in more than two hundred principal jobs throughout
the system. We created about fifty more openings annually as we added
new schools and terminated principals who had failed to perform up to
our standards. Although we fired fewer than 3 percent of principals
each year, even with that number we shocked the establishment. No
one at Tweed, not even thirty-year veteran Eric Nadelstern, could recall
when a single principal had been dismissed for incompetence. Those
few who had been fired in the past had committed serious crimes or
were derelict to an appalling degree.

A sizable portion of our new principals came out of the Leadership
Academy, and many started work in new or reconfigured schools under

Nadelstern's guidance. To promote the development of good teams, he fought to limit school size to fewer than four hundred fifty students. This kind of enrollment could be served by roughly twenty-five teachers. Any more, Eric believed, and a principal would struggle to support and monitor each one adequately.

Although he favored accountability, especially when people are allowed to help set the standards by which they will be measured, Nadelstern would never share my strong interest in test results. He preferred to look at other ways to measure performance, like a portfolio that showed a student's work over time. While that kind of analysis might work well at an individual school, I found it far too complex and subjective to work across the entire system. In the debates we had at Tweed over the Autonomy Zone, he would argue that testing should only count for 40 percent of an evaluation. In the end, we would settle for a somewhat higher percentage, while adding other factors into the mix.

In his new job, Nadelstern made himself a collaborator with his principals and not a top-down manager. Our way of thinking about the Zone put students and schools at the top of the organizational chart, and put administrators at the bottom, as service providers. Nadelstern, the master at navigating around bureaucratic impediments, looked for ways to say yes to ideas and requests, whether they related to new hires, new methods, or new course materials. By the end of the first year, twenty-five of the original twenty-nine Zone principals met or exceeded their goals in every category. (They were especially successful at raising attendance and reducing conflict in their schools.) The four who missed one or more of their targets got a second year to recover, which they all did.

In its second year, the Autonomy Zone program was expanded to include forty-nine schools. Finally, in 2006, it was widened to welcome all applicants. More than 250 schools were added, despite opposition from the principals union. Suddenly, in more than 300 schools, principals were no longer the weakest force but the central one. Their union, of course, was dominated by *assistant* principals, who far outnumbered the building heads. And while the assistants wouldn't have a say in whether a school joined the Zone, they would be affected if their bosses gained more power. Fortunately, the principals union didn't have the ability to slow us down, and Randi Weingarten made some positive remarks about the Zone because the teachers who had been part of it generally liked it. It was a pleasant change in tone, especially considering the lengthy battles she had been fighting with the city over renewal of the contract that expired in May 2003.

THE STORY OF THE CITY'S RELATIONSHIP WITH THE UFT WAS written in work rules that exceeded a thousand pages and long-term benefit packages created when the city gave teachers better pensions and health insurance, more vacation days, and other concessions. Much of this was done to avoid big wage increases, which would show up immediately in the school budget and might prompt a voter backlash, especially when accompanied by new taxes needed to fund the increases. Everyone who participated in the process understood the dynamic, and yet it was almost never discussed openly. Instead, the two sides negotiated in private and argued with each other in the media, where each hoped to sway public opinion to its side.

In early 2004, we knew that the negotiations we were about to begin over a new contract would be difficult and stressful. We wanted big changes and thought this would be our best chance to achieve real reforms. Even if Mayor Bloomberg were reelected, he would be a lame-duck, second-term mayor by the time of the next renegotiation. Our relations with the UFT were already strained from the 2003 UFT spring meeting, when Randi had launched her attack on our program. A speech I had made challenging "the three pillars of mediocrity in the union contract"—"life tenure, lockstep pay, and seniority-based decision making"—also upset her. Randi was out of town on the day I gave it, and letting her imagination run wild, she thought I had tried to attack the union while she was away and couldn't respond.

As if things weren't testy enough, Eva Moskowitz, the fiery chair of the City Council's Education Committee, had decided to hold hearings on the various union contracts governing our schools, focusing especially on the most important of them, the teachers' contract. Eva was as smart and politically savvy as anyone I had encountered. She was a Democrat who represented the Upper East Side but had little patience for the traditional Democratic interest groups like the unions. She cared deeply about education and believed the bureaucracy and unions were the greatest impediments to much-needed change. She could be maddening to deal with, always blunt and persistent, and often aggressive when she called you to testify before her committee.

When I first met Eva, right after I started in 2002, she told me straightaway, "You should think of yourself as having been appointed as premier of the former Soviet Union." Although I laughed when she said this, I knew she was trying to impress on me, as she later wrote, that I couldn't "fix the country's problem by being a better bureaucrat. . . . A monopolistic system of education could not achieve the radical change [I] wanted." I didn't know well enough then to tell her that I agreed, so she remained skeptical about our management and impatient with our early agenda and me. Often she would call or e-mail me, sometimes quite early in the morning, pointing out that something at this or that school wasn't working, or that the regional office had screwed up something, or that our capital plan was unfair to her community.

She also held lots of formal hearings where she would rake members of my team and me over the coals for what she saw as our many shortcomings, including, for example, the poor state of arts education. My favorite was the one she held on the inadequate supply of toilet paper in some schools. Because kids often used the paper to clog the toilets, schools sometimes didn't leave much of it around. But this didn't matter to Eva. She still bludgeoned us over the lack of toilet paper.

Given my own experiences with Eva, I was certain Randi would go ballistic over hearings on the teachers contract. For Randi, the contract was sacrosanct, and it was unimaginable that a politician would attack, much less ridicule, it in a public hearing, but that's just what Eva did. She handed out pamphlets labeled "Contracts for Dummies" and used charts and other visual aids to show how dysfunctional the contract provisions were—highlighting things like how a good new teacher could get bumped out of a class, midyear, by a more senior one, and how the process for terminating a teacher was more cumbersome and protracted than the public could possibly have believed. The hearings attracted lots of reporters, and the white-hot headlines lasted for weeks, making the contract provisions appear, as Joe Williams, a *Daily News* reporter, summed it up, "silly and counterproductive." Randi, not surprisingly, was furious.

Although the hearings had not been our idea, Randi knew we had cooperated with Eva, and several of my staff and I testified. Randi also told me she was upset that the mayor supported Eva's hearings on his weekly radio show and criticized the other council members for having "pandered" to the UFT. The mayor's radio show, my and my team's testimony before Eva's committee, and my earlier speech about the flaws in the union contract were all part of our very determined effort to explain to anyone who would listen why the changes we sought in the contract were essential.

Randi decided to declare war on Moskowitz and let me know that she was furious at us as well. She brought out the big guns in the labor movement to support her, making clear that this wasn't just a dispute between the UFT and Eva. In fact, when Randi testified before Eva's committee, she had Brian McLaughlin, the head of the Central Labor Council, which represented three hundred public and private unions in the city and had 1.2 million members, sitting silently next to her. Things got so heated that some witnesses would only agree to testify anonymously for fear of retaliation.

When the hearings were over, Randi tried to get the City Council to remove Eva as chair of the Education Committee. This provoked a bitter internal fight, but the effort ultimately failed. Randi then decided to go after Eva politically, which she did in 2005, when the UFT was instrumental in defeating Moskowitz's bid to become Manhattan borough president. After that, politicians would often say to me, "I agree with your criticism of the union contract, but I'm not going to get Eva'd." This meant they wouldn't support me publicly, for fear of retribution.

THIS WAS THE BACKDROP AGAINST WHICH OUR CONTRACT negotiations were taking place. As usual, these negotiations were conducted in private meetings, typically held at the UFT headquarters in lower Manhattan, where a group of city officials sat across a big table from a union contingent led by Randi. City Hall was represented by labor chief Jim Hanley. The Department of Education group was headed by our director of labor policy, Daniel Weisberg. Because I hadn't wanted it known that I was considering bringing in a big-gun labor lawyer, I had interviewed Dan in a remote stairwell at Tweed where we both sat on plastic chairs under the glow of a bare lightbulb. To his credit, Dan was unfazed by the stairwell interview and eager to work for a school system that had provided him with a good education in the 1960s and '70s.

Dan and Randi had first met in neutral territory, over drinks at the River Café in Brooklyn. That night he spoke frankly about our goals for the negotiation. We wanted, among other things:

- an end to the system that permitted senior teachers to claim jobs in specific schools based solely on seniority, even if it meant knocking out a more junior teacher from her classroom

- a salary schedule that allowed us to reward teachers for performance rather than the amount of time they had on the job or for courses they took

- a return of teachers to hall duty, lunchroom duty, and bus reception

- a streamlined disciplinary process for teachers

- more teaching time in each day

- two days of pre–Labor Day preparation so that kids could start school immediately after Labor Day

- modifications in the process and standards for terminating teachers that would make tenure significantly less binding

Some of these changes—starting before Labor Day, hall duty, etc.—were intended to address specific problems that needed fixing. But the big ones—teacher assignment, pay, and tenure—went to the heart of the trade union, job-security model that we wanted to dismantle. We sought to give school leaders, not union rules, control over who worked in a particular building. We wanted to pay more for teachers whose students were making progress, to pay less for those whose students weren't, and to terminate those who weren't performing at all. No school district had achieved this kind of labor reform, and we knew it would be tough.

As Weisberg laid out our priorities to Weingarten, he explained that many of them were intended to make the people in the system accountable, but in a fair way. After all, principals who cannot hire the teachers they want and dismiss those who are truly incompetent would be hard-pressed to make the kind of improvements we were demanding. In fact, it would hardly be reasonable for us to set up a system to evaluate their performance if we didn't free them from the constraints that had handicapped them in the first place.

Similarly, he explained, we thought it was unfair that teachers were granted assignments and pay increases almost exclusively on the basis of seniority. What about younger teachers who had proved, by the achievements of their students, that they were extra-talented, dedicated, and successful? Why did they have to wait in line behind less-accomplished colleagues who just happened to enter the system a few years, or even a few months, earlier? Shouldn't the system reward excellence and innovation? And what about the lemons and the teachers who inhabited the rubber rooms?

While sipping her drink, Randi went down the list Dan had shared and told him that we wouldn't be able to make much progress toward any of our goals. She wouldn't consider a change in the tenure policy, which gave teachers with more than three years' service near immunity from firing. And she was almost equally dismissive about our other proposals. As far as she was concerned, all the power and benefits the UFT had secured for teachers were well deserved and off limits. In her view the protections and seniority rules amounted to a form of compensation, which provided her members with privileges that made up for the disparity between their pay rates and the higher wages paid to teachers in nearby suburbs.

Dan reminded Randi that the pay gap between city teachers and those in neighboring districts was narrower than it had been in the past and that we were willing to close it further. The mayor had made clear that he wanted to attract good teachers and was prepared to do something most mayors wouldn't do—pay higher salaries, rather than pensions and other benefits that typically weren't adequately funded. In other words, we were willing to pay for the changes we sought. Randi obviously wanted the additional pay, but she wasn't interested in meaningful givebacks.

Hoping to support Dan and move the negotiations along, I sought to establish trust with Randi. In one-on-one meetings and phone calls, I tried to get her to agree that we wanted the same things for the city's children—better schools and a better future for our students—and to encourage her to take some risks. "You could make history," I would say as I urged her to perform a Nixon-goes-to-China type of turnaround. I really believed then, and still do, that, with the nation's eyes focused on New York, and given her great ability as a labor leader, Randi could have chosen to set an example for all of the country's big-city teachers unions by helping to shape real reforms that would reward the best teachers and push the worst out of the profession.

Profession was the key word here. Teachers *are* professionals, with real individual talents, who require discretion in their work, and not assembly-line workers performing identical repetitive tasks. They didn't need a union that would require management to pay them all the same and enforce rigid, micromanaging work rules. They needed a professional association, or union, that would help them develop new abilities to meet ever-changing student needs and devise ways for them to earn new rewards, including greater public esteem for their accomplishments with our students. Nothing would have done more to change the public schools, I told Randi, than to move teachers from a trade union model to a professional group model.

The trouble, of course, was that the UFT had been in combat mode with the city for its entire life, and most members couldn't imagine anything different. Randi might accept the idea that we were motivated to do right by the students in the schools, but she insisted that her job required that she oppose me on the main contract issues. "You have a role to play, and I have a role to play," she said. Her role required that she protect tenure, seniority, and a lockstep pay schedule that rewarded longevity on the job. In her view, as she explained it to me, her members expected her to preserve these hard-won protections—that's what a union was supposed to do. If she pushed things too much in our direction, the contract would be rejected. She had a good sense of how far labor-contract reforms could go, she would say, and we needed to trust her. Having supported mayoral control in the first place, she added, she was already viewed as too compromising by many teachers, and if she chose to do something historic by cooperating with our labor agenda, she would soon be replaced.

IN THESE BATTLES WITH THE UNION, THE MEDIA PLAY A MAJOR role. They provide the lens through which the public views the competing claims of the combatants. One of the things that is hard to imagine until you actually experience it is how important the media is in New York, and how all-consuming media relations can become for a high-visibility agency like the Education Department. With four daily newspapers, several weeklies, and a handful of television stations all heavily focused on everything we were doing, especially when it came to our dealings with the unions, the city is like no other media market in the country. The pace is frenetic, as you respond to numerous inquiries each day, many on short deadlines when you have to give answers often before there is sufficient time to get the necessary information. Even in a high-pressure job like mine, the time between 4 p.m. and 7 p.m. each evening was invariably unnerving. And what the press says matters enormously. When it comes to a large, complex agency like ours, the public pretty much forms its views on the basis of what the media reports, even more than what the facts may be.

Here the union had a decided advantage. It had been around for years playing the media game and knew, and had worked with, many reporters before we arrived on the scene. In addition, with so many of their people in the field and so many friends among the longtime bureaucrats at Tweed and in the regions, the union had access to lots of juicy, often confidential, information that it could provide to reporters. Sometimes the union would selectively leak to a single reporter, who would then have the story on an exclusive basis, a practice that made the union very popular and powerful with the press. Besides, this was New York, and many reporters tended to be traditional liberals and thus instinctively sympathetic to the unions.

I knew that tough media coverage goes with public service, and I certainly couldn't claim to be the most objective person when it came to evaluating reporting about us. But it seemed to me that things sometimes got a bit out of hand. In particular, I thought the *Times*' reporting, during our struggles with the union over the contract, was pretty hard on us. Not only did the paper appear quick to buy the union's claims, but it decided to run multiple articles attacking our new small schools. While some of this reporting struck me as fair—a few schools were experiencing real problems—much of it seemed highly one-sided and overly hyped. The *Times* even opened a Web site to display this reporting. During a meeting with its education reporter, I asked why the paper was "featuring new small schools with problems when overwhelmingly they were doing so well." He responded, "In the newspaper business, we don't report on the planes that land, only those that crash." I said, "But when it comes to the education of poor kids in America, the news is the planes that land!"

Right in the middle of all this, I happened to attend a party on the Upper West Side for a *New York Times* editor I knew who had just returned from an assignment abroad. Quite a few people at the party were journalists whose children attended public schools on Manhattan's Upper West Side. These schools, like P.S. 87 and P.S. 199, were among the best in the city: they had good teachers, lots of parental involvement and support, and private resources they could call on to supplement their public dollars. It was a friendly scene, but I felt some discomfort because of the *Times*' coverage. Despite my efforts not to let the press get under my skin, I couldn't help but think that the kids we were fighting for were the ones the *Times* needed to care about—poor and minority students, who were getting shortchanged in the public schools. Why weren't they with us more often? I suspected they didn't really believe we cared about the kids, something a conversation with Michele Cahill had appeared to confirm. Michele had been pushing back against what she thought was an unfair *Times* article when the reporter said to her, "Michele, you don't get it. You really care about education and the kids, but that's not what this is about. It's about politics."

At the party, my wife, Nicole, couldn't resist responding when asked what she thought of the paper's coverage of me. Acknowledging that she was hardly neutral, Nicole said she thought the paper often seemed to present the UFT view of the world and thus appeared to run down many of our initiatives, and asked why that was. The response she got from one person there surprised us: reporters' view of our policies weren't motivated by politics, or even necessarily pro-union sentiment, this person remarked. "Our kids are in good schools," we were told. "We don't want changes that might hurt those schools." We took this to mean that, as we tried to get greater equity for schools in poorer neighborhoods, some reporters were concerned that it could come at the expense of their children's schools. This honest comment reminded me that journalists, of course, are human beings who may well be driven by factors that they might not always recognize in their day-to-day reporting. But it also provided me with an important insight—that the more we sought to get money and good teachers into the poorer neighborhoods, the more the middle class would push back on our reforms.

Maybe it was a mistake, but for all we were doing to try to better their schools, the kids in the wealthier neighborhoods couldn't be my highest priority. I believed they were generally well looked after by their existing schools and their parents' ability to keep them sound. Right or wrong, these parents were able to provide extra resources for their kids' schools and usually knew how to work the system to get their concerns addressed. And we were doing a lot for them. For example, right from the beginning, we gave their schools greater control over the curriculum they used, and we expanded the gifted and talented programs they favored. We also tried to open more schools as the existing ones, which were in high demand, became overcrowded. And several times, when parents in more affluent communities were unhappy with a principal in one of their schools, we made a change at their behest.

But truth be told, I worried more about the kids who didn't have parents who were their vocal advocates, or with important jobs and access to City Hall or Tweed. I repeatedly drove this point home when I spoke with people at Tweed or in our field offices, telling them that, while they should always be "responsive to the complaints and concerns of any parent, they should also remember that some of our kids don't have parents or others who can advocate for them. It was our job to provide a voice for those otherwise voiceless kids. The people who did that," I would add, "were my heroes."

Although I was concerned about the political threat posed by middle-class parents who opposed some of our reforms, I remained confident that they liked enough of what we were doing and Bloomberg's policies overall to stick with him in the next election. I kept telling this to the people at City Hall, while also reminding them that huge numbers of parents, who also were voters, sent their kids to schools that were not as high-performing as the ones that served the wealthier parts of the city. Lacking the power to make their schools better under the old system, they could only hope that Bloomberg's approach—education as an influence-free zone—might work. We certainly needed their confidence and support if we were to get the time necessary to make positive changes in enough schools to show that reform could succeed.

I also hoped we would get some support from individual classroom teachers, even if their union opposed the mayor's education agenda. As trusted figures in every neighborhood, teachers are influential. People listened to the teachers they met at parent-teacher conferences and on open school nights. If enough individual teachers spoke well of what we were trying to do, their words might blunt the UFT's efforts to discredit us.

Despite these hopes, I kept being reminded that the press listened when the UFT spoke and paid special attention when union officials attacked the mayor or his administration. We saw this dynamic in action when, during our negotiations, Randi Weingarten declared that the mayor had "decided he can't improve the schools" and therefore "slapped teachers in the face" with an eight-page contract that we had proposed in early 2004 to replace a contract that was more than two hundred pages long. The city's media outlets had a field day with Weingarten's words, playing up the conflict without looking at the facts.

No one paid much attention to the fact that Weingarten had herself suggested that the old, lengthy contract could be radically streamlined (although she had only wanted to do it on a pilot basis) or that our preference for a shorter contract had nothing at all to do with whether we had decided that we couldn't improve the schools. Also, we knew that many teachers liked the idea of a simpler document. Several had told me personally that they would gladly have given up some of the privileges they enjoyed under the contract in exchange for a system that rewarded their extra effort and success. But in the midst of a negotiation, Weingarten would use every opportunity to take umbrage on behalf of her members and attack our leadership.

After the dustup over the eight-page proposal, Weingarten went after us for our plan to ban social promotions for third graders. Mayor Bloomberg had taken office in part on the promise to end the widely employed practice of sending kids on to the next grade even when they were failing academically. Schools advanced failing students in part because educators wanted to spare them the stigma of being held back and in part because the system ran more smoothly if almost everyone was promoted. However, several educators and advocates for poor and minority children opposed social promotion because it denied many of the neediest children a true education. A child who doesn't master third-grade work is unlikely to learn what's required in fourth grade.

Third grade was the right place to begin ending social promotion because it marks the point when students move from "learning to read" to "reading to learn." And too many of our kids couldn't read. Sound as our reasoning was, when we crunched the numbers, the press and public learned that, if previous results on third-grade tests were a reasonable predictor, some sixteen thousand children could be held back. This was many times more than had been held over in the past.

As people began to voice their alarm about the idea of sixteen thousand kids repeating third grade, we rushed to answer their concerns. We explained that we would be providing a new and stepped-up summer program and that some of those kids could gain promotions by passing the test after summer school or by having their teachers submit an appeal showing that they had learned the materials even though they hadn't passed the test. We also believed that third graders were already doing better under our reforms, so the number wouldn't be so high. And besides, if the kids couldn't read, how could they survive in the fourth grade, where they would have to read?

But these considerations were ignored, as the UFT vocally opposed our plan and offered a counterproposal that would establish fourth-grade classes, each with no more than fifteen kids, for those who had failed their third-grade tests. It sounded good—and, of course, meant we'd need an additional thousand teachers (and then more for other grades), all of whom would be new dues-paying members of the UFT—but union officials never explained how, regardless of class size, kids could do fourth-grade level work when they hadn't learned to read by the end of the third grade. It's not as though there's extra time in fourth grade for a teacher to teach third-grade materials as well, especially to struggling students.

The press once again had a field day recounting the heated debates spawned by our proposal, and the frenzy over social promotion reached a boiling point when it was referred to the Panel for Education Policy, which had been created to replace the old Board of Education and had the power to block our proposal. When three panel members who had been appointed by the mayor indicated that they would oppose our new policy of holding back kids who couldn't read, Bloomberg faced a difficult choice. He could replace them, see his policy approved, and listen to the howls of those who would call him autocratic. Alternatively, he could step back and hope these panel members might have a last-minute change of heart or else go down in defeat. Never inclined just to hope when he could act instead to accomplish his goals, the mayor fired two of his appointees and replaced them with loyalists. The borough president of Staten Island followed by replacing the panel member he was authorized to appoint, which guaranteed majority support for the end of social promotion for third graders.

The decision to replace the rebellious members of the panel was announced on a Monday afternoon in March 2004. The entire panel met that night at the High School of Art and Design, where I, serving as chairman, was obliged to explain that some members were departing and new appointments had been made. Having learned of the mayor's decision hours before, our opponents were primed to protest, and they did, shouting, among other things, "This is social promotion!" as I spoke. When we took up the policy, a long line of people talked against it. After hours of testimony, I tried to move the panel toward a vote but was met with cries of "We want democracy, not this hypocrisy." I invited more people to speak, and, after a marathon of criticism, the panel voted to approve the change.

As political theater, the firings, the panel meeting, and the fallout they generated were memorable. Weingarten told the press, "I have never in my life seen this kind of heavy-handedness. . . . To be able to do what is similar to the Watergate Saturday night massacre on a Monday night, it does call for changes to the state law." In fairness, firing the panel members was an aggressive move. But Bloomberg had acted unilaterally because, as he said earlier that day, "Mayoral control means mayoral control, thank you very much. They are my representatives, and they are going to vote for things that I believe in." He had the authority to act, and he wasn't going to let some controversy prevent him from doing what he believed was right.

As it turned out, despite all the commotion over social promotion in 2004, the plan we put in place, including the enhanced summer-school program for third graders, worked well. Far from the sixteen thousand kids predicted to be retained, the actual number, after appeals and the summer-school program, turned out to be a third of that. The world hadn't fallen apart, and kids were now advancing because they earned it, rather than having just shown up. In subsequent years, we were able to end social promotion in all grades, from four to eight, virtually without notice or objection.

We learned an important lesson about change management from this experience. Sometimes, if you have the courage and perseverance to fight through the initial resistance to change, it becomes easier to do something similar the second or third time around. In my experience, too many school districts are unwilling to do what Bloomberg did here—spend political capital and take the heat in the beginning so they can get more done over time.

8

A Deal Worth
Fighting For

Smack in the middle of the social promotion battle, when things were already very heated, we got hit with the only real scandal of our administration. Peter Plattes, the husband of my deputy, Diana Lam, was hired as a teacher in the Bronx and reporters began to ask questions. I soon discovered that an independent investigator with jurisdiction over our department had tracked Plattes's hiring and determined that several people in the system had felt pressured to approve it. As a veteran teacher, Plattes may have been qualified, but that was not the relevant issue. What mattered was the charge that Lam had skirted procedures designed to prevent favoritism and conflicts of interest in hiring.

Lam was a tough and committed educator, but I heard reports from others that she could be opinionated and difficult to work with. She had also made herself a target for members of the UFT who objected to the way she implemented our curriculum. I liked her grit and had found her effective, if sometimes undiplomatic.

On the first day of the controversy, Lam insisted that she had done nothing wrong and that her husband, who had a different last name, had been hired by people who didn't know he was married to a deputy chancellor. When consulted, Mayor Bloomberg initially decided we should stand behind her, since she was a member of our team and deserved a full hearing. I agreed with his decision and told the press I had "full confidence" in her. The mayor's office refused to comment.

Thus began one of the most challenging periods of my term as chancellor. Although Lam insisted she hadn't intervened to help her husband get the teaching post, the inspector found that several witnesses contended she had pushed her husband's application. The case was further complicated by the fact that Plattes had left the job within weeks of his start date and never cashed a paycheck. He and Lam had tried to head off the scandal by saying he had always intended to volunteer. Lam also asserted, somewhat inconsistently given the claim that Plattes was only a volunteer, that the Education Department's top lawyer, Chad Vignola, had given the hiring "a green light." By this, she meant that our legal counsel had told her that Plattes could be hired even though he was her husband.

The more we dug into actual events, the more convoluted they seemed to be. When the evidence did not clear Lam in a conclusive way, we could see that the controversy might distract us from our work and subject the mayor to criticism on an ethical matter. As the *Daily News* published one of its trademark screaming headlines—"Educrat Pulled Strings in Hubby Hire"—it became clear we needed to act. Mayor Bloomberg had the final say. We talked and agreed that Lam had to resign. This kind of alleged favoritism represented a throwback to the old days where cronyism and patronage ruled and would undermine everything we were doing if we tolerated it on our watch. I traveled to meet Lam on the West Side of Manhattan and gave her the news. It was a brief and painful conversation, which she followed with a public announcement of her resignation. It was not a graceful exit.

Diana felt she had been wronged and insisted that our attorney, Chad Vignola, had approved her husband's hiring, and she spoke again about Vignola's "green light." Given the media frenzy we were facing, Chad agreed that we needed to make a quick decision, and, under the circumstances, it would be best for him to leave rather than have the controversy drag on. His resignation was a real loss for us.

In the aftermath of the Lam controversy—where the press had made it seem that, given my initial support for her, the mayor had overruled me—some commentators focused on my relationship with him, with the suggestion that I appeared to work in his shadow. The *New York Times* declared, "Mayor Keeps Hands Off, But His Boot Is Keenly Felt." The commentary reminded me of a strange exchange that had taken place shortly after my appointment in a meeting with the *Times* editorial board. "How are we going to know when you disagree with the mayor?" one of the editors had asked. "The only time you'll know I disagree with the mayor," I replied, "will be when it's a point of principle and I have to resign." In this instance, there was no disagreement between the mayor and me over whether Lam should go.

Under the pre-Bloomberg education system, with an independent but relatively weak chancellor, the press had grown accustomed to frequent battles between the head of the schools and the mayor, whoever he was. These conflicts made for dramatic headlines and fit right into a journalistic tradition that favors a fight over almost everything else. Under the new system of mayoral control of the schools, however, I was not an independent chancellor answering to a Board of Education. I was an appointee who reported to the mayor. Although I possessed far more operational authority than my predecessors, I didn't have the freedom to contradict, criticize, or challenge my boss unless I was ready to depart over a point of principle. In more than eight years, such a point of principle never arose. If anything, my respect for the mayor, his policies, motivation, and decency only increased during my time working with him.

Soon after the social promotion vote and the Lam scandal, Randi Weingarten saw an opportunity to strengthen her hand by teaming with Diane Ravitch to call for a rollback of the mayor's power. In a column they coauthored for the *New York Times* bemoaning "Public Schools, Minus the Public," they said a mayor "should not have unchecked power to hire personnel, make contracts and set policy." In their view, there had been a "collapse" of school safety, a serious decline in services to students with disabilities, and a "rush to fail third graders." Underneath all of these mistakes, said Ravitch and Weingarten, lurked a serious problem of too much power in one man.

The specific complaints couldn't withstand scrutiny. For example, the spike in school crime—an increase of fewer than three incidents per month—had already been reversed, and crime would continue to decrease significantly during our tenure. However, the weakest part of their argument was the one they placed at its foundation—that the mayor had too much power when it came to running the schools. In the old days, when authority was splintered and the chancellor had limited power, citizens may have had access to local education officials, but they weren't able to affect the system in any real way. Under the system of mayoral control, the people of New York held the ultimate check, because they could throw the mayor, me, and every other person he appointed out of office on Election Day in November 2005. In addition, both the legislature in Albany and the City Council had broad constitutional and legal authority over us—the legislature could eliminate mayoral control if it wanted—as well as extensive oversight powers (something I was repeatedly reminded of when called to testify before both bodies). In these fundamental respects, we were like any other city agency under the mayor's authority, except that, given the broad powers the state legislature had over us, we were actually subject to more checks and balances. But none of the facts stopped the critics from shouting about the mayor's supposedly unchecked power.

As Ravitch and Weingarten double-teamed us, the UFT also began to prepare for a political-style campaign that appealed to the city's voters and parents by portraying teachers as the protectors of the children. In April 2005 the union paid to plaster subway cars with posters featuring a grade-school teacher in Harlem and the words, "I never became a teacher to get rich. I'm just asking for a fair contract and the support I need to educate our kids." Next came a TV advertising blitz, with commercials that repeated the phrase "fair contract." The message was clear. The teachers were in it for the kids, and since Mayor Bloomberg and his administration were not fair to teachers, they were also unfair to kids.

The mayor's political team was concerned about the union attack because, in the contest for public support, the UFT enjoyed some huge tactical advantages. Their members were in regular contact with the parents of the children in their classrooms. And while they might criticize education in general, parents work hard to get along with the teachers their children see every day and can feel quite loyal to them. A good parallel might be the way that voters scorn Congress as an institution but faithfully reelect individual representatives because they are known and trusted. Even the worst teachers in the most dysfunctional schools enjoy some support from the communities they serve. When called to support "our teachers" or "our school," many people will answer.

As the competing demands of politics and reform collided in the mayor's office in the spring of 2005, Bloomberg came under enormous pressure. Many of the people around him worried that an acrimonious fight with Randi over the contract could hurt his reelection campaign for mayor. At one key point, Bloomberg was met by a near-frenzy of alarm at a meeting of the Partnership for New York City, where two hundred of the city's most influential business leaders join forces to promote economic development.

In most cities, a group like the partnership would look askance at a public union seeking to maintain privileges and powers, but New York is not most cities. Our municipal unions are much stronger than unions most anywhere else, and they weren't afraid to play hardball with a recalcitrant mayor. Desperately worried about how a teachers' strike might disrupt business, cloud the political situation, and damage New York's reputation as a city on the mend from 9/11, the partnership executives asked Bloomberg, "Does Klein know what he's doing?" and "Shouldn't you to step in?"

"Do you want Joel to resign?" answered Bloomberg, after he had heard enough.

"No," came the collective answer.

"Then let's change the subject."

Bloomberg refused to cave on the contract demands, despite the fact that many members of his own tribe, so to speak, kept warning him that my positions could cost him reelection. Someone who had observed Bloomberg's performance at the partnership, and who was evidently frustrated with the mayor's continued support for me, told the press that I had threatened to resign if he didn't support me. This "leak" suggested that the mayor didn't agree with my agenda, but that I was pressuring him with threats. Although I had never done anything remotely like that, and deeply believed there was no reason to doubt the mayor's commitment or resolve, I have to admit that, if Bloomberg had abandoned me during these negotiations, as many people wanted, I probably would have felt it was time to go. But he didn't. He wanted what we wanted.

The union's pressure continued unabated. In June 2005, it rented out Madison Square Garden and packed it for a flag-waving rally.

Twenty thousand strong, the teachers who attended cheered politicians who planned to challenge Bloomberg in the coming election, including then-congressman Anthony Weiner and Bronx borough president Fernando Ferrer. The speakers gave the word *fair* a good workout, prompting roars from the crowd with attacks on the mayor and me.

The attacks were mostly political theater, intended to inspire the rank and file. But for those of us on the leading edge of the school-reform effort, this was theater of the absurd. Shortly before the June rally, the State Education Department announced the scores on the fourth- and eighth-grade English language arts tests, and the city went up 10 points in grade four and down 3 points in grade eight. The fourth-grade gain was the largest ever and reinforced the view that our reforms were working in the lower grades, where they were likely to have their initial impact. Then, on the day before the Madison Square Garden rally, the release of the results of citywide tests had shown substantial gains in math and English language skills in all the tested grades—three, five, six, and seven. At the high end, fifth-grade students had upped their English scores by almost 20 points over the previous year. In math, they scored more than 15 points higher. Overall, more than half the students in every grade scored at or above grade level. As far back as anyone could remember, this hadn't happened in New York. Combined with the results on the state's fourth-grade English test, this was an impressive set of numbers that was obviously helpful going into a mayoral election in November. Then, shortly before the election, in late September, the state test results for math came out and showed a 9-point gain for us in fourth grade and a slight dip in eighth. This further strengthened our claim that our reforms were working. For me personally, these state and city test results were an enormous relief. I knew they were the last before the election and would be on the minds of voters—especially those with kids in the schools—when they went to the polls. I had spent many sleepless nights worrying about them, while also anxious about our contract battles with the UFT.

Despite the size of our gains, critics immediately challenged them. Manhattan borough president C. Virginia Fields, for example, who was running for mayor, suggested we cooked the numbers by preventing some kids from taking the test. Eva Moskowitz wanted us to verify that the tests given in 2004 and 2005 were comparable. These claims were groundless. The state test results had been handled completely by state officials and validated by outside experts. And the city's results had gone through a careful process run by career employees supervised by Lori Mei, who had been around long before I arrived, and had also been validated by experts from the testing company. For obvious reasons, the members of my team and I stayed far away from anything concerning the test results. Had we tried to influence them, which of course would have been inappropriate, that fact would have become public in a nanosecond. But this was an election year, and the UFT contract negotiations were under way, which meant that suspicion was a safe haven for politicians.

Our supporters, including many around the country who had backed President Bush's No Child Left Behind law, saw proof for their policies in our progress. They found further evidence that the No Child law was working elsewhere across the country, as many states reported making progress. In July, U.S. secretary of education Margaret Spellings was so confident in these reports that she declared, before a national education conference in Denver, "Our commitment is paying off."

As time passed, critics of No Child found much to complain about. One Harvard professor's study showed, for example, how richer districts were able to avoid penalties that were imposed on poorer ones. In addition, many people continued to argue that state tests aren't a reliable indicator of student progress because they were too easy and teachers were just getting better at figuring out what would be on the test and focusing on teaching those materials in class. But none of the critics could explain away the positive findings of the National Assessment of Educational Progress, a well-respected test that is given in the same form, on a sampled basis, in all fifty states every other year. The 2005 results for New York City came out in December and showed some strong gains in both math and English, with major improvements among black and Hispanic students.

In the context of our successes—raising test scores, opening new schools, creating more options for students, improving safety, installing better leaders—it was becoming increasingly difficult for anyone to argue that we weren't working hard for kids. And despite the UFT's public relations campaign, independent polls showed modest but continued improvements in the public's overall view of city schools. A Quinnipiac University poll released in September 2005 found that the number of New Yorkers saying they were satisfied with the schools had almost doubled in the Bloomberg years, from 12 percent to 21 percent. Of course the number remained far too low, but it was moving in the right direction. The same poll showed that a majority—52 percent— supported the mayor's handling of education, and four out of ten people expressed approval for my work. (The rest were roughly split between "disapprove" and "don't know/no opinion.") And mixed in with the complaints and advice and challenges, every day we heard from parents the simple but welcome comment that things were getting better.

With the public generally supporting us, but the calendar propelling the city toward November's mayoral election, the UFT's leaders began letting it be known that its members might be asked to strike. Few things put more fear into the hearts of parents and voters than the specter of teachers on the picket line and children trouping home because their schools are closed. To increase the political pressure, the union ordered lapel buttons with strike slogans, and teachers began talking to friends and neighbors about the possibility of a walkout. Teacher strikes are illegal in New York City, but it is well accepted that they still could occur nonetheless. (Many New Yorkers remembered the teacher strikes of 1968 and 1975, both of which had been extremely disruptive.) In the event of a strike, parents and business leaders would surely press city officials to settle whatever issues were outstanding just so life could get back to normal.

At Tweed, we were determined not to yield to the union's threat. We knew we had to hang tough on the contract negotiations and felt confident that the voters would recognize how much the schools had improved and would support the mayor. In three short years we had:

- eliminated the balkanized community superintendent structure

- created the position and hired parent coordinators for each school

- implemented a core curriculum in math and English language arts

- supported reading and math instruction with coaches for each school

- started a groundbreaking training program for principals

- revolutionized school management through our Autonomy Zone

- reformed our high schools by closing failing schools, replacing them with new, smaller ones, and providing much more choice for students

- implemented one of the most aggressive charter school initiatives ever seen

And we were getting results. Still, we felt we needed a lot more time to see our reforms have greater effect, and to push new initiatives that we thought were essential, starting with the changes to the contract. That's why Bloomberg's reelection was so important to us. When I announced that I intended to stay on the job if Bloomberg was reelected, the *Times* noted that a second term of office would make me the longest-serving chancellor in almost fifty years. With so much turnover at the top, it's no wonder the bureaucracy had successfully defeated every attempt at meaningful change. No one ever stayed long enough to follow through on a significant plan.

Our policies and results were proving that Bloomberg was making good on his promise to improve the schools, which had been his top goal. In the same time period the city had begun to recover from the terrorist attacks of 2001, and the economy had started to rebound from the tech stock bust that began in 2000, which meant tax revenues were on the rise, and the city's programs were receiving budget increases. One month before the 2005 election, a poll reported in the *New York Times* showed that people felt pretty good about themselves and the city. Republicans thought the mayor was a genuine stalwart of the GOP, while Democrats believed he was secretly one of them. This was just about right for a man running as a Republican in a city dominated by Democrats.

As Election Day drew near, a teachers' strike was perhaps the only thing that could have derailed Bloomberg's reelection. Here we got some help from the panel handling the arbitration over the contract dispute between the union and the city. Under agreed-upon procedures, when negotiations break down, either side can ask that a so-called fact-finding panel make recommendations to resolve the dispute. Although nonbinding, the panel's recommendations carry significant weight with the press and public and can put pressure on the parties to reach an agreement.

When the negotiations stalled, the UFT decided to ask for fact-finding, presumably thinking that, as in the past, it would be helpful to the union's position. Throughout the summer of 2005, both sides had presented facts, testimony, and arguments to the arbitrators in support of their various positions. On our side, we brought in education-reform leader Michelle Rhee, founder of a nonprofit organization called the New Teacher Project, which prepared recent college graduates who lacked education degrees to become teachers. Rhee's organization was highly selective and turned out smart and motivated people willing to take on assignments in the toughest schools. Under a contract with the city, she had placed more than one thousand idealistic and talented new professionals in our system.

Poised and well prepared, Rhee was a compelling witness. Addressing the conditions her newly trained teachers faced, she pointedly told the arbitrators that, as newcomers, they were vulnerable to a seniority system that placed them last on the list for every job. She explained the bad impact for kids of rules that permitted the least competent veteran teacher to bump the most promising new teacher out of certain jobs, even midyear. Rhee also outlined the rules that prevented the firing of bad teachers. She submitted persuasive data to support her arguments and showed that poor and minority children, who still had rather limited access to schools other than the ones in their neighborhoods, paid a high price for the union's insistence on the policies that made it difficult to get and keep good teachers in their schools.

The arbitration panel issued its decision on September 12, 2005. It suggested pay raises that could reach as high as 15 percent over the course of three years. That was less than the amount sought by the UFT, but still generous. In fact, the increase would push the starting salary for teachers well above $40,000. Maximum base pay would reach $100,000, which, for the first time, compared well with nearby suburban districts.

In exchange for the money, the arbitrators recommended that the teachers make a series of commitments. First, and most significantly, the seniority system that allowed veterans to insist on being hired, even if it meant bumping newer teachers out of their positions, would be ended. No one could be hired in a school without the principal's agreement. Second, the panel called for a system that would facilitate the reinstatement of hallway and lunchroom duty and other assignments like greeting elementary-school buses. (Having witnessed chaos during class changing and in the lunchrooms at several schools, I viewed the return to hallway and lunch duty as vital to the safety and order of schools.) Third, the panel recommended that we create a position of master teacher, for which we could pay $10,000 more per year for additional duties supervising new teachers. For us, this was the camel's nose in the tent when it came to merit pay.

The panel also proposed that teachers provide ten minutes of additional class time per day to help justify the pay increases. By itself, this was not a lot of time, but the mayor had gotten and paid for an additional twenty minutes per day in the last contract, and we persuaded the UFT to let us combine all the extra minutes, which amounted to one hundred fifty per week, and use them for four additional periods of thirty-seven and a half minutes, with class sizes limited to ten, for kids who were struggling and needed extra help. Although this idea would create some logistical challenges—since different kids left school at different times—it would help about a third of the kids in the system get additional, focused instruction. Next, the arbitrators proposed significantly limiting the use of grievances by teachers, meaning less time would be taken up with process and more time would be available for teaching. Finally, the panel endorsed the notion that the teachers should come to work for two days prior to Labor Day each school year. This meant that, for the first time, we could start school for the kids immediately after Labor Day, rather than on the Thursday of that week.

Nothing the arbitrators recommended was binding, but their proposals did represent an independently charted path to a potential contract. Randi Weingarten complained about the time her members would have to give the city in exchange for their pay raises. But with the mayor's poll numbers surging, and the neutral arbitrators' report now public, Randi must have known she would face an even stronger negotiating team across the table if she rejected the proposed package. And although she told me the deal would be controversial, she aggressively sold it to her members. On October 2, 2005, the union's leadership endorsed the new contract, and the members approved it with a 63 percent majority vote on November 4, 2005. By UFT standards, that was close, and Randi deserves a lot of credit for getting it done. The 2002 contract had garnered 94 percent support. According to the press, those voting against were expressing both their dissatisfaction with the offer and their unhappiness with the UFT leadership.

We had fought very hard, for almost two years, for these changes. We didn't get all we wanted, but the contract would ultimately be viewed as the moment when the Education Department's relationship with the city's teachers turned in a new direction. For the first time, privileges based on seniority were reduced, a $10,000 pay increase for master teachers based on merit was authorized, and the massive, complicated contract became a little less massive and a little less complicated. As a result of these changes, principals would have more power in their schools. Most important, they could select their own teachers, something that was extremely rare in public schools at the time and something that, not surprisingly, most principals view as critical to their ability to run their schools.

In agreeing to this deal, we knew we would be paying a substantial price. Although no teacher could be forced on a school ever again, they couldn't be fired, either. We had proposed that a teacher have eighteen months to find a job, and if he didn't, we could terminate him. But the arbitrators rejected our position. As a result, we had to create a group of what were, in effect, permanent substitute teachers who would get full pay without full work. Although we strongly believed that was preferable to forcing these people on schools that didn't want them, over time this pool swelled in numbers, costing the city more than $100 million annually. By early 2014, there were more than a thousand teachers in this group—one quarter of whom had been brought up on disciplinary charges, one third of whom had unsatisfactory ratings, and more than half of whom appeared not to have applied for a job for several years. Many of these people have remained in this group for seven or eight years now, while drawing full pay and benefits. As I said earlier, no one—*no one*—gets fired.

On balance, however, the deal was a strong one for the city, and three days after the teachers union accepted the contract, the mayor won reelection by 20 percentage points. The margin was so wide that it surprised Bloomberg himself. His core support came from the people his campaign manager had identified as the "middle middle." These were middle-class moderates—male, female, young, old, black, white, Latino, and Asian—whose main concerns included public safety, economic stability, and education. These voters had resisted campaign appeals that painted Bloomberg as an out-of-touch billionaire and, instead, affirmed the work he had begun.

Having run on his own dime, accepting no donations and no political favors, Bloomberg was again free to pursue his agenda without the kind of compromises ordinary politicians might feel compelled to make. In the weeks following his election, top aides at City Hall let it be known that he would put new efforts into the recovery of the devastated area where the towers of the World Trade Center once stood, seek improvements in transportation and public health, and try to boost development that promised new jobs. And he remained committed to education reform as his top priority.

At his second inaugural address, a man who had once been criticized for his wooden style of public speaking seemed buoyant as he declared, "We have gone through tough times and come out stronger. Our population is at an all-time high, crime is going down, student achievement is going up, jobs are being created, new homes and parks are strengthening and revitalizing our neighborhoods." He then pledged to "lock in and extend" the school reforms we had begun. He specifically referred to doubling the number of charter schools as well as the number of children in full-time kindergarten, while continuing the revival of high schools. Most important, from my point of view, he said our reforms going forward would be built on three core management principles—"leadership, empowerment, and accountability." By embodying the basic concepts of our Autonomy Zone, and expanding them to the entire system, this description provided a bold vision for our future efforts. In the end, the mayor said, education remained "our most important obligation."

After the address, the mayor's critics predictably complained about his plan to stay the course on education. They said we hadn't listened enough during his first term and that we were sticking with ideas that remained unproven. Randi Weingarten said that our reform effort would "fall flat on its face" if teachers "don't feel like they are part of the team." In a way, we agreed with her on this last point, and we were already sending new leaders into the field to rally those who really were willing to join up and do their part.

From the start, I had a deep belief, one that only intensified over time, that most teachers cared more about what was going on in the schools—and how our policies and programs were affecting them on a day-to-day basis—than they cared about abstract policy arguments between their union and us. I never bought Randi's view that "the union is the teachers." Sure, I didn't like the union's attacks on me and wished I could have better connected with our teachers so they could feel what I was about and where I was coming from. But I sensed that, day in and day out, our reforms were playing better in the schools than in the headlines. That's one reason why I believe school leadership is so important: the more our principals could get teachers supportive of, indeed excited about, the reforms as they affected their schools, the better off we'd all be.

9

Making Leaders

"It's like the Navy SEALs. The first week first is critical and crucial and it's gonna make you, or it's gonna break you."

Caught on camera for a public television documentary, Rafaela Espinal-Pacheco was talking about her experience as one of seventy-seven aspiring principals in the first class at the New York City Department of Education's Leadership Academy. Like others in the group, she had been pushed to the limit by the demands of the program, which called for long days and nights of study and constantly challenged her with new ideas.

At age thirty-two, Rafaela had worked her way through an undergraduate degree in bilingual education and a master's degree in reading instruction. She had taught for eleven years in some of Brooklyn's tougher neighborhoods. Nothing in life had been handed to her, so the fact that she considered the academy tough meant that we were giving her the rigorous training she would need.

Every member of Rafaela's class came to the academy with the qualifications and talents to succeed. Ranging in age from twenty-six to sixty-six, they had been drawn from every part of the city, and beyond. More than a dozen ethnic and racial groups were represented, and about seven out of ten were female. All had three or more years of experience as teachers, and every one of them had left college and graduate school with a grade point average of 3.0 or higher.

We demanded the best candidates because they would shoulder heavy burdens, especially given their relative lack of experience and our expectations for school leaders. In other settings where major turnaround is required—the auto industry, for example, or other business or corporate situations—veteran leaders with demonstrable success would have been recruited to spearhead the effort. When it needed a savior, Apple brought back Steve Jobs. Before that, Chrysler turned to Lee Iacocca, one of the most successful managers in the global auto business. Our contract with the principals union prevented us from assigning the top veteran principals in the system to the schools most in need of transformation. As mentioned, in 2002, we had tried to use pay incentives to encourage high-performing principals to take on these tough assignments, but the principals union blocked our proposal until 2008. We thus had to train a new group of enthusiastic principals from scratch.

With these challenges in mind, the academy admissions officials put considerable weight on an applicant's interview and admitted only those who demonstrated the intelligence, commitment to excellence and equity, understanding of the core business of schooling, communication skills, and strength of personality necessary to lead a school effectively. A wallflower, brilliant as he or she might be, would never stand up to the challenge of running a city school. And those who believed kids from poor neighborhoods could never meet the same standards as those from richer neighborhoods wouldn't have a chance.

The academy's curriculum had been designed by its academic dean, Sandra Stein, working with Bob Knowling, a master at leadership development. Sandra knew schools and, before she joined us, had developed a problem-based curriculum at Baruch College that had been very successful in training principals. With her guidance, the faculty put the first academy class under intense pressure, assigning management problems to solve, with strict time and budget limits. Thirteen of the original ninety soon recognized they weren't cut out to be principals and resigned. The remainder immersed themselves in a fourteen-month program designed to provide expertise in budgeting, personnel management, instructional leadership, parental involvement, and nitty-gritty items like purchasing and scheduling.

This was not a traditional university program for training principals. We designed it to emphasize real-world experience and included extensive role-playing exercises to train our aspiring principals to deal with unhappy union representatives, disgruntled teachers, and irate parents. Each trainee was directed to focus on herself and her own leadership development. This raised very personal issues for the trainees, and, when visiting, I could sometimes see their discomfort as they struggled to work things through. I always reminded the trainees that "unlike the human eye, a great leader can see within as well as outside." Their personal growth would be critical to their ability to succeed. We gave the class extensive mentorships with our leading principals so they could observe the best, learn from them, and obtain constant feedback about how they were handling situations as they arose in the real world.

Once on the job, our new principals would be expected to use every resource—teachers, other staff, money, time, parents, and students—in furtherance of school and student improvement. This idea of constantly reviewing resource allocation in pursuit of continual progress is common to business and industry, where competition creates the necessity for alertness and improvement. Teachers, accustomed to closing their classroom doors and acting as independent agents, typically had little interest in such a process and often resisted principals' attempts to implement goal-setting and accountability. Our faculty at the academy discovered that our trainees were uncomfortable at times with the notion that they would be empowered to set standards, assess performance, and review the progress of their teachers.

We told them that we *wanted* them to disrupt the culture in the schools, but many worried about challenging the collegial tradition that made teachers feel secure. At a moment when the first class seemed poised between the exciting prospect of revolution and fear of the unknown, they traveled to Crotonville, north of the city, to attend a series of seminars at General Electric's Jack Welch Leadership Center. Formally a management training facility, the center was actually like a small university. More than ten thousand people attended courses there every year. Much of the curriculum was built around the so-called GE Way, which Welch formulated to cut bureaucracy and breathe life into the company as it began to falter in the early 1980s.

Welch turned GE around in part by firing employees who failed to perform and increasing the rewards given to those who excelled. Determined that General Electric remain a leading company in every field it entered, he also sold off losing businesses and invested heavily in those he believed could be winners. During his tenure, GE's revenues increased tenfold. *Fortune* magazine dubbed him Manager of the Century. In the years after he left GE, Welch devoted himself to sharing what he knew; his desire to contribute had led him to serve as chairman of the advisory board of our Leadership Academy.

Shortly after we announced the Leadership Academy and Jack's role as chair of the advisory committee, we took our entire leadership team to Crotonville for a weekend retreat. Jack spent the weekend with us, talking to people informally and participating in the formal sessions. Everyone was amazed at what a regular, natural guy he was. He never hesitated to say what he thought, but he did it in a way that put people at ease. He immediately observed that most of the career people at the meeting described themselves as "instructional leaders," a reflection of the fact that they were educators focused on instruction "By qualifying your leadership role with the word *instructional*," Jack told them, "you're diminishing yourself and your role. You are leaders, pure and simple. Your leadership extends way beyond instruction, as important as that is. You lead people and are responsible for the entire organization. Everything you say or do reflects on that. If you don't own the full scope of your authority—and your responsibility—you will fail."

I was grateful that Jack had said this and so many other helpful things during the weekend. People kept coming up to me and saying how valuable his comments had been and how, contrary to expectations, they had enjoyed having him there. When I thanked him as we were leaving, he shocked me. He said, "I learned a lot, but I'm not going to spend another weekend with you." I asked him, "Why?" And he responded, "Because these people don't know how to have fun, and I don't like to spend time with people who don't enjoy themselves." When I thought about his comment, I realized how serious people had been during the weekend and how little they had seemed to enjoy themselves. Educators tend to be very serious when they get together, and that's unfortunate. It's not that the work isn't very serious—it is—but people who don't have fun and enjoy themselves often end up taking themselves, rather than the work, seriously, and that can retard professional growth and development. I couldn't help but think how insightful Jack was. Because of his comment, we spent much more time relaxing, socializing, playing sports, and even doing karaoke at our future retreats. We had fun—and we also found our time together more productive.

Jack evidently got over his initial reaction to educators and later agreed to more face-to-face encounters with principals training at the academy. "I'm the first to admit that I have never taught in a schoolroom," he began, as he sat down with one group. An intensely focused man with bright blue eyes and a pronounced Boston accent, Welch occupied one of about thirty chairs arranged in a big circle. "I'll be the first to say that I know nothing about all the troubles you go through every day," he continued. "It's a lot easier being Jack Welch, with all the bullets in your gun when you go to work, than it is going in and looking at a bureaucracy and all the things you see and everything you have to fight with every day."

Welch's empathy opened up the group, who were candid about the issues they faced. Many feared becoming so overwhelmed by the demands of their jobs that they would lose sight of their main concern: children. Rafaela Espinal-Pacheco said with concern, "It sounds like we're talking about products when we are talking about children."

"But they *are* products," answered Welch, who viewed the progress of each student as a measure of a school's effectiveness or productivity.

"They are children, and they are products," continued Espinal-Pacheco, accepting, at least in part, that educators would be judged by how well their students perform. Yet she was worried about an overemphasis on test scores, which were stressed as part of No Child Left Behind and by our reform agenda. "You rely on scores," she warned, "instead of on developing the child."

This was a common criticism voiced by those who were skeptical about the federal No Child Left Behind initiative and wary about our reforms. At the federal level, and in New York City, teachers and administrators and, ultimately, students, were being put under pressure to show improvements based on year-to-year comparisons of test scores. The anxiety over all this measuring and scoring was understandable. Every child arrives at school each day with his or her own unique abilities, experiences, strengths, and weaknesses. Some benefit from an abundance of care and attention at home and enriching activities outside of school. Others feel all but starved for nourishment of every type, including the attention of loving adults. Given the wide variation in abilities and backgrounds, our critics asked, How can we trust any test to give us a sense of how a child is doing in school?

Teachers wanted us to understand that they faced classrooms that are each unique. As most will tell you, one year they will work with a classroom full of energetic, interested students and the next year they find themselves struggling to light a fire under a group that rarely becomes fully engaged. In neither case would class test scores alone serve as a fair reflection of a teacher's performance. A teacher assigned to a room full of bright kids might slack off, knowing that her students would ace their exams. Teachers dealing with an overabundance of students requiring remedial attention might offer extra help every afternoon and still fail to get their classes fully up to standards.

Educators had to deal with the paradoxical reality that, all too often, the very best teachers wound up with the kids who needed them the least. Under a contract that barred pay based on performance, the only way an excellent teacher might distinguish herself was through winning an assignment to a better school or to a class for high-performing students. In these settings adults were rewarded with the eagerness and ready cooperation of students who always did well on tests. Although no one could blame a teacher for seeking this kind of distinction, the system would necessarily deprive kids in struggling schools of access to the very best teachers.

Our Leadership Academy trainees understood all of the confounding factors that made accountability difficult, and they too harbored fears of being measured and judged. With Jack Welch they spent a considerable amount of time discussing how students with learning disabilities could drive down the aggregate test scores in a building. Schools in poorer neighborhoods tended to serve a greater proportion of these special-education students, which meant an extra burden for anyone laboring to show that an entire school was improving. None of the attendees knew yet where they would be assigned, but they were already anxious about this problem.

"One of the more important things we could do," one of the would-be principals told Welch, "is to not include special-ed scores in building scores."

Excluding special-education students from the test pool might ease the anxieties of some principals and teachers, but as another seminar participant warned, it could unfairly isolate those who deserved greater attention. "What happens if those kids get pushed aside and nobody really cares about them?" he asked. A principal could conclude that "as long as my other scores are good, I don't have to worry about telling that special-ed teacher that I have to get in there and observe you and your kids and make sure you are doing the best you can do for those students."

Alarmed by the possibility of being judged on the basis of test scores, while trying to make sure every child, even those with low test scores, is well served, Rafaela Espinal-Pacheco interrupted to ask, "What do we need to do?"

"You have to get incentives aligned with what you want to have happen," said Welch. "Think through, as new leaders, how to solve the problem. You won't solve the problem by cheerleading. You will only solve the problem through driving behavior. And in order to drive behavior you have to align it with some incentives. You pick the incentives."

As head of a global company with billions of dollars in annual revenues, Jack Welch had had access to every imaginable sort of incentive to drive the behavior of GE employees toward his goals. He also balanced these carrots with the stick of dismissal in the event of repeated failures. Private sector bosses, and even some in government, could discipline workers with demotions or reward them with pay raises, bonuses, promotions, and many other benefits in exchange for increased effort and success. Welch knew that our people wouldn't have these "bullets," as he called them. Instead, they would have to inspire their people and, when necessary, convince those who couldn't adjust to go elsewhere.

DISPERSED MAINLY TO SCHOOLS WHERE THEIR PREDECESSORS had either been fired or resigned under pressure, the first graduates from our Leadership Academy started their service in the fall of 2004. Rafaela Espinal-Pacheco found herself at P.S. 147, a prekindergarten through fifth-grade school in Brooklyn with about two hundred fifty students. The school ranked just above the bottom third on the English language arts tests and had long suffered from a lack of parent support and involvement.

Aided by an eager assistant principal, Rafaela attacked many of P.S. 147's problems all at once. She ordered new paint for every room and began an extensive campaign to make parents and students feel both welcomed and respected. She increased supervision for teachers by sitting in on classes and offering feedback, first in the form of a few words written on Post-it notes, then in more formal memos filled out in duplicate.

Although Rafaela thought she was providing support and guidance, her teachers were divided between those who welcomed her energy and ambition, and those who resented her as meddlesome and demanding. One teacher, Marina Capelletto, praised Rafaela for energizing parents; others said they felt as if they were being policed or pushed to conform to a cookie-cutter style. One fifth-grade teacher, Eunice Lindenberg, noted, "We actually don't like the notes. We prefer a personal comment. We're not books, we're people. We expect a conversation." Another teacher said, "We feel like a computer, or a computer program, not like teachers. We're people, too."

The frustration ran both ways as academy principals adjusted to their new jobs. One of Rafaela's academy classmates, Larry Wilson, said he encountered "certain naysayers" who believed that he didn't deserve the job as principal of Bread and Roses Integrated Arts High School in Harlem. He felt that some of the assistant principals whom he had inherited refused to support his initiatives and that several teachers treated him as "some golden child" who had never paid his dues. They couldn't believe that he had been selected for the academy and given his assignment on the basis of merit instead of political connections.

An arts-focused school for four hundred fifty students, Bread and Roses had opened in 1997. Designed to serve students not fluent in English or with other special challenges, the school's first class had been comprised of students rejected by other schools. Bread and Roses, a name borrowed from a slogan used by labor union organizers in the early twentieth century, offered small class sizes and a curriculum deemed relevant to the lives of its students, who were mostly poor, black, and Latino. The school had never ranked high in test scores, attendance, or graduation rates.

A gregarious and energetic man with a big moon-faced smile, Larry Wilson had been a journalist before he joined the New York City public school system, where he had worked in administration for eleven years. Coached by his mentor principal, he chose to be a highly visible leader, posting himself at the school's entrance to greet students every morning and again in the afternoon to see them leave. Departing from the spirit of the founders of Bread and Roses, who had stressed creativity and individuality, he required students to wear uniforms to school, and he imposed strict attendance requirements. He also convinced seventeen teachers to go to other schools (the dance of the lemons, which was still permitted when he got there), and he replaced them with new hires who would help him build a team committed to raising expectations.

Wilson spent hours each day roaming his school, monitoring students and teachers and relentlessly pushing them for greater effort. He worked with neighborhood leaders and the police to keep the peace on the sidewalks as students moved to and from school. But although he always seemed to be optimistic and in charge, he confessed to his academy classmates that the job was often exhausting and enervating. "It's nice to hear I'm not the only one who's not sleeping," he said during a meeting where the new principals shared war stories after a few months on the job.

The majority of the new principals could relate directly to the experiences reported by Rafaela and Larry as they, too, had inherited long-standing problems and were faced with teachers who were sometimes obstructive. In the worst cases, our new leaders were confronting truly dangerous situations. At M.S. 22 in the Bronx, rookie principal Shimon Waronker's first goal was to establish basic safety in a building where gangs terrorized both students and teachers.

Shimon was a devout Hasidic Jew who spoke fluent Spanish and had a background in military intelligence. When I wanted to place him at a school that was virtually all Latino, I was told by supervisors in the field that it wouldn't work. We proceeded anyway and Shimon went to M.S. 22, a vortex of chaos. Drugs were dealt quite openly and gangs clashed in the hallways. In some classrooms Waronker saw just a handful of students where thirty or more should have been. In others the teachers shouted themselves hoarse just trying to bring the students to order. One of the city's so-called Dirty Dozen schools, which together accounted for 60 percent of all the crime in the system, M.S. 22 was patrolled by the police. When Shimon took his initial tour, he saw two officers arrest a student who had beaten a teacher. His tour guide said little about what was happening because, in this school, arrests were practically an everyday occurrence.

On his first day as principal, Waronker quickly realized that the teachers at M.S. 22 deserved credit for the simple act of showing up. Although he would eventually convince almost half of them to go elsewhere, he moved slowly because he didn't want to act before he understood the extraordinary challenges faced by the teachers. One day, early in his tenure, students attacked six teachers in separate incidents. Police were called twice, and on both occasions handcuffed students and took them away in squad cars. Shimon knew that his school community was in crisis and responded by making sure that everyone saw him standing at the door, smiling and joking, as they left the building at the end of the day.

"There was a message" sent by his behavior, said Shimon, as he told the story to his academy classmates. He wanted students and teachers alike to see "we're in control. When they saw me smiling and laughing, everyone relaxed." Difficult as it was for Shimon to remain calm, his handling of the situation reassured everyone and helped him build greater long-term trust with those he was trying to lead. M.S. 22 had seen six principals come and go in two years, he explained. "The greatest challenge has been to build trust. They need to know I'm going to stick around."

As predicted, given his religion, which he proudly displayed by wearing a beard and a yarmulke, Shimon had initially provoked some skepticism among the mainly Latino students and teachers. Many in the community were recent immigrants, and the poverty rate was so high that 97 percent of the students received free or subsidized lunches.

Although he looked and sounded different from others in the school, Waronker was a tough-minded army veteran and walked with a certain confidence. An immigrant himself, he had spent the first eleven years of his life in Chile.

As he took over the school, Shimon offered everyone the same level of respect he required from them, and he always acted decisively. A dress code, strictly enforced, instantly helped to improve order and discipline. Borrowing from a strategy used by many effective principals, Waronker identified teachers he thought were underperforming and gave them an ultimatum: they could accept a transfer or they could stay and improve. Most of the poor performers departed. (Quite a few were close to their pensions and simply transferred to get in enough time elsewhere to qualify.) Waronker hired replacements willing to put in long hours, work collaboratively, and support his leadership. During his first year, Shimon did everything he could to change the culture of the school. He raised expectations in the classroom and refused to accept disruptive behavior in the hallways or on the streets nearby. When Halloween arrived, relying on his military training, he posted teachers on the roof of the building so they could observe and even photograph students who might intend to carry out the type of vandalism that had occurred every October for years. Actions such as these signaled to students and the community that a new day had arrived. No one attacked the school.

Shortly after Waronker's Halloween victory, I decided to visit and show my support. Although the school seemed reasonably calm and orderly, I was shocked by a class of sixth graders. With Thanksgiving approaching, the teacher asked a student to read something like the following about why we celebrate the holiday: "The Pilgrims were enthusiastic about their new land because they found sufficient food for their families. For this, they gave thanks." The student couldn't read "enthusiastic" or "sufficient," so the teacher pronounced the two words for him, and then called on someone else to read. As the next student began, I asked the teacher if I could interrupt and ask a few questions. He said fine, and I asked the first student if he knew the meaning of "enthusiastic" or "sufficient," and whether he had any idea why we celebrate Thanksgiving. He said no to all three. I knew then that Shimon had a long turnaround challenge in front of him.

Waronker had been sent to M.S. 22 because the school needed someone strong, and he stayed for four years, having by then groomed a successor to take over while he pursued his doctorate in education. He may have preferred a less demanding spot, but in the end he would say the rewards matched what he put into the job, as test scores increased, attendance rose to 93 percent, and a French-language-immersion program along with a karate program became instant hits. What he accomplished over time was so impressive that it earned him front-page attention in the *New York Times*. The article was a great morale booster for the academy-trained principals. For me, it reinforced the belief that, even in the most challenging schools, great leaders can make real progress. The hard part was getting more people like Shimon.

On the other end of the assignment spectrum, a handful of our new principals had the privilege of opening their own schools, complete with faculty, from scratch. In Brooklyn, academy graduate Alexandra Anormaliza started a new international high school in the old Prospect Heights High School building. Designed to educate students who spoke English as a second language, Anormaliza's school resembled the original international high school opened by Eric Nadelstern at LaGuardia Community College in the 1980s. Like Nadelstern, Anormaliza sought teachers who would be creative and collaborative as they fashioned programs to help students with incredibly varied language and academic skills. She established a cabinet of key advisers, including several teachers, and formed a team that enjoyed working together to succeed. One of her teachers, clearly delighted by the new school, described Alexandra as "a thoughtfully subversive" leader who helped him to succeed even though "there's a lot about schools that doesn't make sense."

As we received more and more positive reports from teachers and the new principals themselves, we began to consider the Leadership Academy a success, especially because it seeded the system with principals who understood and made good use of our reform agenda. In their first year of service, a handful of the new principals failed, either because their efforts fell short or because they met too much opposition. One, assigned to run J.H.S. 8 in Queens, ran into a buzz saw of union opposition and was transferred to an elementary school in the middle of the year. At the notoriously tough Sheepshead Bay High School in Brooklyn, another academy principal faced a similar situation and wound up moving into an assistant principal's post in another school.

Considering that they were generally given the toughest assignments in schools most needing improvement, we expected that some of our Leadership Academy principals would fail as others had before them. But the opponents of our reforms—I called them the status quo crowd—pounced on every instance of an unsuccessful assignment to dismiss the entire academy effort. Ignoring the fact that the program was funded by private grants (not a single tax dollar), public advocate Betsy Gotbaum declared that because of the few failures the expensive endeavor should be subject to serious review. The teachers union, incredibly, bestowed a mocking "shame award" upon one of our academy principals. Diane Ravitch's partner Mary Butz told the *Times* that "given the fact that the entrance criteria—nomination, interview, selection—was so rigorous," the academy must have failed to properly train those principals whose placements didn't work out.

I knew that many of the critics were largely pushing back against these principals because they were demanding more from teachers. Waronker and Wilson set high standards and pressured uncooperative and disengaged teachers to go elsewhere. Under constant attack, the academy became, in the words of some reporters, "controversial," and I decided we had to respond. A little research turned up the fact that more than 90 percent of our seventy-seven academy graduates stayed on the job through the first full year of their assignments, which was better than the 84 percent rate for the nonacademy principals who began working in the city schools at the same time. I presented this evidence during a meeting of the incoming academy class of 2005–2006. With the press in attendance, I promised to keep the academy open and to find additional private funding because we believed it was producing the type of leader we would need over the long run. I was making clear that neither a little controversy nor some bumps on the road to big-time change would deter us.

Many who joined in the debate over principals tried to frame it around choosing between young, energetic leaders trained by our deep immersion academy and older, veteran educators with long tenures as teachers and assistant principals. We refused to see the situation as a matter of a single choice. With well over two hundred openings each year, we could hire all the academy graduates and twice as many additional principals, and give each one a chance to succeed or fail.

Although years would pass before an independent analysis by two professors at New York University confirmed their success, our first two academy classes surpassed the other new principals even though they were given the most difficult assignments. The difference was revealed in the English language arts tests administered each year in elementary and middle schools. The greater progress shown by the schools led by academy graduates persisted for three years, the full length of the study.

This outcome seemed all the more remarkable to us when we considered that most of the principals who followed the traditional path to their jobs had worked as assistant principals and, on average, had three more years of experience as classroom teachers. The only advantage enjoyed by the academy grads was in school size. They worked in the type of smaller schools we generally favored. Their success confirmed our belief that, when dealing with challenging students, smaller was better.

In total, the Leadership Academy has trained some five hundred people in its fourteen-month-long aspiring-principals program and, as of the 2013–14 school year, about 16 percent of the principals in the city schools came from the academy. In comparison with principals hired in the traditional way, from the ranks of the assistant principals, the academy's graduates have a substantially higher percentage of minorities, especially African Americans. Many academy graduates who served as principals later went on to become supervisors in New York. Toward the end of my tenure, as budgetary pressures led us to train fewer aspiring principals in New York, the Leadership Academy became national in scope, partnering with states, school districts, and not-for-profit organizations interested in principal training. It is currently active in twenty-four states and enjoys a reputation as one of the best training programs in education. The NYU study in 2009 summed it up well: "The NYC Leadership Academy has succeeded in bringing new principals to some of NYC's most challenging schools and curtailing their downward trends in performance." It added, based on the data, "There is some evidence that even more improvement lies ahead."

This had been our first major initiative, launched early in my first year. Although it generated controversy, the academy approach brought lots of new, dedicated, high-performing talent to the city's schools. I believe today, as I did when the program started, that this is essential to successful transformation. Schools can't succeed without great leaders. I once said that if I could have one skill where I could be better than anyone else, I would choose to be the best "principal picker" in the world. It sounded funny, but I wasn't joking.

BY EARLY 2006, OUR INITIATIVES AND RESULTS WERE GETTING lots of national, and even international, attention. The press, from *The Economist* in London to local community papers, was taking notice. *USA Today* said that New York's "rule-breaking strategy has begun to turn around what has long been considered one of the nation's worst and most reform-proof school systems." Politicians and school-district leaders were also following us closely. In the spring of 2006, Los Angeles mayor Antonio Villaraigosa came to New York to learn about what we were doing. School officials had already come from Philadelphia, Chicago, Denver, and many other cities, on similar missions. I advised Denver superintendent Michael Bennet (now a U.S. senator from Colorado) that if I had "one core thing" to recommend, it was that "you make your principals the front-line team, and don't allow a layer of bureaucracy between you and them." (This was something he could do more easily than I, because there were far fewer schools in Denver than in New York.) I told him, as I told anyone who would listen, that school leaders are the key agents of reform and that his principals needed to "know and feel him personally, not through the people in the layer below him."

Bennet agreed and spent enormous amounts of his time with his principals, building their confidence and support. As a result of this and other changes Bennet made, including following our playbook on creating new schools and adopting a strong accountability system, Denver experienced sustained improvements in academic performance.

During this period the newly elected D.C. mayor, Adrian Fenty, got so excited about what we were doing that he brought the entire D.C. City Council to tour the New York schools, hoping that they would be encouraged to eliminate the D.C. school board and give him the same control over schools that Bloomberg had. The trip went so well that the council agreed to support mayoral control for D.C. Others were not only adopting our policies, they wanted to copy the form of governance that Bloomberg had championed.

Having secured mayoral control, Fenty asked me to recommend a chancellor for D.C. I immediately suggested Michelle Rhee, whom I had come to know through the work her organization had done in teacher recruitment for New York and from her testimony during the arbitration process surrounding our 2005 contract negotiations with the UFT. I told Fenty that Rhee would be controversial. She was young, she had never been a principal—much less a superintendent—and she was a Korean American who would face resistance leading a school system that served mainly African American students. If he wanted real change, however, she was the right choice.

Fenty chose Michelle and stood by her as she made some of the boldest and most important reforms the nation has seen. Most significantly, Rhee negotiated a truly groundbreaking contract with Randi Weingarten, who, by then, had left New York to run the national union, called the American Federation of Teachers, in Washington, D.C. The agreement brought to reality the accountability and incentive structure we both believed the system so desperately needed. It provided for a demanding five-category evaluation of teachers—they would be ranked from highly effective to ineffective—along with big bonuses for those at the top and dismissal for those at the bottom.

In addition to visits from other school districts, many prominent foundations supported our movement with grants and awards that recognized progress. One of the most important of these was the Broad Prize, which was endowed by philanthropists Eli and Edythe Broad. The award is given annually to an urban school district that shows the greatest improvement, based on sophisticated statistical analyses of test scores and other metrics. New York was a finalist in 2005 and 2006 and, in September 2007, we won. Mayor Bloomberg, Randi Weingarten, Caroline Kennedy, and many others from our team were in attendance. When giving the award, Broad said, "The strong leadership by the mayor, the chancellor, and a progressive teachers union has allowed the nation's largest school system to dramatically improve student achievement in a relatively short period of time."

But while New York was becoming a model for school reformers, we continued to face relentless criticism at home from the teachers and principals unions. Their ally, the public advocate, even blasted us on the day we won the Broad Prize. We knew most of that criticism was politically motivated, or an effort to protect the old way of doing things for the adults in the system, and we took it in stride. But it still influenced public opinion in the city.

We paid greater attention to the criticism we were hearing from teachers who said that we were putting too much emphasis on test scores. What those nervous teachers couldn't know was that we were already listening to them, and to our academy principals, who were telling us that test scores should be compared on a fair, apples-to-apples basis, and that they should be just one element in our assessment of students, teachers, schools, and principals. The academy people had begun their careers already wary of demographic variables that made it unfair to use direct comparisons between schools in different neighborhoods, as the No Child law required. They didn't reject accountability but urged us to adopt the most complete and sophisticated means possible to determine how well schools performed. They also recommended that, in addition to a robust system for accountability, we should provide more support for schools and teachers that were struggling. In other words, accountability should be used less as a club to impose consequences and more as a flashlight to illuminate what was working, identify where there were challenges, and figure out how to address them. These views were echoed by many nonacademy principals as well. They also made a lot of sense to us.

10

Overcoming
the Fear Factor

With hundreds of new schools and a corps of fresh principals invigorating the system by 2007, we were finally ready to address the biggest factor in the education equation: teacher quality.

As difficult as it is to say, especially when so many prefer to focus on the backgrounds of students and family support of schools, nothing matters more to the child in the classroom than his or her teacher. We have all encountered both exemplary and awful teachers, and our common experience tells us that a great teacher can rescue a child from a life of struggle.

But what makes for a great teacher? For generations, educators operated on the belief that great teaching was mostly an art, which the talented refine in the privacy of the classroom over many years of work. Like old-fashioned doctors in solo practice, superior teachers gained great wisdom in their daily work, which they added to their extraordinary personal qualities—creativity, character, intelligence—to yield the consummate educator. Think Sidney Poitier's Mark Thackeray in *To Sir with Love* or Richard Dreyfuss as Glenn Holland in *Mr. Holland's Opus.*

The trouble with the romanticized idea that teachers should be self-directed, creative, and wholly autonomous professionals is that it all depends on the individual. Yes, some educators grow and develop on their own initiative. But this model assumes that all teachers will naturally progress and negates the possibility that any educator can be coached or challenged to improve. And because teaching happens behind closed doors, this conventional wisdom protects less-competent teachers from being assessed and, if necessary, removed. Truly awful teachers can effectively commit malpractice (like bad doctors) against thousands of unsuspecting students throughout a thirty-year career and still collect the same pay, benefits, and pensions as their most effective peers.

Right from the beginning, the mayor and I realized that efforts to reinvigorate our existing teaching force would be controversial. But our endeavor was aided by the high incidence of turnover—especially in high-poverty communities—that allowed us to focus on recruiting top-quality people to fill vacated spots. The mayor raised salaries significantly and, under the terms of the contract we signed with the UFT in 2005, our teachers earned roughly what their peers made in more affluent suburban communities. We also partnered with Teach for America and the New Teacher Project to bring in high performers who didn't come from the traditional education schools. In time, we would come to recruit almost one quarter of our new hires from these nontraditional sources. Many of these teachers came to us because they had heard the buzz about what we were doing.

This recruitment effort paid off handsomely. An analysis by James Wyckoff at the University of Virginia found, "There's a really dramatic shift after 2003 to a really different workforce in New York City [schools] than there had been in place before that." In particular, Wyckoff determined that the SAT scores and college grades of our incoming teachers were significantly improved and that we substantially closed the gap in qualifications between teachers being hired in the wealthiest and poorest schools.

But we still employed a huge number of teachers who had been in the system for years, and we had to get them on board with our program as well. Having met hundreds, if not thousands, of them, I knew that the vast majority had entered the profession filled with hope. Sadly, many had been beaten down by the bureaucracy and its top-down rules—or, worse, by dictatorial, ham-handed principals—to the point where they were just trying to survive until they qualified for pensions.

Other teachers I met just seemed complacent and showed no interest in changing. Quite a few would start their conversation with me by saying, "Chancellor Klein, I've been a teacher for twenty years." Invariably this statement was followed by a recitation of the system's ills and all the reasons why things could never get better. The clear thrust was that the teacher had seen it all. I was the new kid on the block; they'd ignored previous chancellors and would ignore me as well. When they shut the classroom door, they would do what they always did.

This kind of thinking drove me nuts. Although I knew from experience that many teachers constantly strove to improve, there were still too many who felt they were doing just fine and either needn't or wouldn't change. Others had just given up, and, as they told me, would have retired if possible. The absence of enthusiasm and curiosity expressed by these teachers influenced the culture of many schools. I tried to stay focused on those teachers who could be effectively engaged and kept hoping that, if we could reignite their passion and show them a world in which kids were making progress because of their efforts, they would become allies in a dramatic reformation of the classroom. But before we could start on raising the interest and quality of the existing teachers, we had to get them to agree that change was necessary, possible, and preferable to the status quo.

Our guiding notion was that every school should be a community of learners. Under this model, students, principals, teachers, support staff, and parents would all act as lifelong students, continually seeking new knowledge and sharing the excitement of learning. In this kind of school, life itself would be defined as a learning process, with every day bringing the possibility of a new skill or idea. Teachers would seek out and share new concepts for their classrooms. Students would use the skills they acquired to discover material beyond what is presented to them. In this way, everyone would learn to adapt to a world that, like it or not, requires us to change, grow, and improve constantly in order to work and thrive.

A simple example that I observed repeatedly brought this point to life for me. In most schools that I visited, each teacher prepared her own lesson and did her own thing in the classroom, without any input or feedback from colleagues or supervisors. In a few schools, however, I would see teachers working in groups during their lunch hour or prep period, often with a principal or assistant principal participating, discussing what they were doing—and what was working. This sort of collegiality and commitment creates a powerful, enduring impact. I wanted to see it happening everywhere.

Nothing in our community-of-learning ideals represented a departure from the dream of all mainstream educators. Lifelong learning is almost a universal value in the profession, and for this reason we imagined that most teachers would become our allies in changing the system. There was one hitch, however: any meaningful way to improve teaching system-wide would require more than enthusiasm and commitment by the teachers; it would also require an effective system of teacher accountability and real data to structure professional conversations about teacher improvement. Accountability is essential. It tells people where they stand and, if implemented effectively, shows them how to improve. When necessary, accountability enables them to be removed if they don't meet standards.

No one likes to be monitored, evaluated, or corrected. Accountability can have painful dimensions, no matter how it's done, a lesson I personally learned whenever the mayor called me on the carpet for, in his words, "screwing things up." But we couldn't improve academic outcomes if we didn't improve teaching, and this would require evaluating teachers, enhancing their strengths, addressing their weaknesses, and removing those who weren't qualified.

Knowing that I would need the trust of the city's teachers to get them committed to our reforms, I thought I would start a dialogue with them, both in writing and in person. I had some very positive experiences with principals by using this approach. Groups of them gathered for informal sessions with me at Tweed, and they all attended an annual meeting. Early on, I started sending out a "Principals' Weekly" e-mail that kept them updated on policy and strategy. As a result of these various efforts, over the years, I found increasing, if imperfect, support from the principals. Many would tell or e-mail me how much they appreciated, as one principal put it, "knowing I had your support and even in such a huge system you were actually reachable." Another wrote, "You have been for me the first Chancellor that seemed like a 'regular person,' who invited principals to talk and really listen." I heard this kind of thing repeatedly, and although I knew it would be harder to engage with eighty thousand teachers than with fifteen hundred principals, I was determined to try.

My hope was that, as I invited teachers to group gatherings, brown-bag lunches at Tweed, or meetings in schools, we would get to know one another as human beings. (I confess, I hoped some would say to themselves,

"Hey, that Klein's not the jerk I thought he was.") Since it was physically impossible for me to meet eighty thousand teachers face-to-face, I decided that, in addition to lots of small meetings, I'd write e-mails to them all as a group. What was to stop me? After all, I was their boss. Shouldn't we be able to communicate?

The letter I wanted to start with began something like this:

> Look, folks, let's be honest with each other. Our school system is filled with people who came into teaching to improve the lives of kids. They didn't come to fail. They didn't come to make a boatload of money. They wanted to help kids.
>
> But by and large, the system's not working. And it's really not working for the kids in the Bronx, Central Brooklyn, and Northern Manhattan who need it the most and don't have the option of going someplace else to get the education they need.
>
> The problem is not that we don't care, and there's no question some of our kids can be challenging to educate. It's that we have to do things differently. Whatever else is true, we surely should not make excuses and should together take a hard look at what we're doing—at what works and doesn't work. Already things are improving significantly in some schools, and we can all learn from their example. None of this will be easy. It's going to involve some growth, and some pain, and we may make mistakes. But if we do it together, with rigor and confidence, it's the best hope we have.

The letter was never sent. As I learned, no chancellor had ever sent a substantive letter to the city's teachers. Some may have mailed holiday greetings, or thank-you notes, but, as it turned out, the UFT did not allow me or anyone else at Tweed to approach teachers directly on any matter that touched on their actual work. There would be no brown-bag lunches shared in the teachers' lounge or coffee and conversation in the meeting rooms at Tweed without union supervision. These matters were all subject to collective bargaining and, therefore, I was informed (first by the union and then by my own attorney) that I couldn't discuss them directly with the teachers.

This was a real loss. Over the years, I had come to know several teachers personally and, as a result, they had a very different view of me from that held by many of their colleagues. For example, I got to know quite well a longtime physical education teacher and committed union activist who had initially e-mailed to say that, like me, he had grown up in public housing and was an avid New York sports fan. We e-mailed over the years, and although he opposed some of what we were doing, and wasn't shy about letting me know as much, we remain friends to this day. When I stepped down, he wrote me an e-mail saying: "Sadness doesn't really express how I feel about your decision to leave the DOE. Though many of my colleagues shouted for joy when they heard the news, I for one shed a tear for a man who really cared about children and emphasized quality education. Though all your hard work and perseverance didn't always work out the way you had hoped, you were the maverick who led in a passionate way to change the status quo and give the DOE a direction that only a creative mind like yours could have instituted. I salute you." If only I could have had the chance to develop that kind of relationship with all of our teachers.

Unfortunately, I never did. Several years after we started doing annual surveys as part of our accountability program, I found strong support from the principals and parents, but not the teachers. In 2010, when we surveyed my performance in four areas—resources, oversight, curriculum, and student progress—the principals gave me an average 76 percent approval and 19 percent disapproval rating; the parents gave me an average of 64 percent approval and 14 percent disapproval; and the teachers gave me an average of 39 percent approval and 46 percent disapproval. I thought the teachers' results had to be due, at least in part, to the negative influence of the union's constant attacks on our programs over the years and the fear and scorn instilled as a result. I just wish I had had the ability to explain to them directly what we were doing and why and to hear and address their reactions. I know we couldn't have won them all over, but at least they would have judged us based on real information.

DENIED ACCESS TO THE TEACHERS, WE HAD TO FIND OTHER ways to make change happen. We decided that the best approach was to marshal the facts about the need for accountability—by showing how different schools and different teachers were getting very different results with essentially the same kids—and then seek to rally the support of the city and especially the parents. If we couldn't talk directly to the teachers, we would talk to anyone who would listen, including our principals, with whom we already had built a relationship of trust.

Before directly tackling individual teacher accountability, we first would focus on school-level accountability, by motivating principals, who now had the power to choose their own teachers and assistant principals, to take the steps needed to improve their workforce as a way to accelerate student results. Then we would provide tools to aid principals in evaluating their teachers and to help teachers improve their craft. The more help we could provide to principals and teachers, the better we would be.

We took a major step forward when we created a new office to promote accountability and teacher development and hired a highly regarded lawyer and law school professor to run it. I had met James Liebman in the mid-1980s when we were opposing lawyers in a school desegregation lawsuit in Kansas City. The case involved complicated legal and policy issues that ultimately went to the Supreme Court. (Sadly, despite years of litigation and the tons of money that the court required Missouri to pour into the Kansas City schools, the system continues to perform poorly.) Jim and I had also worked together opposing the death penalty in a case before the U.S. Supreme Court. When I became chancellor, he watched what I was up to from the perspective of a friend who also happened to send his children to P.S. 87 in Manhattan. At school events he sometimes heard his neighbors criticize the Bloomberg administration and parts of its school agenda. Although he acknowledged that I had been aggressively explaining our agenda on television and at public meetings, he thought we had not done enough to engage communities like his, and this was costing us support among upper-middle-class and middle-class people who should have been supporters.

A few days before the November 2005 mayoral election, Jim wrote me an e-mail saying that, although he had "never voted for a Republican," he would be voting for Bloomberg "based largely on what he and you have done with the NYC schools." He also wanted to offer some insight into our high-school school-choice process, which one of his kids was then going through. Although he liked the expansion of the choices, he thought we had to do more to make sure that the choices were "accessible to all families, including ones less privileged than ours," and he was concerned that some communities had more good options than others.

Jim was shocked to hear back from me in a matter of hours and even more surprised when I asked him to come talk to me. Soon, at a restaurant near Tweed, he was explaining how I had erred in dealing with the mothers and fathers on the Upper West Side who stood on the sidelines at soccer games with him and shared their feelings of frustration about the schools. In his view, these people wanted to have influence and would support us in return, but in our rush to reform we hadn't considered their need to be heard. "You have not been creative enough on the political side," he said, "especially when it comes to providing transparency and access." Although we certainly wanted these parents' support, I thought Jim's views, while heartfelt, were a bit naive. Of course we could have done more, but I felt our outreach to parents had been quite extensive. I was on television all the time and spent many nights at community meetings listening to parents sharing their views about our policies and their priorities. In my experience, moreover, although people always say they like to be heard, the truth is they mostly like to have their views adopted. I had been in many meetings—with politicians, parents, advocates, and others—where I'd listen carefully but still didn't agree with what was being proposed. When they saw I was unmoved, people would often get even more upset.

To Jim's credit, he never abandoned his interest in outreach, and years later he would still say we had been wrong not to rely more on retail-level politics. Whatever the right answer, I admired his commitment to his position, and I appreciated the intelligence he applied to every problem, which is why I challenged him to join us and help develop a fair and rational system to determine how schools really were performing and how we could help them improve.

At first Jim said no, thinking we were only interested in testing kids and rewarding and punishing educators based on the results, rather than using the results to, in his words, "get inside the black box" of why some educators and schools succeed and others don't. Besides, he was happy in his academic work and not the kind of person who would relish wrestling with big bureaucratic and political challenges. But I don't easily take no for an answer, and I was confident that Jim had both the smarts and background to design a system that would be fair, credible, and effective. In light of our conversations, I also knew he would make communication and outreach a priority and would work hard to sell his program to our schools and communities. We both believed that our assessments of students, teachers, and schools had to be fair and diagnostic, and seen to be so by schools, their staffs, parents, and communities. After a little more talking, I more or less dared Jim to put his money where his mouth was. He took the job and started work in January 2006 with a single administrative aide and a chief of staff.

Although Liebman thought he would basically be an adviser, we found much more for him to do, and within months he was in charge of our fastest-growing department, devoted to gathering data on student performance and giving it meaning. At his request, I gave him a second mandate, which was the development of tools and materials that could help improve those schools and their teachers shown to be underperforming. His office would be called the Division of Accountability and Achievement Resources. To Jim's dismay, however, the press almost always left off the second part when they reported on his work. They called it simply the Division of Accountability and they gave him the nickname "Accountability Czar."

With his name now synonymous with accountability, and given his personal devotion to fairness, Jim was sensitive to complaints and took some of the criticism he received to heart. More than once he told me he wasn't cut out for the task I had given him, but I encouraged him to stay on. He ended up working closely with Kristen Kane, who was now my chief operating officer. Together, they were a formidable team, with Jim as thought leader and Kristen as organizational guru.

Jim focused especially hard on developing programs to produce information more meaningful than test scores alone. Eager to prove he could use data to help teachers do better, he identified and collected all of the reports ever developed on individual students, from their immunization profiles to their attendance records and academic reports. As soon as it was all organized, and the legal and privacy concerns addressed, he made the data available, as appropriately needed, to everyone in the system. For the first time in history, classroom teachers could access profiles of every child they taught and look for patterns in their achievement, or lack thereof. In some cases, teachers discovered that the school enrolled a student in a class he had actually completed in some prior year, but no one had noticed. In retrospect, it's impossible to believe teachers hadn't had this information before.

After rolling out the student information system, Jim rapidly expanded his division, eventually building a staff of two hundred. Many of his folks were new hires, but he also turned to some longtime department employees whose skills had gone unappreciated. These numbers experts, including some who had doctorates, had been collecting information for years without anyone asking them to put it to use. Once they adjusted to the give-and-take in their new environment, many blossomed as their work was recognized as valuable. Spending time with Jim's people was always exciting and informative. I often visited their offices in Tweed late in the evening, where I would find many of them still working even though the rest of the building had emptied.

Jim's team of old-timers and newcomers developed a series of programs and services—most of them online and readily accessible—that would not only give teachers information about their students, but also help them find new books, study materials, lesson plans, and other resources to improve their work. These programs aided faculty collaboration by enabling teachers to find colleagues with similar interests who might have developed useful classroom strategies or materials. For parents, Jim's team developed a separate online service that gave them access to lots of important information about their kids and schools that they had never previously known. Jim told me that, when he signed on to this service for the first time, he discovered that, unbeknownst to him, his own son had skipped three days of classes just before the Christmas break.

Obviously curious about the impact of Jim's efforts, I often asked our supervisors in the field, as well as parents and teachers, to tell me about their experiences with his projects. The reaction was overwhelmingly favorable. Not every teacher or parent took advantage of the new services, but those who did found them helpful. Our monitoring system told us that tens of thousands of teachers and hundreds of thousands of parents were logging on. It was exciting: people were getting information about kids and using it to help them improve.

In order to support schools and teachers further, and to help address the concern that we were too focused on test results, Jim and his team developed a process for an in-depth, on-site evaluation of each school, called a Quality Review. To ensure fairness and effectiveness, we hired the Cambridge Education Group, a well-respected U.K. company with U.S. offices, to conduct the studies. The approach, modeled on the highly regarded Inspectorate Program used in Britain, involved a thorough analysis of school policies, practices, and management based on discussions with principals and teachers, studies of written materials, and classroom observations. The main question asked was whether adults at the school had a clear sense of how each student was doing and a coherent instructional strategy for each. The reviewers would provide a report to the school, assessing its strengths and weaknesses, and make recommendations for improvements. The report would also contain an overall grade (initially Well-Developed, Proficient, or Under-Developed). We published these reviews on our Web site so anyone could read them. Principals and teachers would get valuable feedback about how to improve and, for the first time, parents could find out what independent experts thought about what was happening in their kids' schools.

Jim's work proved that we were serious about the "achievement resources" function of his division. His office worked hard to overcome the fear factor that made so many teachers wary of change. One especially important initiative was helping principals create one, and later several, "inquiry teams" in each school. Using Jim's data and information collected at their school, groups of educators engaged in a structured analysis of why lessons got through to some of their kids but not to others and of how to be sure teaching translated into learning for all kids. Jim's team discovered that students who were the focus of inquiry teams did better later on than similar students who did not get that collaborative help.

We were also serious about the accountability part. Of course, No Child Left Behind required that we report on every school, every year. But, factoring in our own assessments and the fears of educators like those in the Leadership Academy, we had become fully cognizant of the dangers inherent in measuring different schools with different populations in a standardized way. We were determined to fix this basic unfairness in the No Child accountability approach.

To do that, Jim devised a system that compared similar schools with one another. Based on key demographics for elementary schools, and mostly on test scores for middle and high schools, we compared every school with the twenty just below it and the twenty just above it. This comparison approach was applied identically to the highest-performing schools and the lowest-performing schools. We would then evaluate the schools, largely on their students' average year-to-year progress. We also looked at what percentage of the students made a year's worth of progress at each school. In essence, we focused on whether a school was improving when compared with its peer schools and whether its kids were progressing, and not on absolute performance.

In Jim's words, "we were measuring what the school did for the child, not what the child brought to the school." Eighty-five percent of an elementary school's overall grade depended on this sophisticated progress-based analysis, 10 percent rested on a survey of teachers, parents, and students, and 5 percent on student attendance. For middle schools and high schools, progress on tests was a smaller part of the grade, with the rest based on how many credits students earned in core courses, graduation rates, and the like. Each school received a grade, A though F.

While not perfect—no accountability system ever is—Jim's design was a big advance over the No Child approach and, by any fair measure, a good-faith effort to compare similar schools in order to determine which were moving their students forward and which weren't. Even the frequently downbeat *New York Times* was ultimately impressed:

> Commendably, the Bloomberg administration devised a way to control for demographically driven differences that enabled it to reach the bedrock question of how much a given school actually improves student learning from year to year. Despite its imperfections, the system found that schools with similar populations of poor and minority children posted vastly dissimilar results. This, in turn, allowed officials and teachers to zero in on a school's weaknesses, with positive results. The data show that over the last two years, nearly 80 percent of the

lowest-performing schools improved their ratings after receiving help in the areas where they were weak.

By clustering the schools with others that were similar, we also were hoping they could learn from one another. We asked our principals to investigate the practices of schools making more progress than they were. Many did, but there was a problem: some of the principals of schools with lower rankings refused even to inquire and chose instead to remain defensive.

The first Progress Report for the city's then fifteen hundred schools were issued in November 2007. Most got A's and B's, but there were also quite a few C's and D's. Fifty -two were graded F. A quick look at the details showed that everything about those failing schools was awful. Instead of making progress, they were moving backward; even on the attendance and survey components, they usually performed poorly. As we predicted, adults at some of the failing schools responded with anger and resentment.

The public, on the other hand, seemed pleased with the reports. A Quinnipiac poll found overwhelming support for the A–F system. Seventy-five percent of public school parents who knew the grade of their child's school thought it was fair. Still, our critics were relentless in their attacks on the evaluations. They argued that the letter grades were too simplistic, that the formula we used was too complex, and that we relied too much on testing. The City Council held hearings in December 2007, and Jim took quite a beating, both from council members and from a room full of people who hissed and booed him. Although more positive about the overall structure of our accountability system, the editorial writers at the *Times* felt that summing the results into a single grade could stigmatize a school with high-performing students who didn't record year-to-year improvements as great as those at similar schools. This had an element of truth—the hardest schools to compare were those at the very top, where small differences could have a big impact—but it was hardly a valid reason for abandoning the Progress Reports. It was, instead, an argument for refining and improving them, which we constantly did.

Despite the criticism, the Progress Reports worked out quite well. Parents came to rely on them, and many schools did try to learn from their better-performing peers. My favorite story about these reports resulted from a meeting with a reporter who had written several articles about how they were unfair or problematic. While we were talking, I asked her where she was intending to send her own child to school. She replied, "Well, I was hoping to send him to our neighborhood school, but it got a C on its Progress Report."

After the first two years of these reports, two independent studies by economists at Columbia University and the Manhattan Institute found that students in schools graded F or D actually did significantly better on their math tests in the very next year. These same schools reported better English language arts test results, too, but those gains were roughly equivalent to the gains seen in schools that earned higher grades. The authors of one report wrote, "Our results suggest that schools may have responded to the F sanction by improving their performance and that there is no reason to believe that the sanction of a low grade harmed student achievement."

The studies were consistent with the repeated findings of researchers who had looked at a similar grading system in the state of Florida that had been adopted in 1998 under the leadership of Governor Jeb Bush. There, too, schools tagged with an F had improved markedly when compared with peers that received higher grades. Governor

Bush and I had discussed evaluations when I visited him in Tallahassee before we implemented our system. I was impressed by his command of the issues, and the strong results that Florida, previously a laggard among the states, was beginning to show.

How did low-scoring schools manage to improve under the accountability system? Much of the progress was due, no doubt, to the increased efforts of empowered principals who had greater control over hiring and budgets, and who were able to work with teachers to improve their practice. But we also believed that the bad grades became a motivator for the schools, which looked around for ways to do things better. Also, we had no doubt that some of the achievement-support programs that Jim Liebman's division offered to the schools had contributed as well.

One key part of Liebman's "inquiry team" initiative brought teachers together to observe one another in action and then offer constructive ideas for improvement. At the heart of this effort was an idea borrowed from social science experts who practiced "low interference observation," or LIO. Colleagues trained in LIO would watch a teacher with his or her class but offer no judgments or opinions. They would then meet with the teacher to describe what they saw occurring, but again avoid making causal connections or assessments.

The purpose of these exercises was to provide feedback to teachers, who could not observe themselves, in a supportive way that would not cause them to respond defensively. Only when the group agreed on what had happened in a classroom would they begin to ask questions to discover why. After answering those questions, they could consider how to make things better. For example, if colleagues agreed that the teacher was ignoring the less-engaged students—a common occurrence—they would point this out and suggest the teacher make a conscious effort to call on those she had been ignoring.

Many corporations, most famously Toyota, had achieved great improvements with worker-led observations and supportive problem-solving follow-ups. As Jim studied teachers who used these methods well, he realized that his inquiry teams, which were typically comprised of no more than five participants, created a kind of community that rigorously encouraged growth. The groups also broke the isolation that many teachers had assumed was protective but was, in fact, debilitating in its effect on their practice. In the safe context of a caring peer group, teachers who had secretly struggled now made progress. "The people who weren't doing great when they started out, but who were willing to learn," said Jim, "were the key to success."

AS PART OF THEIR OVERALL ACCOUNTABILITY APPROACH, LIEB-man and his colleagues also devised a way to invite more than a million New Yorkers to play a role in improving education. After gathering student names and home addresses, which had been scattered in files across the city, Jim developed an extraordinary stakeholder survey on school quality. It asked about everything from academic standards, to school safety, to parental engagement, to principal support for teachers. Ultimately the second-largest survey in the country, after the decennial federal census, the New York City school evaluation survey was filled out by an astonishingly high percentage of the people who received it. Eighty-five percent of teachers and students answered the questions and sent in the form. The response rate for families, who received the survey at home, exceeded 50 percent. Consistent with his beliefs, Jim viewed this work as an example of proactive democracy. Instead of waiting for people to organize themselves around a cause and use the political system to pressure the bureaucracy, he made it possible for citizens to express their concerns directly, and for us to discover what a great many people thought we should do more or less of.

Although we had nothing to compare them with, the first survey results, which came in 2007, showed a high level of support for individual teachers and most schools. A full 90 percent of the parents checked a box that indicated that they were "satisfied" or "very satisfied" with their child's teachers. Similarly high numbers of parents said they were happy with the opportunities they had been given to be involved with the schools their children attended and that they received adequate communications from the school. In other words, the overwhelming majority rejected the ideas that city teachers were ineffective and that the schools represented an impenetrable and out-of-touch bureaucracy.

Many people in my position would have been quite happy with the survey results. I worried that they presented an unrealistically rosy picture. Of course we *had* made progress. But I also knew that people are inclined to be overly generous when responding to questions about familiar people and institutions. In the case of the schools, parents and teachers often wanted to believe that their schools were better than they were. In addition, over time, schools learned to game the system some by telling staff, students, and families to rank their school high because it would then get a better grade. These factors led me to make some adjustments as I interpreted the results.

But despite the caveats, there was still much we could and did learn from the surveys. Support for the schools was highest among teachers, parents, and even students at the elementary-school level. It declined as we looked at results for middle schools, and then high schools. But even at the higher grades, the positive rating never dipped below 60 percent. The downward trend could be understood as a natural phenomenon— just about everyone is more excited about school in the early grades. But we noticed, deep in the numbers, support for something we had included in our Children First agenda from the start: smaller schools, which we knew enhanced connections. At every grade level, both students and parents identified more positively with schools that enrolled fewer students.

The idea that smaller is better was reinforced as people shared their priorities for the future, with 24 percent of respondents putting smaller class sizes as their first choice. This was hardly surprising, but there were contradictory attitudes to also factor in. Whenever I asked a parent whether she would prefer her child in a class of twenty with a poor teacher or twenty-eight with a great teacher, she would always choose the latter. Still, overall, parents were focused on smaller classes.

Next on the wish list of parent survey responses came "more or better enrichment programs," then "more hands-on learning" and "more preparation for state tests." A full 10 percent of the survey responses put more test prep for students as their first choice, which was ten times the number urging us to reduce the effort we put into this activity. This surprised our critics. Teachers unions, civil rights groups, the National School Boards Association, and more than a dozen other organizations had come out against too much testing and test prep. They argued, among other things, that the questions on standardized tests could be skewed against students from minority communities, who might not have the same vocabulary as their white peers. Poor children could be disadvantaged by the stress in their families, and children of immigrants could face difficulty due to their limited English-language skills. Among teachers, the common refrain was that they opposed "teaching to the test," which was how they described lessons that were supposed to raise scores without regard for meaningful education.

"Teaching to the test" sounds terrible, and any teacher who simply posted the questions that they thought would appear on an exam and drilled his or her students until they memorized the answers should be drummed out of the profession. But good teachers can, and do, teach students the skills and knowledge they need to master, which also helps them pass their exams. Math teachers who teach to the test in this way make sure their students know how to handle the different types of questions a test will present, like solving a long-division or quadratic-equation problem. Successful English teachers school their students on the style and substance of an essay the examiners will expect—one that is well written and well reasoned. As James Samuelson, a New York City high-school teacher, wrote in the *Wall Street Journal* in an article called "The Pleasures of Teaching to the Test": "Testing is good for the intellectual health of students. It is also an excellent way for teachers to better understand the academic challenges their students face." Of course, the tests must be demanding and assess skills that go way beyond rote learning. That can easily be done, even with a multiple-choice answer, so long as, in Samuelson's words, the questions "ask students to evaluate evidence and make inferences." Instruction that enables students to do these things hardly deprives them; on the contrary, it empowers them and can help to build a positive cycle of competence that is reinforced in every successful testing experience.

The parents who told us they wanted more test prep understood the value of high scores and good grades. They may have agreed that tests were not a perfect measure of a student's abilities. But they also knew that their kids would be tested, one way or another, throughout their lives and that, to succeed in this world, we all need to do our best on exams, even if they aren't perfectly fair. By suggesting that schools must choose either testing or good teaching, our detractors in New York and reform critics around the country offered a false dichotomy that was so old and timeworn it had become a cliché.

We faced another false dichotomy with those who argued that students couldn't do just as well at either a large, impersonal high school rich in course offerings or a smaller, friendlier one with fewer opportunities. Diane Ravitch took this view in July 2006, when a writer for the *Washington Post* contacted her for an article on our small schools. She told the reporter, Nahal Toosi, "Since they have a small faculty, they don't have depth of staff in subjects like math, science, can't offer advanced courses, also don't have the range of electives or extracurricular activities, or a choice of foreign languages, or such things as debate club, chorus, etc."

Toosi went on to describe a number of our more unusual small high schools, including the Academy for Careers in Sports, the High School for Violin and Dance, the Peace and Diversity Academy, and the Food and Finance High School. These were just a handful of the well over one hundred we had opened between the day Mayor Bloomberg assumed office in 2002 and the fall of 2006. In those years the size of the average freshman class at a city high school had been reduced from about three hundred thirty to two hundred twenty. At the small high schools, there were usually one hundred twenty-five or fewer students per grade.

Although these new small schools had fewer elective courses, they focused relentlessly—and successfully—on making sure their students were completing the Regents-required coursework necessary for them to graduate. Not surprisingly, we didn't hear many complaints about missing opportunities from kids who wanted first and foremost to learn what they needed to know so they could pass their courses and graduate. Instead, we heard from hundreds of students and parents who were grateful for schools where everyone was recognized by name, and no one got lost in the crowd. And of course, the critics of small schools ignored the fundamental point that the students at these schools had affirmatively chosen the school, and that each of them could have gone to a nearby large school, which typically had many openings. In other words, anyone who wanted the benefits that a large high school could provide could readily get access to it. That's what school choice is all about.

Years would pass before the first big, independent analysis would confirm that small high schools made a huge difference. It would come in 2010 from a nonpartisan research institute called MDRC, which focuses on education, health-care, and social-welfare issues. Employing a demanding research design that matched students using the naturally occurring lotteries produced by our high-school admissions process, the researchers found that students who attended the new small schools were far less likely to fail more than one core subject and far more likely to stay on track to graduate. The difference held through to the end of high school, with 69 percent of small-school students getting their diplomas on time, compared with 63 percent of their peers at larger schools. Subsequent studies by MDRC and other independent researchers who applied the same kind of rigorous methodology found even greater success at our small schools, with an almost 10-point higher graduation rate across the board, including for racial and ethnic subgroups.

With our small schools helping to narrow racial and income-group achievement gaps, and the entire school system showing improvement, we were demonstrating what we had always believed—that progress could be made in a big urban school district in relatively short order. This record was certainly a part of the reason why so many of the people who responded to Jim Liebman's annual survey gave their schools high marks. Our progress also made us both an inspiration for those who hoped to fix troubled schools and a target for those who lined up against us. Since we still planned to do much more, however, we could only expect the opposition to increase, perhaps into an even more significant backlash.

No major backlash came, however, from rank-and-file teachers. Sure, the UFT voiced its complaints and continued to challenge our policies and me. And certainly many individual teachers remained wary of what we were doing and critical of me. But day to day, the survey results showed, most were satisfied with what was happening in their schools and the support they were getting from their principals—conclusions that were reinforced by subsequent survey results. Ultimately, those are the things that matter.

11

Relentless

By early January of 2007, Mayor Bloomberg was set to an-
nounce more sweeping changes to the public school system. Rumors
swirled that we planned to turn over core management functions to
private companies, but we refused to comment before the offical announcement, even as leaks to the press stirred up critics prepared to
pounce. "This is so reckless," Randi Weingarten told Juan Gonzalez at
the New York *Daily News*. "We've been hearing all sorts of rumors
about privatizing the system and a radical restructuring. How many
more of these restructurings must we go through?"

You usually know something is wrong in an organization when the
news of a big policy push is leaked to the press. A longtime fixture at the
News, Juan Gonzalez had access to countless sources around the city, but
his story about the next phase of reform was almost certainly based on
inside information from someone in the bureaucracy or the UFT. Considering the negative way the article framed what we were doing—as a
"reckless" giveaway of authority to private companies—his sources were
almost certainly opposed to our plans, especially those that might bring
people from outside the public education monopoly into the picture. But
his portrayal—which, unfortunately, set the stage for much of the public's
response—was incorrect. Although we sought new supporters for our

schools, we had no intention of turning over responsibility for any part of the Education Department to private interests. Instead, our plan was to redouble our effort to make the system more effective by giving schools an array of support organizations with which to work and letting each principal choose which would be best for him or her.

This initiative grew out of the enormous success we had experienced with our (renamed) Empowerment Zone (formerly the Autonomy Zone), which we had started under Eric Nadelstern's leadership in the beginning of the 2004 school year, and which had enabled principals to operate with far more freedom and greater accountability. We began by announcing that we would close the ten regional offices that we had created in 2003. These offices had been an improvement, but they didn't achieve the kind of efficiencies we thought possible. They had also failed to deliver the level of administrative, instructional, and institutional support our principals needed. I knew that the regional offices were falling short because I was in regular contact with hundreds of principals. Many had created, or joined, mutual support groups where they were able to vent their frustrations, crow a bit about their achievements, and exchange ideas. Shimon Waronker belonged to one that called itself the Banzai Group (after the Japanese war cry), and he made sure I joined them for dinner at least once every school year.

The Banzai Group believed that the regional offices could be improved on many levels. As we learned soon after the offices were created, the regional officials still operated from the top-down model, too often positioning themselves as the authorities who should dictate to the principals. To illustrate the problem, Shimon described a visit from a regional official who came to his school for a meeting and insisted that he "stay right where he was" instead of dealing with a crisis in a classroom. "You'll never be a good principal," she had told him, "if you respond to every fire." Well, the emergency was, in fact, a small fire caused by a student who had taken a lighter to a bulletin board. Shimon ignored his supervisor to make sure everyone and everything in his building was safe. The episode convinced him that at least this one regional bureaucrat was not equal to the assignment she had been given.

Few of the regional managers—most of whom had grown up in the old system—fully understood and embraced the service and facilitation role we had envisioned for them when we created their offices. We believed that everyone outside of our school buildings, right up to the chancellor, was supposed to focus on making the system work better for the principals, teachers, and students in each school. This idea of leadership with an emphasis on service and support—but not control—was difficult for many people to grasp, especially when they had spent their careers giving orders in response to requests for help.

Under the leadership of Kristen Kane and a more recent hire, Chris Cerf, who later went on to be Governor Christie's education commissioner in New Jersey, we prepared plans to create thirteen new "school support organizations," including the Empowerment Zone, to provide services to the schools, such as professional development for teachers and consultative advice for instructing especially challenging populations like special-education students and English-language learners. They would also facilitate collaboration among the schools they served, which would be organized into small networks that could learn from one another. These organizations would each pitch the schools for their business. Four were to be led by four of the former regional heads. Each was asked to differentiate itself in terms of services to be offered to the schools. They hired their own staffs, designed their themes, including leadership and community service, and set their own prices for the packages they provided. (Some offered "premium" as well as "regular" service packages.) Although they weren't used to competing for schools, rather than having them be assigned, the former regionals generally responded well to the challenge.

We also reached out to the nonprofit community that had worked closely with us over the years to create nine new "partnership support organizations." Among our partners were New Visions, the Center for Innovation–Public Education Association, the City University of New York, and Fordham University. I was especially gratified that the universities agreed to participate, since I had been trying to get them more involved with our schools for years.

We advised our principals of all thirteen options, told them they had to choose one, and gave them funds saved from closing the regional offices to pay for the organization they would join, which typically charged between $25,000 and $40,000 per year. The services included mentoring, professional development, specialized services for challenging populations, and the like. With so many different organizations offering different services at different prices, the principals had lots of options. To help them select, we held a fair at the Grand Hyatt New York on Forty-Second Street, where the principals could meet with and question all thirteen organizations and narrow their choices. Each of the thirteen organizations set up a booth, handed out literature describing its services, and gave away pens and other mementos to help promote brand awareness. The principals came with a mixture of excitement and perhaps some trepidation at their new authority. I spoke at the outset and stayed to watch the excitement build as the principals engaged with the support organizations, trying to figure out what was best for their schools. In making their decisions, the principals talked with their colleagues, especially those hoping to engage the same organization. Although we said that, to provide some stability, the principals' original decisions should be for two years, we also made clear we would allow exceptions if things didn't work out. (Each year, as it happened, a dozen or so schools changed support organizations.)

Almost to a person, the principals were thrilled by the autonomy and choices we gave them. In exchange, we required that each sign a performance agreement, setting out the criteria by which they would be measured and the results for which they would be held accountable. Although the agreements were several pages long, the key provisions focused on the accountability metrics from our A–F Progress Report and our Quality Review system, both of which they were becoming increasingly familiar with. No one had ever imagined anything like this kind of management structure in public education. The combination of opportunity and accountability made the principals feel more respected, empowered, and excited about their jobs. And no support organization could get complacent, or dictatorial, because, if it did, a principal could make a different selection. Many observers in the education-reform community were astonished. In a world where a top-down management structure had always been the only model, we were turning that model entirely on its head, and doing it not as a pilot program or experiment, but for every school in the largest school district in the country.

Eventually, more than five hundred schools would choose the Empowerment Zone, supported by a small organization of professionals whom Eric Nadelstern had assembled. Many already were taking part in it; others were drawn by the fact that it was a light-touch, relatively inexpensive option that allowed principals to use the money they had been granted for other programs, too. The Empowerment Zone became, by far, the largest support organization. About a thousand other principals chose one of the organizations run by the four former regional superintendents. Lastly, about one hundred fifty schools chose one of the nonprofit "partnership support organizations," with New Visions getting almost half.

The principals made their selections based on the individual needs of their schools, with newly appointed principals choosing a group focused on leadership training, for example, while those who supervised schools with large numbers of English-language learners chose groups designed to promote specialized expertise in that area. The market appeared to have worked well, and the response from the principals was overwhelmingly positive. My team at Tweed, which had worked hard to pull this initiative together, couldn't have been more excited. We knew we had done something big and bold and had implemented it well.

Recognizing that we were nearing the end of Bloomberg's second term—the close of his administration as originally scheduled—we had planned a year of many changes and had to keep moving. Our next focus was a big play on pay for performance. We had negotiated hard with Randi Weingarten, who had agreed to a school-based program that gave all teachers a bonus if the school as a whole met its improvement targets as set by our accountability office. We had hoped for bonuses based on the performance of individual teachers, but the union had rejected that approach out of hand. The plan we adopted applied to two hundred of the lowest-performing schools, and provided for what amounted to a $3,000-per-teacher bonus. Although a school was allowed to form a committee to decide whether the amount of the bonuses should be differentiated based on individual performance, that rarely happened.

We raised tens of millions of dollars from philanthropies to fund the program, and many schools met their targets and received bonuses. The program lasted for three years, and the teachers who received the bonuses loved it. It was subsequently evaluated by researchers and found to have no effect, meaning that the schools eligible for bonuses did no better than a comparison group of schools that wasn't eligible for bonuses. I was disappointed but not entirely surprised. I continue to believe that bonuses tied to an individual teacher's performance would work. In D.C., where bonuses range up to $25,000 per year, and are awarded on an individualized basis, the program appears to work well. Soon after the studies on our initiative came out, Roland Fryer, a Harvard economist who had done one of the studies on us, did another study of a pay-for-performance program in a high-poverty school district near Chicago. In that one, he found significant effects from an $8,000 bonus and even larger effects if teachers were given $4,000 at the beginning of the year and had to pay it back if they didn't meet their achievement targets. With the research still contradictory, the debate over performance pay continues to rage. Count me as a supporter: it works well in the private sector and, properly done, should work in the public sector as well.

In the very busy 2007–2008 school year we next focused on the one aspect of teacher accountability that we were allowed to change without the union's consent: granting teachers tenure. Created by state law, tenure had become all but automatic in practice, with 99 percent of teachers achieving this status after three years of teaching. As mentioned previously, tenured teachers had such iron-clad job security that firing one required years of legal battle and hundreds of thousands of dollars in costs.

We believed tenure should be, as I said when announcing our proposal, an "honor, not a routine right." We designed a more thorough performance-review process, based on a teacher's impact on improving student test scores as well as direct in-classroom observations. We worked with our principals to make sure they implemented this new process effectively. As a result, significantly fewer teachers got tenure after three years (eventually the number came down to about half), many were extended for a fourth or fifth year, and the number denied tenure outright, while still not large, increased substantially.

This tenure initiative grew out of the work that Jim Liebman had started on school-based accountability. Using the most sophisticated statistical analyses, we put together a team under Amy McIntosh, a Harvard Business School graduate who had joined us after a successful career in the private sector, to develop fair and equitable comparisons of different teachers' effects on student performance based on test scores. Built into the teacher data reports was the recognition that different teachers working under the same circumstances with the same kinds of students would make different amounts of progress. Much to our astonishment, soon after we announced our tenure initiative, the UFT went to Albany seeking legislation to block it. It was hard to imagine that this obstruction would succeed—surely a teacher's effect on student progress is at least a legitimate factor to consider in lifetime tenure evaluations. But the UFT's power in Albany should never be underestimated. Although the Republican head of the Senate, Joe Bruno, personally promised both the mayor and me that the Republicans would block the legislation, he had to renege on his commitment. A few of his more vulnerable colleagues simply folded under UFT pressure. Remarkably, the law that passed prohibited us from using a teacher's effect on students' test results in tenure decisions, leaving principals to rely solely on infrequent classroom observations. Fortunately, a few years later, with pressure from a new program instituted by the Obama administration, this law was repealed.

Our final—and in many ways most controversial—proposal for the 2007 school year involved a new funding plan that would allocate money to schools on a per-student basis, with those students facing greater challenges—English-language learners, special-education students, poorly performing students, and students from low-income families—getting additional dollars. Educating them was more costly. We hoped the extra money would encourage schools to recruit more of these kinds of students, knowing they would get higher budgets if they did. We also gave them extra points on their Progress Report grades when they posted strong gains with these students.

Under the then-existing budgeting system, money was generally distributed based on student head count, but there were lots of "special"—typically meaning politically driven—deviations. Most significantly, teacher salaries were built into the budgets so that a school received enough money to cover their salaries regardless of what the salaries turned out to be. This meant that high-performing schools in wealthier neighborhoods were able to hire the most-experienced teachers in the city at the highest salaries without any impact on their budgets. This is precisely what happened as seasoned teachers clustered together, leaving the schools in poorer neighborhoods mostly to newcomers. As a result, one school would spend $600,000 for seventy-five teachers and another in a poorer community would spend $400,000 for the same number—with the difference being the cost of the more seasoned teachers. The budgets they received simply ignored this $200,000 difference, awarding the school that spent $600,000 a budget line for that amount, and the school that spent $400,000 a budget line for the lesser amount.

We believed our planned change—rolling up all the money and allowing it to follow the individual student—would make the system fairer for the struggling schools and poorer kids by allowing the schools to use the additional funds for other educational purposes, including hiring more teachers to lower class sizes or increasing intervention programs for students who needed extra help.

Union officials immediately let us know this would be war. They wouldn't tolerate any method of budgeting that took into account the actual cost of teachers. And to no one's surprise, parents in upper- and middle-income communities immediately raised a protest over our funding proposal because they feared their children's schools would lose if others gained. They were right, of course, that this was a zero-sum game, and if the differences in teacher salaries were taken into account, their schools—with higher-salaried teachers—would inevitably get less nonsalary funding than they would have received if teacher salaries continued to be ignored in the budgeting process.

With parents up in arms, we went around the city trying to respond to their concerns. Robert Gordon, a talented lawyer with a background in school reform, whom I had brought in to design the plan, prepared a detailed manual and attended many community meetings to explain why the changes were fair and reasonable. He was shocked at the ferocity of the responses. In the hope of turning down the volume, we decided to create a floor of funding for each school, based on where it stood in 2008, so that no one would be worse off. By holding some schools harmless, so to speak, we would only be able to use new monies to address the prior funding inequities. This solution quieted some nerves but did not silence our critics entirely. The unions and the more affluent parents were now joined together in their attacks on us. I learned, once again, that equity can be costly.

To add insult to injury, in January 2008 we made a totally bone-headed move that cost us dearly. We had brought in some consultants, largely paid for by private philanthropy, who had done an analysis of our bus routes and concluded that we were wasting hundreds of millions of dollars by not routing buses efficiently. We were eager to make the changes in the fall when the weather would have permitted, but we kept getting delayed. We finally decided to change the routes in late January, and, unfortunately, the weather was very cold at the time. As we should have expected, when you reroute buses for tens of thousands of kids, there is lots of confusion. For two weeks, the papers were filled with pictures of kids and their parents freezing while waiting for buses.

This was not a pleasant time. The mayor, while defending us—we were right to reroute the buses and save the money—was understandably furious. The City Council held hearings, and it was open season on us. The council's complaints about our various initiatives were now colored by the busing debacle. All I could say was that we had blown it. Had we ever. This was the most self-injurious thing we did during my tenure, and the opponents of our reforms made good use of it.

SCHOOL CHOICE, WHICH WOULD EMPOWER FAMILIES AND RE-quire educators to compete for students, remained at the top of our agenda, but it could be done meaningfully only if we increased the supply of high-quality options for all students. After all, what good is it to have the freedom to choose if all the good schools are filled beyond capacity?

In addition to our small-school initiative, we knew we had to ramp up our charter schools by working with existing or new partners. So far, our charters had outperformed other public schools, although not every charter was stellar, and a few had been closed for poor performance. The problem was that, as of 2007–2008, we had just sixty charters in the entire city. They served only a tiny fraction of our more than 1 million students. But even with this small number, many veteran educators felt threatened by them. When they heard the word *charter*, they imagined profit-making companies taking over public school functions, driving costs down through wage and spending cuts, and making a killing while delivering inferior education. Nothing like this doomsday scenario had happened in New York City or anywhere else, even though charters had been around since 1992.

Studies on their *effectiveness* had produced contradictory findings, but no one had documented a significant example of operators reaping huge profits. If anything, corporations founded to run charters had struggled to break even.

In part to assuage those who feared profiteering, we decided to work only with nonprofit charter operators. While this decision mollified some, it did nothing to soothe the teachers union, which remained adamantly opposed to charter expansion. The charters took kids away from the traditional public schools, and most weren't unionized. That was reason enough for the union to oppose them. It didn't matter that tens of thousands of parents—mostly poor and minority—wanted charter school placements for their kids but couldn't get them because there weren't remotely enough seats.

As we tried to expand our new small high schools, we ran into additional opposition. In particular, we faced criticism from politicians and parents who objected when we targeted failing schools for closure, even though we planned to immediately open smaller replacements. Sometimes, as with Canarsie High School, our critics said we were racially biased because we closed a school primarily attended by minority students. This, of course, made no sense because the replacement schools would be attended largely by minority students from the same community. The schools we had closed were all predominantly minority because those were the schools that were performing miserably in a system in which almost three quarters of all students are minorities. The union helped to stir up this opposition, no doubt motivated by the fact that whenever we shut down a school the teachers there had to apply for new jobs. Only some of them would get hired by the replacement schools. The others had to find spots, if they could, in one of the other (now) almost sixteen hundred schools or else join the pool of substitute teachers we had established under our 2005 contract with the UFT.

Although we tried over and over to explain that we were providing better options to the very same children who were being failed by the system, we were unable to generate strong support. Too many blacks and Latinos were worried that a group of mostly white reformers might be acting on the basis of subconscious or even conscious prejudice. This problem was especially acute in the black community. I discussed my concerns with several black leaders, including a popular radio personality and musician named James Mtume who came to understand the realities of the situation and to support many of our efforts.

Mtume, patient and wise, explained to me that mistrust ran deep in the black community, and there was no easy way to eradicate it. If we closed a school that many blacks themselves had attended and loved, they would immediately suspect our motives. If we were going to insist on accountability, and fire people for nonperformance, they assumed black principals and teachers would be the first to go. Isn't that what always happens when people are fired? Mtume introduced me to Howard Fuller, a charismatic black leader who, as school superintendent in Milwaukee, had fought successfully for school choice for minority children by opening more charter schools and providing vouchers for kids who wanted to attend private schools. After that, Fuller went on to create the Black Alliance for Educational Options to push school-choice policies for blacks nationally. Mtume knew my views echoed Fuller's, so he thought I could learn from him about how best to get community support for them.

Although Fuller acknowledged that he was also controversial, he explained why it was different for him: since he was black, with a long history in the civil rights movement, his motives weren't suspect. He advised me to be patient but persistent. Mtume tried to help me gain trust, allowing me repeatedly to appear on his Sunday-morning call-in radio show, the most listened-to black program in New York, to respond to concerns. After these programs, people in the street would often stop to say hello or talk about the show. Mtume also thought I could benefit by partnering with a high-visibility black leader. Aiming big, as was his style, in the spring of 2007 Mtume suggested I meet with the Reverend Al Sharpton.

Once a polarizing figure, Sharpton had evolved into a well-respected and powerful national leader. He hosted a daily radio talk show, which aired in many major cities, and as probably the most visible and important leader of the black community in New York, he wielded real influence with public officials and ordinary citizens. I had known him some during my years as chancellor and found him to be fair and, if he wanted, helpful. But given the long association between the unions and the civil rights movement, I worried that, even if he agreed with what we were doing, Sharpton would be reluctant to ally with me because he might alienate the UFT.

We met at a coffee shop in Manhattan, near Lincoln Center, and found much to agree on. We both thought that American education was shortchanging minority students and that accountability would be essential if things were to improve. Sharpton was appalled by the high-school graduation levels for inner-city black kids and was especially interested in the problem of teacher quality. He believed, as did I, that more should be done to get better teachers into schools serving black and Hispanic children. Here, Sharpton appeared to diverge from the position of the teachers union, which had long resisted giving school officials more power to assign particular teachers to specific schools. He also supported charter schools.

Soon Sharpton and I agreed on the outlines of an alliance, which we would call the Education Equality Project. The founding members would include, among others, James Mtume and Howard Fuller, along with the mayor of Newark, Cory Booker; Geoffrey Canada of the Harlem Children's Zone; Arne Duncan, then head of the Chicago public schools and later to become Obama's secretary of education; and Michelle Rhee, then head of the D.C. public schools.

Sharpton and I hoped to make the Education Equality Project a home for people from different social and political backgrounds who backed the reform agenda. We insisted on diversity in our leadership, and we wanted to make sure education became the civil rights issue of our day. At a press conference we held in Washington on June 11, 2008, to announce the formation of the group, I called our failure to educate minority children "the shame of this great nation." Sharpton questioned why civil rights leaders are "silent when only 40 percent of black men are graduating from high school." Journalists got a kick out of calling us an "odd couple" as they reported on our plan. Michelle got their attention when she said, "We are still allowing the color of a child's skin and their zip code to determine their education."

Sharpton and I worked together for about a year, advocating in favor of changes to help assure high-quality teachers for every child including through pay for performance and by making it easier to remove bad teachers. We also argued for more choices for families from low-income communities, including more charter schools. He was a good partner, and although we didn't agree on everything, his was a strong—and, to many people, a surprising—voice for education reform.

In 2009, after Obama became president, Sharpton got more involved with his education initiatives and decided he needed greater independence than the Education Equality Project provided him, so we went our separate ways. The Education Equality Project continued for a while without him but ultimately wasn't able to solve the problem of building greater trust for school reform in minority communities. To this day, I worry that the reform effort is too easily described as a "white guys' movement," and the need for strong alliances with leaders in the minority community remains of paramount concern.

BACK IN NEW YORK, STILL ANTICIPATING THE END OF Bloomberg's administration, we barreled ahead on school closures while opening up dozens and dozens of new schools and pushing our successful charter operators to double down. Quite a few of them responded favorably, and our vision of New York City as a mecca for charter schools started to become a reality. KIPP opened several, as did Achievement First and Uncommon Schools. These three charter organizations were getting strong results, and their schools were considered top-notch by parents. No matter how many schools they opened, they always had many more applicants than they could accept. It was heart-wrenching to watch time after time as public lotteries were held for one hundred new seats out of the thousand or more families that had applied. The families would go together to large gyms or auditoriums, hold hands, and silently pray as names were called. Some cried out in joy. Others wept when their children weren't selected. Even young kids applying for a kindergarten spot seemed to understand this was a crucial moment in their lives.

But none of our charter operators was as aggressive about expansion as was Eva Moskowitz, the former chair of the City Council's Education Committee, who had sparred with me in my early days as chancellor. After the UFT helped to defeat her in the 2005 election for Manhattan borough president, Eva decided to become a charter operator and started a not-for-profit organization called Success Academies. She opened several schools in Harlem and then moved to the Bronx and Brooklyn. We had to push some charter operators to increase their numbers, but Eva always pushed us for more space so she could open more schools. Each year, she started a half dozen or so new charters while other operators opened one or two at most. Her relentless pressure sometimes drove us (especially my staff) nuts, but we all had to admire her determination.

More important, we had to admire the results Eva achieved. She operated her schools in heavily minority communities and served mostly lower-income kids, and her performance numbers were exceptional. Across her schools, she obtained pass rates on annual state exams that rivaled the best schools in the city and state. Some of her schools performed at the level of gifted and talented schools, which, unlike her charters, admitted only the smartest kids in the city based on a demanding test. Think about it: a bunch of mostly poor kids, from some of the city's most challenged communities, were consistently performing at the very top. It forced the question: Why aren't all of our schools doing that? That, unfortunately, is the question that the die-hard defenders of a failing status quo didn't want to discuss.

Rather than celebrate and attempt to replicate Eva's success, the unions and their political allies did everything to discredit her. They claimed she was selective in her admissions and that she got rid of kids who couldn't cut it. The facts didn't support these claims—admissions were determined by an independently verified lottery open to anyone who applied, and her discharge numbers were similar to those at other schools in her community. In any event, small differences in the backgrounds of her students could hardly explain away the stellar results she achieved with high-poverty minority kids. But repeated enough, these kinds of attacks took on a life of their own and negatively affected public perceptions about Eva's schools.

At one point Juan Gonzalez, the *Daily News* columnist, published a piece on Eva and me, which was based on e-mails between us that he had received by making a request under the Freedom of Information law. He argued that the e-mails showed I was doing special favors for her. The only evidence he could offer, which I proudly acknowledged to be true, was that my team worked hard to get her space and address her concerns. There is no question that we wanted to support her as much as we could: she was opening up consistently great schools at a remarkable rate—schools for which there were lengthy waiting lists of kids from our city's poorest neighborhoods. And of course we met with her often, and even helped her raise private money to support the great work she was doing. We also did that with Bob Hughes at New Visions, Sister Paulette LoMonaco at Good Shepherd Services, and Richard Kahan at Urban Assembly, each of whom had repeatedly helped us to open new schools within the traditional system. These were all key partners who were instrumental in supporting work we needed done to create new options for kids who would otherwise end up in failing schools.

The frustrating thing about our charter school opponents was that the facts simply didn't matter to them. Everyone could see, from the beginning, that the charters were oversubscribed, with mostly minority families, especially blacks, seeking admission in large numbers. Eva's schools alone were getting five applicants for every vacancy. Then came two separate studies by professors at Stanford that showed our charter schools getting much better results than traditional public schools. Both studies held demographic factors constant and examined the performance only of students who had applied to charter schools. Those who were admitted were compared with those who were not and went instead to traditional public schools. The second of these studies, done by Margaret Raymond, director of the Center for Research on Education Outcomes, was especially important. She had previously done a national study showing no difference in the performance of charter and traditional public schools. The anticharter crowd cited her work as gospel. In New York City, however, using precisely the same methodology, she found that the charters were getting five months per year more learning in math and one month per year in English language arts when compared with a matched group of students in traditional public schools. That's a lot of learning, especially over the course of the thirteen years that a child spends in school. Raymond concluded, "The rest of the nation can learn from New York's combination of careful school design, strong implementation and vigorous oversight—a balanced approach that has proven it can produce high-quality education options in any setting." Unfortunately, the charter opponents ignored this part of Raymond's teachings.

AT THE START OF MAYOR BLOOMBERG'S SECOND TERM WE HAD taken a big step toward fixing the part of the DOE bureaucracy that served teachers with an initiative code-named Project HR. Officially, the HR stood for Human Resources, but people who worked on it often said it stood for "home run," as they hoped it was going to make a big hit by creating a one-stop service center for the 135,000 people working for the city's schools. We especially wanted to help teachers who needed solutions to real problems but despaired of finding them in a byzantine bureaucracy where phone calls were transferred to extensions that no one answered and people were expected to wait for months to resolve simple issues.

Before Project HR, everyone just seemed to accept that a new teacher might go months without getting a paycheck or access to his or her health benefits. A veteran teacher who had earned a raise might wait even longer to see the money. While they waited, teachers with these kinds of problems were expected to have faith that the system would eventually respond. In the meantime, of course, enormous customer service systems at corporations and even some government agencies were able to process vast numbers of requests with far greater efficiency. Though not intentional, the unresponsiveness of the DOE's bureaucracy communicated to teachers and other employees that the city, which expected them to be accountable, didn't care enough about them to respond to their concerns effectively and efficiently. They saw the human resources system as an obstacle and, on the rare occasions when someone in HR reached out to them, it was someone with bad news, in the form of a complaint or a new demand.

Project HR was ultimately led by deputy chancellor Chris Cerf, who came to work with us after heading a private company called Edison Learning, which helped public school districts operate schools. I knew Chris well, having hired him at my law firm, Onek, Klein & Farr, some twenty years earlier and then had worked with him in the Clinton White House. I brought him in as a consultant in the beginning of the mayor's second term and soon made him a deputy chancellor.

As noted earlier, Chris was instrumental in developing our new system of school-support organizations, and he managed labor relations—obviously not an easy task. He was always looking for ways to strengthen relations with our teaching force. Working closely with a longtime DOE manager named Larry Becker, Chris began by urging our HR professionals to see themselves as problem solvers, and to see the teachers as customers. Union people and outside consultants were tapped for advice, and, in short order, Chris and Larry developed a plan for a commercial-style call center where staff members would have the authority and ability to resolve routine problems quickly and guide people with more complex concerns in the right direction.

To overcome the resistance of the still hidebound DOE, Larry went from office to office to reassure those who felt threatened by the call center's mandate. No one was going to be dismissed or demoted as a result of the new initiative, he told them. In fact, the operators were supposed to make life easier for everyone by proving that HR could be supportive, helpful, and efficient. If they did their jobs well, in-boxes should be emptied throughout the system as backlogs of requests were resolved and a new, rapid-response approach became the norm.

The call center operators, thirty-five in all, had to learn everything about the way the school bureaucracy worked so that they knew whom to contact to answer a teacher's concern quickly and effectively. The questions they fielded would run the gamut—from health coverage, to pay and assignment, to professional development and teacher certification. The work required a steady temperament because, as Larry said, "You have to be just as friendly at five p.m. Friday as you are at eleven a.m. Monday." Our operators had to work so well under pressure that they wouldn't fall apart on days when the calls came in at a rate of four hundred per hour. All this, and they would be timed and monitored by supervisors who required them to be efficient, accurate, and courteous.

With all the pressure, turnover was high in the first months of the call center's operation. Yet we discovered that, with training and support, certain people thrived in this work. They were generally team-oriented people who could empathize with teachers who called and enjoyed helping them. They were the type who were not frustrated by puzzles and understood the valuable role they were playing in raising teacher morale and thereby improving things for kids in our classrooms.

In addition to the call center, which we repeatedly heard was a big hit with teachers, Cerf and Becker set out to correct other HR problems that had festered for decades. To help principals and job-seeking teachers, they computerized the job application and transfer processes for the first time and established a matchmaking system that actually helped put people in the spots where they were needed. As an exten-

- -

sion of this program, they also set up a system that helped principals follow each new hire's progress through the bureaucracy. Other new programs allowed teachers to submit requests for leaves and to file for the pay raises they earned with additional college course work by logging on to a computer system. All of these things had previously been done by hand or through endless phone calls to people who, more often than not, didn't know the answer.

Months after the call center opened, teacher complaints about payroll, benefits, and bureaucracy plummeted. We no longer had to ask that hundreds of newly hired teachers simply trust the system to deliver them all the money they were owed as the weeks and months passed and the payroll office still didn't send a check. Freed of the stress and, let's admit it, the resentments caused by this kind of snafu, teachers and principals were able to focus more time and energy on the work they did with children. To me, that made it a home run.

AS WE APPROACHED THE END OF THE MAYOR'S SECOND TERM, we had one more major move to make: to fund and encourage innovations in the way schools instructed their students. We had done a lot to spur innovation, largely by opening hundreds of new and varied public and charter schools, some of which were uncharacteristically cutting edge for public schools. For example, the Brooklyn Generation School, started as a replacement school for the old, failing South Shore High School, substantially increased the amount of time students spent in school by reconfiguring the school's schedule and adding electives that got students heavily involved in college and career-related activities. Many of these activities took the kids outside the classroom and into the city. The teachers union supported the novel scheduling approach, the teachers were enthusiastic about the model, and the students performed well. The group that worked with us opened schools in several other cities.

Similarly, we opened a high school in lower Manhattan called the iSchool that used technology to personalize the learning experience and to bring in talent remotely through the use of computers. This school became an early national model for blending human capital with technological supports to improve student learning. And we started a unique middle and high school called Quest to Learn, also in Manhattan, that was created by game designers and curriculum specialists using gamelike principles to help students develop the skills and habits needed for the twenty-first-century, information-rich world. When I visited the school, I could tell immediately that it was much more hands-on than the usual classroom experience.

We had also brought in one of the most innovative minds in public education, Roland Fryer from Harvard—the same economist who subsequently studied paying teachers for performance—to work on how best to motivate students. When I met Roland, he immediately said he wanted to come to New York and work with us. This astonished me. Why would he leave Harvard, where he had it made? He spent a year with us, designing programs to incentivize kids to perform better through the use of financial and other rewards. Fryer was utterly unafraid of controversy—his ideas prompted a lot of questions—and completely committed to assessing results rigorously. If something worked, great, let's do more of it; if it didn't work, get rid of it. He was the most entrepreneurial educator I had ever met. While his ideas had limited impact in New York, he saw greater success in Chicago and D.C., and his research ultimately led him to implement some very effective programs in Houston and Denver. Though an economist and statistician by discipline, Fryer's passion remains K–12 education, where he doesn't just do studies, but gets deeply and personally involved in the trenches. I'm proud he got his start in NYC.

Despite these examples, I still felt we had only scratched the surface on innovation. Most important, neither we nor anyone else had really looked at the basic classroom model—with one teacher responsible for twenty-five or so students whose individual abilities varied greatly—that had remained essentially unchanged for more than a hundred years. We knew we had to crack this open. The world was moving fast, and the demands on our children were accelerating as well. If the schools didn't keep pace, our kids would pay the price. Yet education somehow remained, as I often put it, "an innovation-free zone." This was hardly surprising because monopolists, as Timothy Wu reminds us in his insightful book *The Master Switch*, have no reason to disrupt a successful business model. Just as our charter schools were designed to break the public school monopoly, our innovation work was similarly intended to do what monopolists don't do—in short, we had our sights set on "disrupting class," as the visionary Harvard Business School professor Clayton Christensen had titled his book on education.

To begin this project, which we called the iZone ("i" for innovation), I put together an internal working group and asked it to come back with proposals. I got some help from an unexpected quarter. Joel Rose, another former Teach for America alum, had worked with Chris Cerf at Edison Schools. When Chris joined us, he persuaded Joel to come along. In his spare time Joel worked on a model of personalized learning that would tailor a student's experience to the different ways and speeds she learns. He called his concept the School of One. It was so impressive that we made him the head of our innovation working group and began to get his idea ready for piloting.

Having spent time in the classroom himself, Rose focused on individualizing instruction by providing teachers and administrators with daily updates on what materials a student had mastered and which instructional method had worked best for him or her. Rose's model allowed several classes to be combined, with the teachers collectively responsible for the entire group. Each day, different students would be assigned to different instructional programs. Some would work in small groups with teachers. Others worked with online programs or virtual tutors. Each student was assessed every day, and the results of these assessments were fed into an algorithm that determined which mode of instruction the student should receive the next day.

No student could proceed to the next lesson until he or she showed mastery of the current one. As for the teachers, they found themselves dealing with far fewer students, and they could also focus their preparation on fewer lessons since each would teach the same lesson to several different small groups at different times. This kind of specialization by the teachers was unheard of in traditional classrooms.

The School of One started with a summer pilot program in lower Manhattan in 2009. In practice, the summer school came to resemble a high-tech workplace. Each morning eighty students received folders with their individualized schedules—called playlists—that included four forty-minute lessons broken up by lunch and recess periods. They would end the day with a twenty-minute period during which they would answer questions and solve problems that assessed how much they had learned. During the night, the computer software that was the backbone of the program devised the next day's activities for students as well as for the five teachers involved. As the algorithm that the school used to determine which activities to assign to a student got more information about what worked best for each individual, the system kept getting smarter and better. I visited numerous times and was always impressed by how dynamic and, yes, innovative the project was, and how engaged the students were. It reminded me of my trips to Silicon Valley to visit places like Google.

As people heard about School of One, they came from all over the city and country to observe. Foundations invested millions to help it grow and expand. *Time* magazine selected the program as one of the fifty best inventions of 2009, an honor no education program had previously won. Soon we were operating a School of One in three schools during the regular school year, and the early results were encouraging. Joel Rose went on to set up his own not-for-profit organization and began implementing his model in several different school districts around the country. Arthur Levine, formerly president of Teachers College at Columbia University, and now president of the Woodrow Wilson Foundation, began to evangelize the program, explaining: "We know that children learn different subjects at different rates. We know that children have different learning styles, which make different methods of instruction more or less effective for them. We also know that today's new technologies, advancing at a breathtaking pace . . . can enable us to individualize education for each child, gearing instruction to each particular learning style and pace. School of One is based on these realities."

We didn't stop with School of One. We were eager to fund other new approaches, and I knew Shimon Waronker, who had had success in turning around M.S. 22, was thinking about changing the education delivery system. In September 2008, with my support, he took a leave to attend Harvard's Graduate School of Education, where he spent long days and nights studying the origins of the American education model, searching for the source of the problems he saw in it today and looking for solutions. He was joined by several classmates at Harvard who shared his frustration with the traditional American school and yearned for something better.

The current school model, Shimon told me, "is not about teaching and learning. It is about sorting the kids into groups. They tested a kid to see, 'Can you do this?' If you can, you go to the next level. If you can't, too bad." The alternative Shimon imagined would create communities of learning in which four teachers would see the same sixty students through their entire elementary-school experience from kindergarten through fifth grade. The teachers would be led by a "master" teacher who would work with two less-experienced, but nevertheless veteran, educators called "partners" and "associates." The fourth member of each team would be a beginning "apprentice" teacher. Together, the four professionals would set goals, support one another, and lead their students through the grades. They would work collegially, but their pay would vary significantly, with the master teacher making multiples of what the apprentice made.

When he talked about his idea, Shimon spoke excitedly about the relationships that would be formed by teachers who worked with children for six years. He imagined parents becoming far more engaged with their children's teachers, and he hoped that they, too, would see the school as a true community. But no one in this model would benefit more, said Shimon, than the teachers, who would get the chance to learn from one another and rise to higher positions with greater pay and, eventually, more leadership responsibilities.

In the traditional New York City school, individual teachers still had little opportunity to distinguish themselves by earning promotions or pay increases beyond what years of service gave them under their union agreement. In the school Shimon designed, apprentices and associates could move up to become partners, and partners could advance to become master teachers. Each move would be accompanied by a substantial pay increase, and those who reached the master level would then be assigned as leaders of new teams. Starting pay for team leaders would be $125,000 per year. This was significantly more than the most senior teachers in our system were getting paid.

Based loosely on the type of professional rankings seen in law firms or group medical practices, Shimon's design treated teachers as true professionals who were expected to run their own affairs. A principal would be available for support, and to intervene in unusual circumstances. But otherwise, each team would be expected to function as a collaborative unit, with almost complete autonomy. Of course, their students would have to take all the mandatory exams, and they would be subject to the evaluations everyone else underwent. But apart from that, no one would tell the teachers what to teach, or how to teach. Like tiny schools within the larger elementary-school structure, the learning communities would enjoy extraordinary independence and freedom.

When he was ready to return to New York, Shimon prepared a proposal for a school based on his design, which we approved. He decided that his school would be a public school employing union teachers rather than a charter school. He negotiated with the UFT to win its support for hiring and pay scales based on merit and ability rather than length of service. At the same time, he scoured the city's school buildings for space. He eventually found a perfect one inside a public school in a high-poverty community on the border of the Crown Heights and Brownsville neighborhoods in Brooklyn, not far from the Hasidic Jewish community where he lived. He named his school the New American Academy.

In September 2010, Shimon's school opened with just two classes of about sixty students each. These were not children who were pre-screened for their abilities so that New American would have the cream of the crop. Instead, students chose to enroll and were accepted on a first-come, first-served basis. More than 80 percent of the students came from families that qualified for free or subsidized meals. Ten percent needed special-education services. By any measure, this was a challenging group of kids to educate.

Shimon's school had its ups and downs. He had to replace a master teacher in its first year. Still, it received praise from parents who valued its safe, nurturing environment and for the high academic expectations communicated to students. *New York Times* columnist David Brooks chimed in with a positive review. However, when Shimon ultimately received the first results of tests taken by his third graders, they were disappointing. Although relatively few kids were tested, and the school performed similarly to others in the neighborhood, more would have to be done to improve results.

Shimon made some immediate changes and also urged everyone involved in the school to take a long-term view. New American had been set up to see kids through six solid years of consistent education. He would wait until the first cohort had completed the program before reaching any firm conclusions. In the meantime, he would find encouragement in the feedback from teachers, students, and parents, who raved about what was happening at the school. He was also heartened by rising attendance rates, and an influx of students from nearby middle-class neighborhoods where parents had heard about the academy's long-term, relationship-based approach to elementary education and wanted it for their children. From where I sat, Shimon's experiment was just the kind of thing I wanted to encourage.

Soon after launching Shimon's school, I met with Sam Palmisano, the CEO of IBM, and that meeting led to the development of P-Tech, the school that I described in the preface and that President Obama highlighted in his State of the Union speech. This school also became a national model as other cities began to open their own versions in partnership with major corporations. And it's no wonder they've caught on. These schools are providing kids with the kind of practical training that will enable them to get hired after they graduate.

Other technology-based innovations were developed by the iZone, which was led by my deputy chancellor John White, who was yet another Teach for America alum. He proved to be one of the most talented leaders I have ever met. He had been managing our high-school and charter initiatives when I asked him to tackle innovation as well. He did that brilliantly, and, to no one's surprise, other districts soon began recruiting him to run their school systems. In his early thirties, he was hired to head the New Orleans school system and, soon thereafter, he was put in charge of all of Louisiana's schools, where he continues to this day to do cutting-edge work.

Some of the iZone schools tried distance learning by Skyping in expert teachers from other parts of the city or country. Others experimented by mixing online courses with traditional classroom work, a model that came to be called "blended learning." And others tried a digitally enhanced curriculum that teachers would use in the classroom. For a school system that I had once called "an innovation-free zone," innovation was thriving. As Robin Lake at the Center for Reinvention of Public Education put it, the scale and ambition of what we were doing was unmatched: city officials, she wrote, "want to be on the leading edge of this, and I think they are for sure."

12

Change That Endures

From the very beginning, we said we wanted to change the city schools in a lasting way that relied on certain core policies—effective management, accountability, choice, innovation, and more. Our every move was informed by these ideals, and we never wavered.

Some people never accepted that we were motivated by the desire to fix this problem. They continued to insist that we wanted to hand over the public system to private, profit-gouging interests, and they pointed to the donations by philanthropists such as Bill Gates, Eli Broad, and Julian Robertson, as if their support proved the point. These men had each made billions of dollars in private enterprise, but their commitment was hardly proof of a malevolent campaign to hijack public schools on behalf of self-interested corporations. Gates and the others were acting in the highest traditions of philanthropy, trying to make America, which had been so good to them, better for others. It is one thing to challenge their preferred policies on the merits; it is an entirely different thing to seek to impugn their motives. Nevertheless, these kind of attacks were relentless. Critics tried to discredit our efforts by linking them to what Diane Ravitch and others called the "Billionaire's Boys' Club," a phrase that echoed the title of a 1989 movie about rich and depraved young killers.

The boys' club epithet had been used earlier, but it gained real currency in 2009 as Mayor Bloomberg began to pursue a third term of office. Opponents of school reform, including many not directly involved with the schools, had been counting the days to the end of his term and were eager to see Bloomberg defeated. Early in the campaign, Ravitch attacked his supposed "authoritarian mode of governance" in *Education Week.* "It appears," she wrote, "that the Big Money has placed its bets on dismantling public education. Mayor Bloomberg decided long ago, when he took over New York City's public schools, that their biggest problem was too much democracy." She also warned against schools being run by "hedge fund managers [and] dilettantes."

Bloomberg anticipated such criticism, and I doubt it bothered him much. But his decision to run for a third term was made difficult for another reason: he had previously pledged to abide by the two-term limit in the law, and to overcome that limit he would need to seek a change in the law from the City Council. The mayor reconsidered his two-term promise after the country was plunged into economic crisis in late summer of 2008. As the financial capital of the world, New York City was destined to suffer big revenue and job losses as mortgage banking and the rest of the financial industry fell into the abyss. The city's financiers and entrepreneurs would also be called upon to help lead the way to recovery. Considering his unique background in both government and business, Bloomberg decided it was not the right moment to step down and hoped voters would agree. He won a change in the term-limit law from the City Council and embarked on his reelection campaign.

Education was a primary focus of the contest, and Bloomberg could point to real achievements. In seven years the passing rate for fourth graders taking the state math test had risen from 53 percent to over 80 percent, and the gap separating the city's kids from students across New

York State had nearly closed. Although reading scores had not risen so dramatically, they were still better across the board. High-school graduation rates had gone from about 45 percent to 62 percent, even though the state had made graduation requirements more demanding. Bloomberg ran hard on this record.

While the mayor stumped for reelection, my team used the facts and figures to defend mayoral control in Albany, where state legislators were considering whether to renew this authority, which otherwise would have expired on June 30, 2009. As a political body, the state legislature—the lower house is called the State Assembly, the upper house is the State Senate—was subject to all kinds of interest group pressures. In the years since the mayoral control law was passed, this pressure had only increased. I got an earful from legislators who feared that they and their constituents would continue to lose power under mayoral control. I pointed to our accomplishments, arguing that a mayor who approached the schools with a "citywide focus" was more likely to deliver a fairer, better outcome for all. Under splintered control, "those with power, or access to power, typically prevail," which is exactly what had happened in the bad old days.

We knew we had to win this fight. Otherwise, we would get nothing done during a third Bloomberg term. The process was ugly and dragged on past a June 30 statutory deadline, leading to a brief reinstitution of the old seven-person school board. Fortunately, sanity returned, and in August 2009, Governor Patterson signed the reauthorizing legislation into law. We had won on virtually every issue, although the legislature made a few, largely cosmetic, procedural changes to mollify opponents of the renewal, one of which would soon come back to haunt us.

With mayoral control extended, the city's focus turned toward the November mayoral election. Never part of the mayor's political team, I had no role in the campaign. However, this didn't stop others from trying to attack the mayor by attacking me. Randi Weingarten branded me "untrustworthy" for having criticized the teachers contract when she was out of town many years earlier. A state assemblyman said my attempts at reaching out to elected officials were "bogus." Others tried to paint me as autocratic and unresponsive. At a low point in the campaign, Bloomberg's Democratic opponent, Bill Thompson, called for me to be fired and made clear that he would have no use for me if he won.

During the campaign I allowed myself one opportunity, in a press interview, to respond. I said I was happy with our record and pointed out that in education, policy debates can devolve into personal attacks because parents understandably have an intense interest in the outcome. "When it comes to peoples' own children," I said, "they may sometimes want things that aren't equitable." I noted that the mayor and I were in agreement when it came to policies, priorities, and management style, but I didn't say anything about the upcoming election. I had told Bloomberg that I always intended to serve two terms only, never thinking a third would be possible. When I learned he hoped to stay beyond 2009, I assured him that I would serve through a reasonable transition period if he won. But, now in my mid-sixties, I had other things I wanted to do, and I intended to make way for someone who could move the reform effort forward with new energy and a fresh perspective.

AS THE MAYOR AND OTHERS CAMPAIGNED, OUR WORK CONTIN-
ued unabated. Despite substantial progress, the relationship between zip codes and school quality remained strong, and the achievement gaps between blacks and Latinos on the one hand, and whites and Asians on the other, remained large. The effects of this last problem could readily be seen in the makeup of classes at the elite public high

schools. Based on a very demanding special exam, admissions at these schools still skewed heavily toward white and especially Asian American students. Although we had expanded a test-prep program to help students with entrance exams, black and Latino students were less likely than others to enroll in it. When those minority students did attend prep courses, they were still less likely to take the exams and win admission. More broadly, we were far from satisfied when it came to high-school graduation rates for minority students. On-time graduation rates for black and Latino students, although greatly improved, were still unacceptably low.

No doubt, generations of poverty and substandard schooling contributed to the stubborn achievement gap. For African Americans, you could add the historic impact of slavery, racism, and segregation. Some of the young men I spoke to in the African American and Latino communities had concluded that the system was not fair, and, as a result, they looked to alternatives outside the law to win respect, earn money, and feel a sense of achievement. They were plenty smart but didn't think of the mainstream routes to success as realistic options for themselves. Considering the quality of the schools prior to our reforms, it was hard to say they were wrong. Too many became failing students who disrupted classrooms and left school as soon as they could. Thus, the cycle of disengagement and poverty continued.

Unfortunately, many educators still believe they need to lower their expectations for certain children because, putting it charitably, they want to avoid setting them up for failure. Whenever I thought about this defeatist view, I recalled a meeting I attended with parents and teachers in the predominantly middle-class community of Middle Village, Queens, where the schools were not doing very well. When I suggested they should get behind some of our reforms, I ran into a lot of resistance. Some of it was fear of the unknown, which is understandable.

But I was shocked when a high-level UFT representative said, right there in front of hundreds of parents, "Chancellor, if you want better results from the schools, you should send us better kids." What must those parents have thought hearing this from a well-respected teacher-leader?

This point of view defies the facts, not only with respect to what we can achieve with the kids we have, but also with respect to the enduring value of a high-school diploma. Studies have shown that young people who complete high school live longer, healthier, richer lives. They are less likely to be arrested or have unwanted pregnancies and are far more likely to obtain further education or vocational training. Society bene-fits, too. In 2003, economists in the United States and Canada esti-mated that with every 1 percentage point rise in graduation rates for American males, the United States saved $1.4 billion a year in costs related to policing, prisons, and lost productivity.

The advantages that accrue to high-school graduates are so great, and the benefits to our communities so important, that we decided we couldn't wait for the gradual improvements in the overall system to meet the needs of those students who required immediate help to earn a diploma. Pretty early on we had invested $37 million to develop and implement a "multiple pathways" program for high schoolers to find and serve students who were either falling dangerously behind in cred-its, or getting too old to remain in public school. (At age twenty-one, students are no longer legally entitled to a free public education.) This was playing catch-up—compensating for the past failures of the schools—but no issue deserved our attention, and creativity, more. Those kids would never have a second chance; they were the most challenging group in the entire system.

Remarkably, when we started, no one even knew how many of these students there were. My senior adviser, Michelle Cahill, along with her deputy, JoEllen Lynch, began to answer this question by tracking down and analyzing the records of several hundred thousand students. They discovered that, at any one time, some seventy thousand students in their second or third years of high school were significantly behind schedule in accumulating enough credits to graduate. An equal number of students between the ages of sixteen and twenty-one had already dropped out without a diploma, with little prospect of reentering school and completing the academic work needed to get a diploma before they aged out of eligibility for public education. Altogether, that's 140,000 youngsters who would end up facing the prospect of lifelong disadvantages.

Among the falling-behind students were many who had demonstrated real aptitude by completing, for example, all of their math requirements, and more than twenty-five thousand had passed two or more Regents exams. But these same students may have missed several years of mandatory gym classes, taken the first half of American history and then missed a semester, or failed in English more than once. As Cahill told the press, "The transcripts came in a bit of a mess," but with time, her study group was able to discern some important patterns. In many cases, at-risk students failed to get credit for a course they took, or *should* have taken, in their first two years of high school. Many of these courses were required for them to move on to the next level of work. Thus, a cascade of failure could begin in a student's first year of high school and quickly become overwhelming. With a student's credit deficit growing bigger every term, leaving school could seem preferable to extra-long days of remedial work or the humiliation of being an eighteen- or nineteen-year-old in a class filled with sixteen-year-olds.

We believed it was necessary to identify students in danger of falling behind as soon as they suffered their first stumbles, before they got into serious trouble. Some high schools—which we called "beat the odds" schools—were already doing this and getting much better results.

What else did they have in common? They were smaller—no more than six hundred students—and teachers weren't overwhelmed by huge numbers of struggling students. On the opposite end of the spectrum, big schools, where more than half of the incoming students tested below grade level, invariably suffered from the worst graduation rates.

We saw that we could give the most kids the best shot at a diploma by making more small-school options available, and doing what we could to avoid loading up any one school with great numbers of low-scoring freshmen. But as Michelle and JoEllen found, there was much more to be done. Teachers at beat-the-odds schools also followed students closely, intervened early, and excelled at personalized help. Students under their supervision developed what we began to call recuperative power, which made a big difference. Citywide improvements would depend on the leadership of principals, who had to set higher expectations and provide more training and support for teachers.

Fortunately, several of our educators knew a great deal about how to help students who had fallen behind. Double-period courses were already being used in many schools to boost students behind in the basics. Other schools offered extended day, and even extended school-year options to help these students catch up. We expanded the use of these programs. More important, we redesigned and increased the number of Young Adult Borough Centers (YABCs) to offer the courses that undercredited kids, grouped in cohorts of two hundred, needed to graduate. In these centers, no one had to feel self-conscious about mingling with classmates who were much younger. The YABCs would offer classes in the evenings for students who were employed. They also implemented a new initiative, called Learning to Work, where we partnered with community organizations to help YABC students find employment, including internships, so they could develop the skills and confidence necessary for full-time work after graduation. We held several ceremonies celebrating successful YABC students, and when they told their stories, most of us cried.

In time, we would create nearly a hundred new pathways that a student could take to earn a diploma. We revamped the so-called alternative high schools that served students who, for some reason, just didn't fit in well in our traditional high schools. The alternative schools usually were less structured and often provided internships or other practical experiences as part of their offerings. We also opened several specialized transfer high schools—for kids who weren't making it in their original schools—that recruited teachers committed to the success of these students and to developing instructional strategies to help them compensate for their academic deficits. These schools also provided strong youth-development and social service supports and served only students who had fallen behind in their credits and were at least sixteen years old. New full- and part-time programs were created for students to get an alternative credential through the General Educational Development testing system. Overall, these programs not only improved the city's graduation rate, but also helped reduce the dropout rate by more than half under Bloomberg's tenure—from 22 percent to 10 percent. *Time* magazine wrote a lengthy feature on this effort, aptly titled "Stopping the Exodus," and explaining, "New York City has more dropouts than most cities have students. It also has more ways to help them." The scope and dimensions of this work were important, but just as important to us was the message we sent about New York City's concern for young people. We weren't giving up on anyone.

BLOOMBERG WON REELECTION, AND SOON AFTER I TURNED MY attention to the national Race to the Top competition that the Obama administration was pushing in education. This $4.35 billion program grew out of the initial economic stimulus initiative that President Obama and Congress enacted to address the recession. Under Race to the Top, states were eligible for huge grants, but to qualify they had to adopt reforms similar to those we were pursuing in New York City. The federal Education Department also set aside an additional $650 million for what it called Investing in Innovation grants, thereby mirroring our focus on innovation with our pioneering iZone.

President Obama's election, followed by his appointment of Arne Duncan as secretary of education and their adoption of Race to the Top, marked a real shift in national education policy. Together, Obama and Duncan dramatically repositioned the Democratic Party, which traditionally had been much more aligned with the teachers unions' positions. Obama had dropped some hints about this shift during the campaign. I recall in particular his embrace of Michelle Rhee, the Washington, D.C., school chancellor, in one of the presidential debates. Although she was a Democrat, Rhee's very visible and outspoken commitment to reforms based on teacher evaluations and accountability had made her public enemy number one as far as the unions were concerned. Obama's praise didn't go unnoticed. On the other hand, his chief education adviser during the campaign was Linda Darling Hammond, a well-respected Stanford professor, many of whose views were more closely aligned with the teachers unions and often opposed by the reform movement. The question for education watchers was, if elected, which way Obama would go: the Rhee approach or the Hammond approach?

This question was pretty much answered the day after Obama's election when some of his key operatives leaked to the *Washington Post* that I was seriously under consideration for secretary of education. I was flattered, and even indulged in a little fantasy about how much I might accomplish working with a strong Democratic president who clearly cared about improving education for the underserved. But I knew it wouldn't happen. The unions would declare war if the president named someone like me, or Michelle Rhee, to be education secretary. I quickly concluded Obama intended to name his friend Arne Duncan, who was a committed reformer but not nearly as controversial as Rhee or I would have been. By putting my name out there—and letting the unions spend their political capital taking me down—the president could then shift to Duncan, while seeming to compromise.

Duncan got the nod and, working with a very strong team, came up with the proposal for Race to the Top. It was right out of the reformers' playbook, focusing on real evaluations for principals and teachers, the use of data to understand student performance and differentiate instruction, and support for charter schools. Race to the Top also addressed a serious problem in the No Child law. Under No Child, states were able to set their own standards and devise their own tests, which meant they could keep pass rates high by lowering performance requirements. Duncan immediately decried what he said had become "a race to the bottom." He then added, "States are lying to children. They are lying to parents. They're ignoring failure, and that's unacceptable. We have to be fierce."

All of the Race to the Top elements were controversial, but, over time, the one that encouraged states to change their standards and testing requirements became the most contentious. In the past, the idea of a shared set of standards for education, applied across multiple states, would have been a nonstarter because of the widespread acceptance that education policy and funding are state and local matters. But as other countries with national education systems kept exceeding the United States in global assessments of school quality, experts and public officials started to reconsider the American model. In 1996, several concerned governors from both parties joined with key business leaders to start a group called Achieve to study this issue as part of a broader consideration of education standards. The organization paid particular attention to what students need to succeed in the world after high school, whether that meant entering higher education or getting a job.

With Republican and Democratic governors in support, Achieve issued a 2004 report showing that, in general, we could not assume that a high-school diploma meant a student was actually ready to move on to a job or to higher education. In fact, the expectations set by employers, as well as colleges and universities, had risen substantially, even as most state standards for high-school graduation stayed the same or declined. The mismatch between the education supplied by public schools and the skills and knowledge demanded by colleges and universities was so bad that the majority of students entering higher education would need remedial instruction in at least one subject area. Respected organizations like the College Board found that only about one in four kids going to college is fully prepared. And sadly, most of the students who enroll in college never receive a degree. They drop out, in many cases because they feel unprepared and frustrated by having to do remedial work even as their expenses and debt for college loans increase with each passing semester.

Alarmed by the overwhelming evidence that our public schools were failing vast numbers of children, the governors searched for solutions. What emerged from the work done by Achieve became known as the Common Core standards, which ultimately attracted surprising levels of support from both Republican and Democratic governors. As its name suggests, the plan was to establish learning standards—the knowledge and skills a child needs to master in each grade—for math and English language arts that, if faithfully implemented, would produce students ready for college. The Obama administration got behind the Common Core concept too, committing more than $300 million in federal funds to support two private testing groups—the Partnership for Assessment of Readiness for College and Careers and the Smarter Balanced Assessment Consortium—that would provide a choice of tests for the states that adopted Common Core.

Opposition to the Common Core and the new tests came from people on the Left who objected to the strictness of the standards and their likely impact on teacher evaluations and from people on the Right who feared it meant big government interference. Seeing this odd alliance of the Left and Right, I couldn't help but think of the quip attributed to former Reagan education secretary William Bennett: "America will never have national standards, because the Right will never do national and the Left will never do standards."

Despite the substantial political resistance, officials in the large majority of states adopted the Common Core, presumably in part because they wanted to qualify for Race to the Top federal money and in part because they recognized the potential for progress. As of early 2014, more than forty states and the District of Columbia had signed on to the Common Core, but the debate continued to rage, with a few states abandoning the standards and the tests.

Much credit for Obama's aggressive education agenda belongs to Arne Duncan, whom I initially came to know while he was running the Chicago schools. We talked when I was first appointed chancellor in 2002 and consulted frequently over the years. He was doing good work in Chicago, and I was eager to learn from him. After he became secretary of education, he came to New York to highlight the work we had done and show how it aligned with Race to the Top. We visited several charter schools together and did an event featuring the data systems that Jim Liebman had established.

It took some fortitude for a Democratic secretary of education to show so much support for what we were doing, but Duncan never wavered. He also drew national attention to a McKinsey & Company report showing how the country's education woes were depriving the American economy of between $1.3 and $2.3 trillion worth of productivity every year—amounting to a loss of somewhere between 8 and 13 percent of our total annual economy. Over time, this loss could make the country less competitive in the global economy, lower our standard of living, and reduce our influence around the globe. In my view, it would not be an exaggeration to say that the world would become a more dangerous place if we continued to accept mediocrity in our schools.

At the time of the McKinsey report's release, Duncan said that too many schools were "perpetuating poverty." What was required, he added, was a radical reform agenda that would begin with closing the worst schools across the country and replacing them with new faculty and external support mechanisms to assure high standards and demanding instruction—much as we were doing in New York.

With our record and the national education department's like-minded policies, we were quite optimistic about New York's application for Race to the Top funding. The amount of money involved for the state was $700 million, of which New York City would probably get around $250 million. Unfortunately, the state's initial application failed, in no small part because New York State had several antireform laws on its books that conflicted with Race to the Top policies. To succeed in round two, the state would have to eliminate the recently passed tenure law that had barred us from considering student progress in evaluating a teacher's performance and would have to lift the cap preventing the opening of more charter schools. Finally, Race to the Top would require the adoption of a whole new teacher evaluation system—for tenured as well as nontenured teachers—something we very much wanted.

After another grueling legislative battle, these changes in state law were made. But Race to the Top also required the state to win support from the teachers union for its qualifying programs. To accomplish that, the Education Department in New York State had to make some special deals with the union. As a result, the final application was to be laced with caveats that I feared would make it difficult to implement many of the changes, even if the state won the award. I opposed the deals the state had made with the unions, but to no avail.

Several years have passed since New York won its Race to the Top grant, and it has achieved only mixed results. Although Race to the Top led to important changes in the law on charters and tenure, in others areas the anticipated pushback from the union has hampered progress. Most troubling, despite Governor Cuomo's efforts, New York City still hadn't implemented a meaningful teacher evaluation process by the end of the 2013–14 school year, and the union continues to find new reasons to oppose it. That's a big disappointment.

ALTHOUGH RACE TO THE TOP DID NOT ACHIEVE EVERYTHING IT set out to do, my team was ecstatic when it was enacted. Then, all of a sudden, the day-to-day realities of running the school system brought us back to earth.

The first new challenge arose from the changes made when the mayoral control law had been reauthorized in Albany. As part of the overall package, the legislators granted the request of those opposed to closing failing schools to require our department to conduct public meetings and publish so-called educational impact statements before any school could be closed. These statements were supposed to depend on community input as well as professional assessments to estimate the effect of shutting down a school. We planned to close nineteen schools and replace them with new ones.

We worked hard to complete the impact statements and conduct the requisite hearings, but since this was completely new territory for us, we stumbled along the way. After the Panel for Educational Policy reviewed our work and approved all nineteen closings, the UFT joined with the New York branch of the National Association for the Advancement of Colored People (NAACP) to ask the courts to stop us. In their lawsuit, they said our work had been inadequate and the closures would be disruptive to the communities where the schools were located.

I was surprised when the NAACP joined the suit because our effort to close bad schools and open new ones had been, as independent studies confirmed, most beneficial for minority students who got better access to superior schools. All I could conclude is that the old labor–civil rights coalition, so important in the 1960s and '70s, was still strong enough to hold together even if it came at the expense of the very kids I thought the NAACP was supposed to protect.

When a trial court and then an appeals panel found that we had failed to satisfy all the procedural requirements, we had no choice but to accept that our impact statements had fallen short. This was tough. We had planned on these closures and new small-school openings as part of our high-schools admissions process for that year, and many school-placement decisions would have to be undone if we had to reverse course completely. In addition, Mayor Bloomberg, who hated bureaucratic screwups, made his displeasure known. With our back against the wall, we compromised with the union and NAACP by agreeing to keep a few of the schools open and to provide additional supports to schools in danger of closing. As a result, we were able to salvage most of the high-school admissions process. We also learned from our mistakes, and, in the following year, the closures went more smoothly.

A second troubling event had a more lasting impact. It happened as

I had just finished testifying for the state on Race to the Top and took a short vacation in Nova Scotia. As my wife and I drank in the beautiful scenery, I learned that the state had decided to radically change the way its tests were graded by redefining proficiency, and, as a result, our scores (i.e., the percentage of kids passing) would appear to have plummeted. Other school systems throughout the state also saw big declines. For us, the shift meant that instead of 82 percent of our students being judged proficient in math, only 54 percent of them made the grade. In English the number dropped from roughly two thirds proficient to just under half.

When the test scores were recalibrated, our team felt that the state officials had totally mishandled the matter. Two years before, Jim Liebman and I had had a private meeting with the prior state education commissioner and members of the Board of Regents to show them that their cut scores were too low and should be recalibrated, but they ignored us then. When they did finally make a change—requiring more correct answers to get a passing grade—they didn't adequately explain to the press or public that they were simply raising the bar, not disproving the real gains that the city kids had made against a standard that, to be sure, had been kept too low.

Although the new measurement scheme didn't change what we had actually achieved, it did sow considerable public confusion. Only the most well-informed New Yorkers would know, when considering our scores over time, that a new, tougher cut line had been set to separate those students who were deemed proficient from those who were not. Most people would take one look at the numbers and conclude either that we had experienced a big system-wide failure or that we had been cooking the books in previous years. Neither conclusion would be true. There had been no decline in actual performance—but there was no way for us to adequately explain this to all the people who would react negatively to reports on our test results. And of course there were lots of people opposed to reform who cheerfully sought to exploit the situation to undermine our support.

To understand why the gains were real, consider a simple example. Suppose it used to be that making five of ten foul shots in basketball would be considered proficient, and then the standard for proficiency was raised to eight out of ten foul shots. A player who initially made five would be proficient but if, after the standard had been raised, he made seven he wouldn't be proficient. Which is better? Clearly, it's better to make seven shots than five, regardless of whether doing so is called proficient. That, in effect, is what children across the city were doing, but the state's clumsy change branded them failures.

A more detailed analysis showed that, even with the recalibration, New York City had made real progress that year and, as before, substantially outperformed the rest of the state. This was all the more impressive to me since schools outside New York City served far fewer disadvantaged students. Independent researchers confirmed this conclusion. James Kemple, the executive director of the Research Alliance for New York City Schools at New York University, documented continued progress in New York City, noting that "the improvement trend continues even taking into account New York State's recent recalibration of test scores." And Charles Sahm at the Manhattan Institute carried out an analysis showing that, despite the recalibration, the city's five counties (each borough is a county) dramatically outperformed the other fifty-seven counties in the state. Queens, for example, had gone from the fifty-ninth best performing county in 2002 to the fourteenth best in 2010. We found additional support in the National Assessment of Educational Progress tests, which are given every couple of years on a sampled basis in math and reading to fourth and eighth graders. Our scores showed that, since the advent of mayoral control, the city's fourth graders had increased their learning by the equivalent of one year in both English and math. Our eighth graders had advanced by half a year in math.

There was one area where we weren't seeing progress on the national exams, however, and that was eighth-grade reading. Concerned about this, I contacted E. D. Hirsch, a University of Virginia reading specialist who had developed a comprehensive curriculum that was much more knowledge-based than most reading programs in use in America's classrooms. Hirsch, though a genius, was considered highly controversial because of his emphasis on knowledge acquisition, which progressive educators generally thought was about memorizing facts or studying the work of "dead white men." Hirsch maintained that his approach was essential to effective reading comprehension, especially as texts become more complex in the upper grades. He explained that children from poorer communities, in particular, struggle because they generally have weak vocabularies and difficulty making the connections between words in different contexts. Together, Hirsch and I introduced a pilot reading program in the city using his materials. It lasted several years and got outstanding results.

Looking back, I wish I had consulted Hirsch earlier. My years as chancellor convinced me that too much classroom time was being spent on what I came to call self-referential learning rather than real knowledge and skills acquisition. By this, I mean discussions focused on what kids think or feel about something, rather than discussions that enrich knowledge so that a child can develop views or feelings based on the knowledge required for serious critical thinking and analysis. The most disheartening example came in a history class I observed on the Civil War, where the teacher asked, "What caused the war?"

"Slavery," answered one student.

"And what caused slavery?" continued the teacher.

"Racism," said a second child.

When the teacher then asked, "Has anyone here experienced racism recently?" half the students raised their hands and started talking about their own personal experiences. The class never got back to discussing the Civil War.

This kind of approach—tying things to the individual's own experience or feelings—is all too common in public schools today. To be sure, there's a place for some of it, and it's certainly easier for teachers and students to talk about their personal experiences and feelings than it is to try to master the economic forces that led racism in America's southern states to result in slavery while, at the same time, racism in the northern states didn't lead to slavery. But a discussion about personal reactions, whatever its rationale, can never take the place of the real learning—about history, literature, science, you name it—that these students need and that education should be all about.

ON NOVEMBER 9, 2010, THE MAYOR AGAIN SURPRISED THE city, announcing that I would be stepping down at the end of the calendar year and would be replaced by Hearst Corporation executive Cathie Black. On the same date, News Corporation announced my appointment as executive vice president in the office of Rupert Murdoch. I would also run a newly formed education division and join News Corp's board of directors.

The response to my departure was like nothing I had ever experienced and touched me deeply. All four city newspapers—from the liberal *New York Times* to the conservative *Wall Street Journal*—gave my tenure a favorable review. The *Daily News* wrote: "Scour the history of the last half-century, or go back even further if you like. You will find no chancellor who had a greater impact on the New York City schools than did Joel Klein. The city's children are far, far better off today than when he started eight years ago." Joe Nocera, a *New York Times* columnist, wrote a lengthy piece, detailing our achievements and tying my work as chancellor to my antitrust background and the suit against Microsoft. *The Economist*, calling me "an innovative chancellor," also pointed to our results, noting that "Mr. Bloomberg wanted Mr. Klein to shake things up, and he did." The city's residents likewise viewed my tenure favorably. A Quinnipiac poll released on November 23 found that, by 46 to 35 percent, voters said my chancellorship had been a success.

The response from the media and the city's voters obviously meant a lot to me. We had fought hard through many contentious battles. But more powerful and emotionally enduring were the comments and e-mails from people at Tweed, as well as from many people in the schools and the not-for-profit community. People I had never met told me they had come to New York to be part of what we started. Parents and students hugged me when I visited schools or events. And hundreds of principals came to see me or wrote me candid e-mails about what our reforms had meant to them.

Some of these were very personal, like a visit from Frank Cimino, who ran a successful elementary school in Brooklyn for many years. I had met Frank years earlier, when his regional superintendent had berated him for disagreeing with us in the press, and I let him know that he had every right to criticize our policies. We came to know each other well, and he said he wanted to say good-bye in person because he "had to bring closure to the many years of friendship that we had." He told me he considered me "a true friend and mentor" and wanted me to know that I would "forever be an influencing voice in his heart and his soul." He gave me a print his wife had made of a child jumping rope shadowed by another figure jumping beside her, later writing to explain that he had chosen it because it symbolized "the innocent child having fun while the chancellor was jumping along, watching over the innocence of the child (of all the children) and doing all he could to protect them, to educate them and to prepare them for the real world." I treasure that print, along with my memories of Frank Cimino and the many other great people with whom I was priviliged to serve.

13

Choosing Hope

In a note he sent after Mayor Bloomberg won his third term, the writer Steven Brill told me, "You are sitting in the middle of a revolution and I don't even think you realize it, because you are so immersed in it." Though it's hard to assess something you're in the middle of, I did recognize that, in the eight years the mayor and I had worked together, the world of public education had changed profoundly—not as much as I would have hoped, but probably more than I should have expected. The forces protecting the old status quo of no accountability, no choice, and no innovation had not been defeated, but they were in retreat.

At the national level, a progressive Democratic president had selected a committed reformer as his education secretary and, together, through Race to the Top and their innovation program, they had promoted virtually the entire playbook that New York and other reform districts were pursuing, and they had put $5 billion of the federal budget behind it. With the exception of providing vouchers to pay for private schools, the Obama administration's policies were largely the same as those being embraced by leading Republicans, such as the former president, George Bush, his brother Jeb in Florida and Mitch Daniels in Indiana. This is a rare example of strong bipartisan agreement in today's fractious political climate.

The shift in the Democratic Party could also be seen at the local level. Mayors like Cory Booker in Newark, Antonio Villaraigosa in Los Angeles, Adrian Fenty in D.C., and Kevin Johnson in Sacramento were all pushing an aggressive school-reform agenda. This development had enormous importance. Mayors are the elected officials closest to the schools. In urban areas, they are invariably Democrats and often minority members. While they were all aware that their education policies would cost them politically with the unions, they were nevertheless prepared to pay the price because they saw the kids in their cities suffering and knew that business as usual would no longer do.

Even among school superintendents—not a group known for rocking the boat—you could begin to see remarkable change. Near the end of my tenure, I pulled together several district leaders to see if we could agree on a statement of principles for effective school reform. We developed a manifesto published in the *Washington Post* on October 10, 2010. It stressed the importance of teacher effectiveness and highlighted all of the core reform principles behind accountability, choice, and innovation. To my delight, fifteen superintendents, including those leading the schools in Chicago, Houston, Denver, Boston, and Charlotte, signed it. Together we represented districts serving 2.5 million students. I doubt we could have gotten half of them to sign before President Obama was elected.

Yet another indication that the reform movement was becoming increasingly dominant was that other cities and states were recruiting some of my key people to run their programs. Andres Alonso, my former deputy, had been chosen to run Baltimore; Marcia Lyles, another deputy, was selected to run Wilmington, Delaware (and then Jersey City); and John White, also a deputy, was picked to run New Orleans (and soon after to be Louisiana's education commissioner). J. C. Brizard, one of our high-school specialists, went to Rochester (and subsequently to Chicago), and Chris Cerf, another deputy, became education commissioner for the State of New Jersey. (This trend would continue after I left, with Garth Harries appointed to run New Haven; Cami Anderson, Newark; Paymon Rouhanifard, Camden; and Veronica Conforme, Detroit.)

One of the most important reasons for my continuing optimism is the new young talent being drawn into the field of education. In contrast to a dozen years ago, large numbers of America's best and brightest, coming from our colleges and graduate schools, are now deeply committed to education reform. No one has been more instrumental in making this happen than Wendy Kopp, the visionary who created Teach for America. (I serve on TFA's board of trustees.) By scouring our universities for youngsters with strong academic talent and leadership ability, TFA has brought more than forty thousand graduates to teach, for at least two years, in high-poverty schools. Many TFA teachers get the education-reform bug for life and stay active, sometimes as teachers, principals, and even district superintendents and state commissioners. Some now lead or work for major education advocacy groups. Quite a few have run for office or worked with elected officials. TFA continues to bring an additional six thousand new teachers into schools each year, meaning more young talent with strong leadership skills will fill the ranks of committed education warriors.

Maybe I was in the midst of a revolution. But I had no illusions that the battle was over. Those opposed to our approach to reform would regroup and fight on. In New York City, of course, that occurred several years after I left, when Bill de Blasio was elected mayor. De Blasio was sharply critical of many of our policies and sided with the teachers union on many more issues than we did. But the world had changed a lot under Bloomberg, and although the new mayor will be able to roll back some important reforms—and, in my view, do some real damage as a result—I remain confident that significant portions of what we accomplished will continue, and many programs that are reversed will be reinstated later on because they are working. The *New York Times*, although sometimes critical of our initiatives, has written several editorials advising de Blasio not to undo the basics of most of our key accountability and school choice policies. In addition, the new, post-Bloomberg status quo now has its own defenders who will fight unwanted changes. Among them are seventy thousand families with kids in charter schools. These parents are happy with their kids' education. They will fiercely defend charter schools—and a parent's right to choose—on behalf of their own children and on behalf of their neighbors and generations to come.

This is not to suggest that we won't see some major retrenchments in New York and elsewhere—unfortunately, no doubt, we will—but the longer-term view of history looks favorable for those pushing a reform agenda. And in the short run, I have to believe a lot less will get undone because those who have benefited, and continue to benefit, from the Bloomberg-era changes and similar reforms elsewhere—especially the kids and their parents—will fight to preserve them.

AS I LEFT THE CHANCELLOR'S OFFICE AT THE END OF 2010, I spent a lot of time reflecting backward and thinking forward. I tried to be objective about the things we did and didn't do well and, most important, what we should have done differently. I believe our policies were sound and that, with some notable exceptions, we implemented them well. I wished we could have gotten further with the union on contract reforms by eliminating a lot more of the ridiculous work rules and putting in place an effective, well-accepted teacher evaluation system. Unfortunately, the union's recalcitrance, coupled with our inability to muster the political support to overcome it, made that impossible. As I said to the press on the day the mayor announced my resignation, "We should have been bolder."

But there were two things that we could and should have done differently. First, despite my skepticism, Jim Liebman was on to something when he said we didn't engage the public, the city's communities, and our teachers as effectively as we should have. I did a tremendous amount of outreach over the years, personally wrote tens of thousands of e-mail responses to concerned citizens, and attended numerous community events, week in and week out, over my eight-plus years. But if we had somehow been more strategic about this aspect of our work, we might have garnered greater support, and that would have made us more effective. Building trust takes time and effort, something that can get overlooked when you're so completely focused on the fact that, each year, a kid has only one shot at a good education.

I also think we should have figured out better ways to connect with teachers. Although the union blocked us when we tried, on reflection I don't think we were resourceful enough. I believe most teachers want the world of professionalization that our reforms contemplate, not the assembly-line, work-rules model the unions embrace. Sure, compensation, benefits, and reasonable job security matter, but most of those are consistent with a world in which teachers are true professionals, acting with discretion, bringing their judgment to bear, and being fairly evaluated, with a focus on constantly improving their skills and craft.

Second, I'm convinced it took us way too long to get the curriculum piece right. In fairness, when we started there were no Common Core state standards challenging us to rethink curriculum in a major way. Although there were a few states and advocates pushing on this issue,

---

most states, including New York, embraced the kind of child-centered, progressive curriculum and tests that, following state standards, we used in the city. Over time I learned a lot from E. D. Hirsch, the University of Virginia professor; Sol Stern at the Manhattan Institute; David Steiner, dean of the Hunter School of Education (who briefly served as commissioner of the New York State Education Department); and David Coleman, the architect of the Common Core standards for English language arts. They all stressed the importance of knowledge acquisition and careful reading of complex texts as essential to effective education, especially for poor and minority students, who often come to school with weak vocabularies, poor reading skills, and a fraction of the knowledge that middle-class and wealthy kids bring.

This is not about memorizing facts, as opponents of knowledge-based curricula suggest. On the contrary, it is about learning to understand increasingly complex materials and argumentation. Kids with limited vocabularies and domain knowledge—meaning background information in many areas, like science, history, finance, etc.—won't be prepared for the kind of higher-order, complex thinking that the twenty-first-century workplace will increasingly demand. The encouraging news on this front is that the American Federation of Teachers, run by Randi Weingarten, has said it supports this kind of knowledge-based curriculum, and if it gets involved that will matter. Even so, making such a curriculum work well will be extremely difficult. It will require much more from our teachers and our students, and also from our schools of education, which are currently doing a dreadful job teaching content knowledge to their students.

Reflecting on all this, I became persuaded that, although the kind of reform agenda we had adopted in New York would be necessary for continued progress in New York and elsewhere, it wouldn't be sufficient. Even with a meaningful accountability system—one that gives teachers helpful feedback and removes those who don't perform—and more choices, we would still come up short. Today, there are well over 3 million teachers in America and, sadly, too many aren't performing as well as their students need. But we won't be able to replace a large number of current teachers overnight, and self-improvement, even with good feedback, although important, will get us only so far. What will be needed, in addition, are the kinds of tools and supports that will help teachers improve and better engage kids. Making curriculum more demanding without giving teachers the help required for them to deliver it effectively isn't a winning strategy.

For these reasons, it seemed increasingly clear to me that we need a technological transformation in education like those we have seen in so many segments of our economy. The work that Jim Liebman and his team had done in providing teachers with data and support—online materials, affinity groups, inquiry teams, and the like—was an important but only a first small step on this road. Encouragingly, teachers welcomed the help, and there's so much more that can be provided.

In the last few decades technology has transformed many fields—communications, business, entertainment, and health care, to name a few—while education has lagged behind. Yes, computers have made it into most classrooms, and yes, most schools now have some access to the Internet. But students and teachers still lack the tools that will revolutionize their experience and empower them the way that workers and consumers in other fields have been empowered around the world.

Once again, this was an area where Albert Shanker, the visionary union leader, was ahead of his time. In his 1985 article on professionalizing teaching, he wrote, "We need to use the new technology to do what it can do best, so that teachers have the time to do what they do best." After giving examples, like replacing a lecture with a "videocassette on how Eskimos live in Alaska," he concluded, "The technology is here. Either we will seize it and use it to our advantage . . . or it will be imposed on us in some unthinking attempt to replace some teachers without improving the work lives, status, or salaries of the others." Think how much more technology, properly used, could help teachers today than when Shanker uttered those words some thirty years ago.

The more I focused on the absence of transformative education technologies, the more I came to believe that real improvement would require the private sector, which has driven so much of the change in other fields, to get involved. Private enterprise can access the capital and entrepreneurship necessary to bring about such a transformation. Educators themselves could obviously develop some of these programs, as could not-for-profit organizations like the Gates Foundation and the Khan Academy, which provides high-quality online instruction. But I was convinced that, without private capital and engagement, we wouldn't get things done at the scale needed to effect dramatic change.

Perhaps not surprisingly, like everything else with school reform, this is a controversial view. Given that American capitalism has been the principal driver of global innovation, you would think that the education sector would welcome such participation. But you would be wrong. In education, for some reason, the profit motive is often seen as malevolent. To me, this view seems completely ahistorical. Private, for-profit companies—from textbook publishers to architecture and construction firms—have partnered with the schools since time immemorial. More important, I should think school districts and educators would want private firms to invest big sums in developing products that students and teachers could use. After all, no one has to buy any of it. Only if the schools find value in these products will they purchase them. Sure, the people making these big bets want a return on their investments. But, as in any other field, they can get such returns only if they bring something of value to the market.

This view about education technology and the role of private entrepreneurs in the future of school improvement is why I joined News
Corp. Rupert Murdoch shares this vision of how technology can improve educational outcomes for America's kids, and he and his company were prepared to make big investments to bring this vision to
reality. He knew from the outset that it wouldn't happen quickly, and
that there would be the usual resistance to new ways of doing things in
the schools. But he has a good track record in seeing opportunities for
his company, especially because he is willing to take a long-term view
of success rather than focusing on quarterly profits, which so often
drive today's public corporations.

Shortly after hiring me, News Corp. entered this space by acquiring
a company called Wireless Generation. Founded in the year 2000 by
two talented entrepreneurs, Larry Berger and Greg Gunn, who were
sophisticated in the use of data and technology, Wireless Generation
had become a national leader in using information to analyze what was
happening in schools. Beginning with information already gathered by
teachers—including formal test scores—and supplementing it with the
results of quick assessments, the company found ways to track how well
individual students were doing and then advise teachers on strategies
for intervening with those who were struggling.

In buying the company with an investment of almost $400 million,
News Corp. made an enormous commitment to the development of
technology for schools in America and, it hoped, someday for the rest
of the world. Hundreds of millions of dollars of additional investment
was also planned to enable the rapid expansion of News Corp.'s effort
to develop twenty-first-century tools and content for the classroom.
Named Amplify, in part to reflect our commitment to enhancing the
good work done by teachers, the new company will develop tools and
curriculum based on the emerging Common Core standards being im-

plemented by most states. Available on tablets or computers, Amplify's products will ultimately be able to serve every kid in every grade. Our goal is to build a virtual world of learning that teachers, using their own judgment and discretion, can orchestrate in the classroom and students can visit whenever, and wherever, they want.

Amplify is not about technology per se, but rather about the use of technology to improve teaching and learning. Too often in the past, technology was introduced to the classroom with no effect. A computer can help a motivated kid learn by exploring the Internet; it can also get him in a lot of trouble by doing precisely the same thing. Technology, in other words, is agnostic when it comes to education. It's how it's used that matters, and that basic recognition drives everything Amplify does.

We had three main ideas at the beginning, and we organized a separate division around each. The first, Amplify Insight, the old Wireless Generation, is based on the idea that technology can make teachers smarter about their students by providing real-time information to help them customize and individualize the learning experience. In most classrooms today, some kids are way ahead of others, and teachers struggle to meet varying needs. By using straightforward assessments, followed by simple reports with advice on how to address an individual student's needs, teachers can effectively differentiate the learning experiences for each child. I learned a lot about the great potential of this kind of support for teachers from Jim Liebman's work in New York.

Our second idea—housed in a division called Amplify Access—was to maximize individualized instruction and extend the overall time for student learning through one-to-one computing. Here, the advent of the tablet holds great promise. Kids love tablets and, compared with computers, tablets are reasonably priced—and will decline in price while improving in quality over time. But traditional tablets sold to consumers aren't designed for teaching and learning. We wanted to design the right kind of tablet for schools. For instance, our software will enable a teacher to see what's happening on every kid's screen and, with a single tap, restrict the apps that kids can use or shut their tablets down completely. She can also deliver different lessons to different kids, and during class she can do spot checks and quizzes to see whether or not kids are getting the lesson she's delivering. Overall, a tablet with this kind of functionality can help teachers run their classrooms more effectively, help them personalize lessons for individuals or groups of students, and get students more excited about learning.

Finally, our third idea—housed in a division called Amplify Learning—was to develop instructional content that will assist teachers and engage kids. In the end, three things in education really matter a lot: the nature and quality of what's being taught (the curriculum), how well it's being taught (the teacher), and how much of it a child absorbs (the student). Amplify Learning would aim to tackle all three, based on the view that knowledge and skills are both critical for kids. The goal is to help teachers sequence lessons and customize them for their students. We will provide a year's worth of digital lessons that a teacher can adapt to her own personal approach. In addition to carefully planned and sequenced lessons, these materials will include dramatic readings of portions of difficult books, group problem-solving exercises called quests, games that reinforce what a child is learning, and individualized reports for teachers and students about how a child is progressing. The use of these kinds of multimedia presentations, along with sophisticated games that kids love, to support a comprehensive, well-thought-through, demanding curriculum is new in K–12 education. All of it is built to help teachers improve their craft and get kids more engaged in their learning.

Although we are excited by Amplify's possibilities, we recognize that some people would look at tablet-based learning, consider all the various video screens already occupying the lives of children, and see problems. In a nutshell, the concern is that technology takes something away from human interactions and can distort a child's experience. No one should argue that a machine is able to substitute for human interaction or that a game can replace a teacher's ability to help a student over a classroom hurdle. That's why, rather than simply building online courses, Amplify's materials are all organized around the teacher and her ability to have students use them in or out of class. Although online courses have their place, our deep belief is that in K–12 education, the classroom teacher will—and should—remain at the center of the instructional mission.

IN FOCUSING ON TEACHERS AS THE CORE OF WHAT WE DO AT Amplify, we hope to reinforce the paramount importance of recruiting and retaining well-prepared and highly motivated teachers to our public schools. Lots of research in the past decade underscores the importance of great teachers. Summarized by Raj Chetty, a distinguished Harvard economist, the studies show that "being assigned to a highly effective teacher generates substantial long-term gains for students, and conversely, being assigned to a highly ineffective teacher generates significant harm in the long-term." Chetty has noted that good teachers are not only "effective at teaching to the test and raising students' performance on tests, but also that that teacher has longer term impacts on outcomes we ultimately care about from education: like attending college, like earnings, like teenage pregnancy."

We learned quite a bit about this in New York City, where we found that, with proper recruitment, support, and incentives, school systems can increase the numbers of teachers who are both temperamentally and intellectually equipped for the modern classroom. We accomplished this by making the city schools an exciting place to work, bringing in partners to aggressively recruit talented new teachers, and significantly improving our compensation system. When the unions allowed us, we used incentives to encourage good teachers and principals to serve in schools where they were needed most, and we created mentoring and peer group programs so teachers could share what they knew about best practices in the classroom.

But if we are to raise the quality and the performance of teachers across the country, more effort must come from the profession itself. This could begin with an honest assessment of the system that educates and certifies those who become teachers. Today, despite some recent improvements, we are still not getting the best students to go into teaching; most of the college students who go into teaching rank well below the top third of their class and many still come from the bottom third. They often attend college programs that are so weak that they have been described as "an industry of mediocrity" by the National Council on Teacher Quality. The council's 2013 Teacher Prep Review was based on a study of more than one thousand undergraduate programs that train new teachers. Of these, fewer than 10 percent earned a rating of three stars or higher, on a scale of four. Only one, Ohio State, earned three or more stars for programs that educate both elementary- and secondary-school teachers.

Young teachers are not well served by the profession as they enter it. Too often they are hired to provide instruction in subjects outside their areas of academic expertise. This mismatch surely affects both student achievement and teacher satisfaction. Overall, the image of today's teacher in a big urban system is that of an overworked, isolated, and bureaucratically oppressed man or woman struggling to educate students who can be exceedingly difficult to reach. Although many teachers in New York and other big cities defy the odds and do well, too often the stereotype is borne out.

Teaching is a challenging job, as anyone who has stood before a classroom will attest. But if you look carefully, you can find places in the world where teachers as a group enjoy greater success, more job satisfaction, and higher social standing than they do in America. In China, Japan, Finland, and several other countries, teachers are accorded the same level of respect as doctors. In South Korea, a recent survey found that almost half of parents would encourage their child to become a teacher. This view was shared by just a third of American parents.

Among the Western industrial nations, Finland stands out for its consistently high scores on international achievement tests. Ninety-three percent of Finns graduate from high school and fully two thirds of the country's high-school graduates go on to college. These results have attracted a great deal of attention among Americans in part because Finland wasn't always at the top of the heap. Forty years ago, its schools ranked near the bottom in Europe. Their success today began with a commitment to reform back then, showing that sound policies can lead to much better academic outcomes.

The thing that immediately stands out is that, unlike in America, Finnish teachers are drawn from the top 10 percent of their college classes. As one commentator recently noted, "gaining admission to a teacher-training program at Finnish universities is as difficult as winning admission to MIT. Teachers are expected to become genuine subject experts in the fields they will teach." They must earn a minimum of a master's degree before applying for a job, and, when they do apply, the competition is stiff. Once they are employed, Finnish teachers go through a yearlong teaching apprenticeship and, if they succeed, are required to devote two hours per week to professional development throughout their careers, much of it focused on rigorous collaborative inquiry, experimentation, and action-based research of a sort we could only gesture at with our teachers in New York City. Finnish teachers are permitted to try out almost any innovative method they prefer, as long as they meet certain general curriculum standards and collaborate freely to help students with challenges and share what they learn with one another.

The Finnish model teaches us that, if we are serious about improving the quality of the people who go into teaching, we need to begin by asking more of the education schools that train our teachers. Far too many of these schools function as indiscriminate revenue sources for universities and colleges, accepting underqualified students and their tuition dollars for programs that are academically weak. To solve this problem, states could institute rigorous exams—similar to the bar exams for lawyers or licensing tests for doctors—that graduates would have to pass in order to be cleared for the classroom, an idea that Randi Weingarten has also championed. In addition to testing pedagogy, these exams would require prospective teachers to demonstrate real subject-matter knowledge, something that is largely ignored today.

Once a bar exam for teachers becomes the norm, all sorts of services and associations would arise to support the profession and enforce standards in the way that bar associations enforce them for attorneys, and like lawyers and physicians, for example, teachers could be required to take ongoing continuing education courses, and those who sought to specialize in certain areas such as English as a second language might be required to pass additional exams. In time, borrowing a page from Shimon Waronker's New American Academy, new designations, with increased compensation, might emerge—master teacher, mentor, team leader, and so on—and these, too, could benefit from certification tests. With such a system of rigorous professional certification and continuing education, the teaching profession could be elevated above its current status, gaining not only greater respect but more influence over research, teacher education programs, and public policy.

Although I'd like to take credit for this idea, it was promoted almost thirty years ago by Albert Shanker. Shanker was well known because of the teachers' strikes he led in New York during the 1960s and '70s, and he became even more famous when Woody Allen described him as the man who had blown up the world in the movie *Sleeper*. Later in his career, after he left New York to head the American Federation of Teachers, Shanker became a visionary leader on education reform. In 1985, this once dyed-in-the-wool trade unionist said, "Unless we go beyond collective bargaining to the achievement of true teacher professionalism, we will fail in our major objectives: to preserve public education in the United States and to improve the status of teachers economically, socially and politically." He called for a "second revolution in American public education"—the first being collective bargaining, which he had pioneered a quarter century earlier. The numerous changes he proposed were bold and would have moved teaching away from its current, as he described it, "factory model," and made it instead into a real and well-respected profession. Among other good ideas, he pressed for a demanding bar exam–type test for teachers, to require them to demonstrate their expertise in their subject areas as well as in pedagogy. He further suggested that all new teachers serve one- to three-year internships prior to winning a regular teaching position in a school. During this time they would be evaluated on their work with students and fellow teachers, and coached so they might improve.

Shanker urged teachers to embrace his agenda in order to protect their own economic, social, and political status. But he knew this could happen only if the transformation he proposed resulted in a different, and much better prepared, teaching force. Notably, for a union leader, he saw the parallels between the destruction of the auto industry by overly zealous trade union policies and what could happen to public schools and their teachers. In 1993, calling for big changes, Shanker explained:

> In terms of my own motivation on this thing, I wouldn't be saying these things or doing these things if I didn't have the sense that we are at the point that the auto industry was at a few years ago. They could see they were losing market share every year and still not believe that really had anything to do with the quality of the product. Then, when it was almost too late and they were about to go out of business, they pulled themselves together.
>
> I think that we will get—and deserve—the end of public education through some sort of privatization scheme if we don't behave differently. Unfortunately, very few people really believe that yet. They talk about it, and they don't like it, but they're not ready to change and stop doing the things that brought them to this point.

Here we are, more than twenty years later, and these wise words remain largely unheeded. In my view, he is right that the unions need to lead this transformation, and, I would add, schools of education should join them.

What are the overarching lessons to be learned? Whatever else we do, we need to make teaching a well-respected profession that attracts our best college graduates and requires that they have the training in the subject area they will teach as well as in pedagogy and classroom management. To accomplish this, we need to pay teachers well and base their overall salary on merit and performance, not length of service. Let's also give them the tools and curriculum supports that modern technology can readily make available so we can help them be better at their craft and use their valuable time most effectively. And reflecting the professionals that all our educators must be, let every school create a culture of accountability, where every adult strives to do better for every child every day. These are lessons of hope, and they are readily attainable.

Postcript

As I have thought about my return to New York City in 2000,
after thirty-three years away, soon to run the school system that helped
prepare me for my life's odyssey, I couldn't help but be reminded of the
words from T. S. Eliot's poem "Little Gidding":

> *We shall not cease from exploration*
> *And the end of all our exploring*
> *Will be to arrive where we started*
> *And know the place for the first time*

In June 2013, I was asked to give the graduation speech at Bryant
High School, fifty years after I graduated in 1963. In a way, I felt like I'd
never left Bryant. Today's kids reminded me of my class, and my classmates still seemed like the kids I knew in high school. I have relished
my long period of exploration, following anything but a linear path.
And I am glad that it led me to discover that education is what I was
meant to commit myself to. For me the reason is simple: education is
the thread that holds the fabric of our country together and must, therefore, be our top priority.

Soon after I left the New York City Department of Education, the
Council on Foreign Relations asked former secretary of state Condo-
leezza Rice and me to cochair a task force on U.S. Education Reform

and National Security. For the council, which focuses on issues of global policy, to highlight public education in America speaks volumes about how deep and pervasive this problem is. The task force had thirty members, including representatives from the military, schools, business, unions, academia, and civic groups. I was pleased that Randi Weingarten agreed to serve. The report recognized the specific threats to national security caused by an underperforming education system, emphasizing that we are not educating enough students with the skills needed in the diplomatic, intelligence, and foreign service fields, and that more than half our kids are academically ineligible to serve in the military. It also pointed out, as Secretary Rice and I wrote in the preface, that the greatest threat to our national security is if the United States becomes "two countries—one educated and one not, one employable and one not. Such a divide would undermine the country's cohesion and confidence and America's ability and willingness to lead." We explained that "we took on this project because we believe the crucial question for our generation is whether the American Dream becomes the American memory on our watch. We believe and hope that the American Dream can be sustained."

Properly done, education prepares our people for citizenship and provides them with opportunity by helping them to acquire the knowledge and skills they will need to be successful in a world moving at a pace that is almost unimaginable to those of us who grew up in the twentieth century. Several recent developments—including Common Core standards, some improvement in the qualifications of those going into the teaching profession, and the intelligent use of technology—promise to better the status quo. But if these changes are imposed in an ad hoc way, in school systems that are not operated effectively, their impact will be substantially blunted. We know this from our experience with many failed reforms tried in the decades since *A Nation at Risk* was released in 1983.

If things are to change and reform is to work now, we must make important adjustments at the system level. First, in addition to professionalizing teaching, we have to fix our governance structure. Today, there are some fourteen thousand school districts throughout America— from New York City, with over a million kids, to some with fewer than a hundred. As Lou Gerstner, the CEO and organizational genius who turned IBM around in the 1990s, has long argued, this is senseless. Although we may feel historically attached to community control, these myriad small school systems cannot provide the options or the innovation their kids will need. A district with a single high school isn't going to have a P-Tech, the IBM six-year combined high school–college that Lou's successor Sam Palmisano helped launch in New York, even though it probably has some kids who would want to attend such a school.

Related to this romantic notion of the local school district is our continued reliance on elected school boards. Mayoral control is not a panacea. A bad mayor can hurt the schools as much as he or she can hurt other government functions. But mayoral control provides the opportunity for leadership and accountability that can drive change. School boards, by contrast, have often resulted in the politics of paralysis. Most school board elections draw very low voter turnout, making it easier for special interests—like local political machines and unions—to have their preferred candidates prevail.

Second, to return to where I started in the preface, we need to increase choices for all our children. Whether through charters, more choice within the traditional public school system, or vouchers, the competition that has helped many of our colleges and universities will work in our K–12 public school system. If choice is good enough for anyone who can afford it, I'm sure it's equally good for those who can't.

As I reflect on my experience in New York, I have little doubt that our charter school initiative and high-school choice system, including the enrollment process, were among the most important and enduring things we did. Critics point out that not every charter school or school of choice is doing a good job, and that's true. But you could say the same thing about many traditional, community-based public schools, and that doesn't appear to upset the critics nearly as much. In the end, choice among schools won't guarantee a good outcome for everyone— just as choice among hospitals or air carriers doesn't always ensure a good outcome—but choice gives us the best chance of getting the best results for the most people. Again, look at what people who can afford choice do, and let's let others have what they're having.

The biggest problem with choice is that it can't happen overnight. The expansion of high-quality charter schools will accelerate as chains like KIPP and Success Academy learn to expand more easily. In the meantime, the third systems-level change we need is to bring about real accountability for all educators. As long as seniority—rather than excellence—is the polestar when it comes to human capital in public education, we will fail. To me, the basic logic of accountability for teachers defies any reasonable opposition. In a choice-based education system, excellence would inevitably become valued. But until we get there, the education schools and teachers unions need to chart the way to a merit-based teaching profession. Harvard's and Stanford's Graduate Schools of Education, considered the best in the country, both insist on excellence when it comes to hiring their faculties. And I'm confident that most leaders of teachers unions don't use seniority to decide who their key people are. Why settle for less for our kids? The education schools and unions are, so to speak, fat and happy: they have the resources and support to keep on doing what they're doing. But if that happens, they will increasingly find that they are sustaining an educational ecosystem that doesn't work for kids or teachers.

Once again, it was Albert Shanker who saw this issue most clearly. In 1993, he uttered the wisest words about accountability I've ever heard: "The key is that unless there is accountability, we will never get the right system. As long as there are no consequences if kids or adults don't perform, as long as the discussion is not about education and student outcomes, then we're playing a game as to who has the power." Unfortunately, too often in public education today "we're playing a game as to who has the power."

I cannot count the number of people who have told me they agree with what I'm saying about school reform but think I'm being unrealistic because the forces defending the status quo are too strong to overcome. But if all of those people, and others who think like them, got politically engaged in these issues, things would change. Indeed, it was because of Mayor Bloomberg's leadership that more got done in New York than these people would have expected. Surely, if their kids were stuck in the kind of dead-end schools that so many kids in poor communities are stuck in today, they would never be so tolerant.

As I noted at the start of this book, we face a profound choice. We can remain complacent and watch as our country continues to be ripped apart by a growing underclass that finds itself increasingly economically disenfranchised because it doesn't have the knowledge and skills it needs to be successful. Or we can finally say what we've long known. Too many of our schools are failing. We who can choose would never deem them acceptable for own children. That should mean they are not acceptable for anyone's child.

ACKNOWLEDGMENTS

My first thanks go to Michael Bloomberg, who took a risk on me and gave me the opportunity of a lifetime. I will forever be grateful to him, not just for the appointment, but for the outstanding leadership, support, and encouragement he provided.

Several members of the mayor's team were enormously helpful during my chancellorship. In addition to Dennis Walcott, who was a great partner, others deserving special thanks include Patti Harris, Kevin Sheekey, Howard Wolfson, Ed Skyler, Jim Anderson, and Stu Loeser.

I owe a great debt to Margaret Carlson, both for her friendship and for her willingness to recommend me to Bloomberg.

The men and women who joined our effort at the DOE merit particular mention. Some were there when I started, but many came from all over the country. This was an extraordinary group of people, lots of whom made great personal sacrifices in order to improve education for kids. There are far too many to name, but they know who they are, and, to me, they are the heroes of this story.

We received a great deal of help from community groups, foundations, and corporations that participated in numerous ways—from opening new schools to partnering with schools to providing financial support that enabled us to do things we could not otherwise have done. The number of groups and individuals who supported our reforms is remarkable. Only in New York could this happen.

Two seasoned authors, Michael D'Antonio and George Hodgman, helped me organize my thoughts and provided strong editorial help. My thanks to both.

Jonathan Burnham, Tim Duggan, Laura Brown, and the entire team at HarperCollins made many constructive suggestions and showed great patience in dealing with a rookie author.

Several people gave me comments and suggestions on earlier drafts. From among my colleagues at the Department of Education, Michele Cahill, Jim Liebman, and Dan Weisberg were generous with their time and wisdom. So, too, were my friends Marie Brenner, Ernie Pomerantz, and Gerson Zweifach, along with Bob Barnett (who also ably represented me on this book).

My daughter, Julia, is a talented writer who sharpened my prose and brought clarity to my thoughts. My assistant, Rosanne Mullaly, helped in numerous ways, as she always does.

My greatest debt goes to my wife, Nicole Seligman. She is the best editor I know, and her work on this book was invaluable. She is also the best partner I could ever have hoped for. She was my first adviser in dealing with the many tough issues that came before me as chancellor, and her love made it possible to get up every morning ready to tackle the challenges I faced and go to sleep every night knowing that, no matter how rocky things might seem, it would all be fine because she was there for me.

ABOUT THE AUTHOR

JOEL KLEIN served as chancellor of the New York City Department of Education from 2002 to 2011. Earlier in his career, he served as U.S. assistant attorney general in charge of the Antitrust Division of the U.S. Department of Justice, deputy White House counsel during the Clinton administration, and CEO of the U.S. arm of Bertelsmann. He currently serves as executive vice president at News Corporation and CEO of its education division, Amplify. He lives in New York City with his wife, Nicole Seligman.